CHICANA ADOLESCENTS

CHICANA ADOLESCENTS

Bitches, 'Ho's, and Schoolgirls

LISA C. DIETRICH

Westport, Connecticut
London

Library of Congress Cataloging-in-Publication Data

Dietrich, Lisa. 1965–
    Chicana adolescents : bitches, 'ho's, and schoolgirls / Lisa C.
Dietrich.
        p.   cm.
    Includes bibliographical references and index.
    ISBN 0–275–96154–0 (alk. paper)
    1. Mexican American teenage girls—California, Southern—Social
conditions—Case studies.   2. California, Southern—Social
conditions—Case studies.   I. Title.
F870.M5D54   1998
305.235—DC21   97–34750

British Library Cataloguing in Publication Data is available.

Copyright © 1998 by Lisa C. Dietrich

Library of Congress Catalog Card Number: 97–34750
ISBN: 0–275–96154–0

First published in 1998

Praeger Publishers, 88 Post Road West, Westport, CT 06881
An imprint of Greenwood Publishing Group, Inc.

Printed in the United States of America

The paper used in this book complies with the
Permanent Paper Standard issued by the National
Information Standards Organization (Z39.48–1984).

10 9 8 7 6 5 4 3 2 1

Contents

A Note about Vocabulary

I have used the terms *Mexican American, Chicano/a, Latino/a,* and *Hispanic* interchangeably throughout this text. When quoting or citing other research material, I have maintained the specific ethnic label used in the cited source. Although most of the individuals who participated in this research project referred to themselves as "Mexicans," I have substituted the terms Mexican American or Chicano because almost all of the individuals in this study are citizens of the United States.

I have changed the names of the people and places associated with this project to protect their privacy. However, with respect to other terms and vocabulary, I made a consistent attempt to privilege my informants' choice of words. Consequently, the reader will notice that the Spanish word for neighborhood, *barrio,* is spelled *varrio* throughout the text. This is the way that the residents of Varrio Granos referred to their neighborhood.

Acknowledgments

I wish to thank the Research Institute for the Study of Man, the University of California Institute for Mexico and the United States, and the University of California at San Diego for their generous support of my research. I would also like to thank F. Bailey, Suzanne Brenner, Nancy Friedlander, Paula Levin, Ricardo Stanton-Salazar, John Weinzettle, and the girls of Varrio Granos for their thoughtful and challenging comments on previous drafts of this manuscript. While I cannot name all of the many individuals who generously gave of their time and patiently answered my questions, I would not have been able to complete this book without them. Nor would I have been able to complete my research without the constant support and encouragement of my family, especially my husband John who graciously assumed the role of chief cook and bottle washer, while I was working on this book. Finally, I would like to recognize the girls and women who are the subject of this book; they have my deepest gratitude for letting me into their lives.

Chapter 1

Introduction

This introduction anticipates questions about how a twenty-nine-year-old white woman was able to conduct research among Latino adolescents. It also brings to the fore questions about the potentially exploitative nature of anthropological research: Is it possible for a member of the dominant culture to enter a subordinate community and win the trust and approval of its members? Can the researcher in such a situation collect reliable data and judge their reliability? What types of obligations does the researcher owe to the members of the community that she is studying?

In some respects, I was very lucky. I was able to conduct fieldwork in my metaphorical backyard. Rather than fly thousands of miles away to some remote village in the highlands of Papua New Guinea, I chose to focus on the kids that I saw every day. Because I conducted my research close to home, within a socio-political system with which I was familiar, I was able to use my skills to help "informants" in a myriad of ways. I met with school administrators, medical professionals, and social workers on behalf of the teens and their families. I helped the adolescents with their college and scholarship applications. I also provided tutoring, transportation, and baby-sitting services. This type of fieldwork, while allowing me to give back to the community, however, poses its own hazards, not the least of which is the difficulty in producing a sense of closure on the project. I still field phone calls from my friends who need to borrow a computer or want to stop by to chat and check on my new baby. I find that I am updating my files continuously. At times I feared that I would never finish this project. Of course, the relationships that I forged during this project did not necessarily come easily.

To say that it was difficult to gain an entreé into a community that defined itself in opposition to my ascribed status as a white adult woman is an understatement. I had to prove that I was someone who was trustworthy enough and "cool" enough to be accepted as a member of the adolescent set. Toward that end, the fact that I had a car facilitated my acceptance by the teens. Because I had "wheels," I could, and did, drive them to parties, car shows, movies, and amusement parks. While I could never become a teenager again (nor would I want to), I did become a friend and confidante of the teens with whom I worked. I knew that I had truly become accepted when I was attending a "kickback" party and several of the adolescent boys, who did not know me and were obviously uncomfortable with my presence at the party, asked the host who I was. Carlos, the sixteen-year-old host, replied, nodding his head in my direction, "That's Lisa. She's cool. You don't have to worry about her snitching on us or nothing."

While I did try to fit in as best I could (I dressed in blue jeans and T-shirts), I never tried to hide my adult status, my white skin, or my purpose for spending time with them from the teens. My honesty with them not only affirmed my trustworthiness but also proved to be a great means of networking among the teens. When word got out that I was writing a "book," I was all but harassed by teens who wanted to be interviewed.

The girls also became very adept at using my adult status to their advantage by enlisting me to play the role of parentally approved chaperon for various outings. My first invitation from the teens came from Lydia, who wanted to go dancing with her illicit boyfriend. She invited my husband and myself to her family's home for dinner and broached the subject during the meal. Her parents solicited my husband's approval of the outing before granting Lydia permission to go dancing with me (neither they nor I were aware that Lydia planned to meet her boyfriend at the dance club). Lydia's parents, as were many of the people I met while I was conducting my research, were very curious as to why I would want to spend time with a group of Latina teenagers instead of my "own kind." The girls constantly asked me if it was true that I was writing a book about girls, "just girls." They could not believe that people would be interested in reading about them. I, on the other hand, could not believe the lack of research that addressed issues related to Latina teens.

This project is important for many reasons. First, I began this project with a desire to make sense of what appeared to be the self-defeating behavior—dropping out of school, early pregnancy, gang affiliation—on the part of many Latina adolescents. I wanted to explore the logic underlying their life choices and examine the links between the decisions they made and larger societal processes. Second, and no less important, I wanted to interject their voices into the public debate about teen pregnancy and gang-related violence.

While problems of violence, crime, and teen pregnancy are not limited to the Chicano community, politicians and media have habitually constructed these social problems as predominantly minority problems. While teen births within the Hispanic community consistently outnumber those in the white (non-Hispanic) community (Centers for Disease Control 1994), statistics relating high teenage birthrates or increasing numbers of adolescent gang members within Hispanic neighborhoods do not tell the entire story. Chicano adolescents experience a variety of social, economic, and cultural pressures that may orient them toward making decisions such as joining gangs or engaging in unprotected sexual intercourse. It is important to understand why many adolescents are making these types of decisions.

My research focuses on working-class Chicana adolescents. I chose to focus on Chicana girls because very little research directly addresses the issues and concerns of importance to this particular group of adolescents. While my research focuses on one working-class *varrio* in southern California, the issues and contradictions with which these girls grapple are common to many Chicano communities. For example, while adolescence is often idealized as a time of protected self-discovery where individuals progress toward adulthood, many adolescents must cope with structural conditions that do not support this notion of adolescence. The Chicana girls involved in this study find that the interplay and conflict between political, social, economic, and cultural factors often complicate their transition to womanhood.

Public policy addressing social problems such as teen pregnancy and juvenile delinquency has become increasingly punitive in orientation. Teen mothers are treated as lacking moral fortitude. Poverty, substance abuse, violence, and crime are treated as if they are only a consequence of teen pregnancy, rather than also being causal factors contributing to the pregnancy. California governor Pete Wilson noted in a 1995 campaign speech that "the fourteen-year-old unwed mother all too often *produces* the fourteen-year-old predator" (my italics). Girls are increasingly assumed to be autonomous, responsible actors by conservative public policy, which then denies them the ability to act responsibly by interfering with their access to abortion and birth control options. Proposed welfare reform initiatives, wrapped in the cloak of individual responsibility and morality, require that individuals take responsibility for their actions without addressing underlying social inequities. Most publicly proposed solutions to gang violence or teenage pregnancy do not link these "moral" problems with structural/material problems. It is far more difficult to propose solutions to remedy structural problems such as low-wage employment, discrimination, and unplanned urban development than to propose solutions to moral irresponsibility. While individuals do make life choices, these choices are often constrained or shaped by their social, political, economic, and cultural environments.

Many Chicana adolescents find themselves socially "betwixt and between." Neither adults nor children, they occupy a curious social position of increasing individual responsibilities without a concomitant increase in their perceived sense of power or self-determination. This is complicated by the fact that girls' bodies are perceived as markers of moral boundaries in ways that boys' bodies are not (Nathanson 1991). Control over Chicana girls' sexuality is often used to focus male authority and reinforce group identity:

FATHER: I told my girls, if you want to act like a white woman and be all liberated, you gotta pay the price. Everybody's going to think you're a bad girl, and they're gonna look bad at our family.

The girls often chafe under the efforts exerted by their families, school officials, and boyfriends to control them. Many of them find creative means to assert control over their daily lives, their bodies, and their futures. Unfortunately, sometimes their efforts toward emancipation end in pregnancy, criminal records, or drug addiction.

These social problems can then trap individuals into reproducing what has been labeled in public policy as the "cycle of poverty."

Chapter 2

The Pragmatics of Culture

The girls I met during my research led very different lives than the girls I knew when I was growing up as a white, middle-class kid from the suburbs. For example, most of the kids with whom I went to high school graduated from high school and attended four-year universities. Not one of the girls associated with this study attended a four-year university upon graduation from high school. In fact, many of the adolescents I met during my research did not graduate from high school. Nor did I know anyone in a gang while I was going to high school. I don't recall hearing about gangs, gang violence, or drive-bys as a teenager. In contrast, gangs are an integral part of the social scene for the teens in this study. All of the girls I interviewed knew someone affiliated with a gang. More often than not, the gang member they knew was also a family member. Also, as a teenager, I knew of only one girl who "got in trouble" and had to leave high school because of an unwanted pregnancy. The city of Westhills, where I conducted my research, boasts the second highest teen pregnancy rate in San Diego County. As I sit here writing this chapter, three out of the seven girls introduced in Chapter 4 are either pregnant or have had babies.

So how can we explain the differences between their adolescent experiences and mine? Partly it is a result of a changing society. As a twenty-nine-year-old woman, I had come of age eleven years earlier than these girls. However, these girls also look and act differently from their middle-class peers. After all, there are girls today who do not get pregnant, who do go to college and who do not have intimate connections with drugs or gangs.

Which again broaches the question: How can we explain the different life trajectories of these girls? One tendency has been to explain these differences in terms of differences in culture, replacing an outdated and racist biogenetic explanatory model—inferior genes—with an equally racist cultural model —inferior values. This explanatory model, often termed the "Culture of Poverty," has recently enjoyed a resurgence in popularity. This model argues that poor people are poor because they do not share the same standards or values as mainstream society. The Culture of Poverty is the belief in a cultural transmission of a distinct set of values that undermines individual success (Lewis 1959; Liebow 1967; Miller 1958). Thus, the self-perpetuating, pathological culture of the poor, which emphasizes instant gratification, self-expression instead of self-constraint, fatalism, pleasure instead of productivity, and low education motivation, shapes the behavior of the poor in such a way as to prevent them from attaining success in mainstream society. For example, it has been argued that Mexican American children do not do well in school because they are family oriented or are overly dependent on their authoritarian (*machismo*) fathers, thus culturally predisposing them toward failure in an educational system that emphasizes individual achievement (Heller 1966; Madsen 1973; Rubel 1966). Consequently, the means of fixing the problem (i.e., Mexican American children dropping out of school) relies on changing their cultural values, making "them" more like "us," rather than fixing the educational system.

The problem with the Culture of Poverty model is that it makes little reference to the context of culture, in effect divorcing behavior from the material conditions of society. Through the lens of this model, the *varrio* traditions of lavish weddings and *quinceañeras* are seen as indications of the fecklessness and present-day orientation of the Chicano lower classes, when in reality big parties do little to change the socioeconomic position of families.[1] Rather than interpreting cultural values as ways of coping with social and economic conditions which are independently experienced by successive generations of individuals, cultural values are interpreted as causal factors in reproducing these same social and economic conditions.

Proponents of this theory attempt to change the behavior of the lower classes by inculcating "good" values into young people. These good values are usually disseminated by implementing policy changes that are punitive in nature: lowering the age at which juveniles can be convicted of adult crimes and denying welfare benefits to unwed teen mothers. Proponents of these policies erroneously assume that the poor do not share the same values of conventional society. They mistakenly believe that the poor live completely insulated or isolated from conventional culture. While there are cultural differences between socioeconomic classes, as well as various racial and ethnic groups, the poor are intricately bound up with conventional society through a variety of institutions: television, public school, employment, advertising, youth recreation programs, public health services, and social welfare services. Consequently, the poor share many of the same values—social achievement and financial success, family and marriage stability—with middle-class society.

The Culture of Poverty theorists rely on an outdated, mechanistic view of culture where cultural values hover beyond the reach of everyday realities. In this model, cultural values function as immovable traffic signals that direct individual behavior and police social interaction in an uncompromising way. I prefer to envision culture as more processual and dynamic and intimately bound up with material realities.

So what is culture? Culture is best understood as a shared, learned set of values and practices that we use to express our social identities. It is the means by which we communicate who we are or, more accurately, who we would like to be. Consequently, cultural values are constructed in the real world, intimately linked to their socioeconomic contexts, and most thoroughly articulated in social interaction.

The intimate and complex relationship between culture and socioeconomic class is brought to the fore by the girls in this study. While the girls affiliated with this study are subjected to a variety of cultural norms that constrain their behavior—Anglo norms, Chicano norms, the norms associated with being a woman in each of these groups, and norms associated with being an adolescent in each of these groups—their experiences are also circumscribed by class structure within the United States. They live in a country where it is difficult to be poor with dignity. They are acutely aware that the jobs they are able to find—domestic service, minimum wage employment—are disdained by wider society, yet they are criticized for lacking a work ethic. They are encouraged to consume conspicuously by the media, yet they are scolded for their lack of self-restraint. They live in a society where "family values" are glorified in the abstract, yet real support for their families—subsidized child care, job training—is visibly lacking. These experiences, no less than cultural values, also shape their life trajectories. What is needed, then, is a theory that incorporates factors of socioeconomic class into the concept of culture. Subculture theory attempts to correct the overly deterministic Culture of Poverty model by linking the concept of culture with structural factors. The study of youth subcultures highlights the role of particular groups of young people (e.g., hippies, punks, street gangs) who pose collective cultural solutions to commonly experienced problems (unemployment, discrimination, lack of social status). Subculture theory explores the means by which stigmatized groups resist their lack of social status and prestige by reversing the stigmatization through the creation of oppositional cultural forms and practices. Thus, the creation of a new subculture becomes a means of coping with experiences of marginalization and alienation.

For example, Willis's research (1977, 1981b) on British working-class lads and Ogbu's (1974, 1981) research on American black students emphasize student resistance to school from the perspective of an oppositional subculture. The working-class lads in Willis's ethnography reject their school's orientation toward middle-class values by developing an exaggerated masculine identity that categorizes school success and white-collar jobs as effeminate. Consequently, they identify school success as antithetical to their identities as working-class males. The lads collectively resist dominant school culture by flouting school rules and confronting teachers and school administrators aggressively. Likewise, the students in Ogbu's study reject school success as representing white culture. Their negative orientation toward school is further exacerbated by their perceptions that the labor market privileges white workers to the detriment of black workers. Consequently, the black students reject school as antithetical to their racial identity and as a futile means of achieving economic success.

While the analytical concept of subculture is useful, it does have some limitations. The field of subcultural studies has been strongly influenced by Marxist theory. Researchers particularly those associated with the Center of Cultural Studies in Britain, have linked youth cultures to class struggles. The emphasis has been to highlight the use of oppositional cultural forms, pitting middle-class values against working-class values. Cultural systems are seen as mutually exclusive alternatives, rather than intertwined behavioral repertoires. This overemphasis on the oppositional content of subcultures undermines the diversity and plurality of the life experiences of most individuals.

Research on youth subcultures is further hindered by its orientation toward street-based cultures. The study of youth cultures has become almost synonymous with male delinquency. For practical purposes, those involving public policy, youth subculture is masculine street culture. This orientation, however, obscures the complex reality of youth subcultures particularly with respect to girls' subcultures.

The stigma associated with independent girls and street culture precludes many girls from associating with this masculine form of youth subculture; only the most conventionally deviant girls (gang-affiliated girls) are associated with street culture. This tends to render the majority of girls invisible or peripheral to studies of youth cultures. Rather than having any subculture of their own, girls appear in the research as den mothers or sexual objects manipulated by the masculine purveyors of youth subculture. This is particularly true of research done within Hispanic youth cultures (Jankowski 1991; Padilla 1992). Researchers need to break free from the oppositional framework that has traditionally shaped the use of subculture as an analytic tool in order to provide more sophisticated analysis of girls' subcultures.

The girls involved in this study are simultaneously immersed in two cultural systems. That is not to say that they do not engage in some forms of oppositional behavior; nobody wants to be accused of "acting white" or become labeled as a *pocha*. However, while the girls embrace some oppositional values, they do not subscribe to a straightforwardly oppositional subculture. They tend to discuss their experiences of marginality in terms of geographic location (neighborhood), gender, ethnicity, and age. They do not define themselves solely in contrast to Anglo middle-class society. Consequently, many of the girls' values overlap significantly with the values esteemed by Anglo middle-class society.

Rather than rigidly defining themselves in opposition to Anglo middle-class norms, the girls are cultural pragmatists who use their bicultural status to their advantage:

LYDIA: I told my mother it's not like in Mexico. We live in America, and here you are supposed to go out on dates. She thinks that it's bad for girls to go out with boys, but I keep telling her that's the way it is in Mexico, not here.

IRIS: That's the difference between whites and Mexicans. If you were Mexican, your mother would already be a grandmother five or six times over already. We get married young. That's the Mexican way. I got married when I was eighteen, but for us that's not too young to get married.

They often choose to emphasize one aspect or another of their bicultural identities, depending on the circumstances.

This type of cultural pragmatism—picking and choosing cultural values, stretching existing norms to fit the circumstances—is the way that most people live their lives. The girls associated with this study are no exception. They attempt in a variety of ways to create for themselves a comfortable social identity. They must do so, however, within the constraints of cultural and structural limitations associated with their social status as young, unmarried, working-class Chicanas. This book is an attempt to explore the cultural roles and patterns that illuminate working-class Chicana adolescents' behavioral choices, but to do so with an eye toward other characteristics that underlie and help shape these cultural values: economic status, racial and ethnic stratification, and "mainstream" ideals.

NOTE

1. In fact, lavish parties may do more to enhance a family's socioeconomic stability by strengthening social ties to others in the community. Most of the families in the *varrio* did not have the capital required to access formal economic institutions. Since banks required collateral for loans and minimum amounts of money to secure saving and checking accounts, the economy of the *varrio* was based on the sharing of resources. *Comadres, madrinas* (godmothers), *padrinos* (godfathers), aunts and uncles were all expected to contribute to weddings, birthday parties, and graduation parties. Informal loans were secured through the practice of *cadenas*, where several people would get together and contribute a small amount of cash weekly, then obtain the entire pot of money when they needed the extra cash.

Chapter 3

Setting and Methodology

Westhills is a coastal community with a total population of 140,000. It is located between San Diego and Los Angeles, the two major West Coast entry ports for narcotics. At least two of the city's African American gangs claim the downtown area as their drug trafficking territory. Two of the city's Hispanic gang territories also border the downtown area. Unlike other coastal cities that boast trendy bistros and tourist attractions, the downtown area of Westhills is home to pawnshops and tattoo parlors. Many of the community's residents do not venture downtown after dark.

Westhills is a multiethnic community, although the Anglo population is the dominant ethnic group, comprising approximately 74% of the total population. Many of the Anglo residents of Westhills are military retirees. The Hispanic population forms approximately 22% of the population, but it is the fastest growing of all ethnic groups within the city, increasing 105% within the last ten years. The Hispanic population dominates many of the city's public schools, comprising almost 50% of the student population at Westhills High School. The city itself has three separate *varrios*, referred to as "the ghetto" by many of the community residents. Two of the *varrios*, Varrio B Street and Valle Bajo, have developed within the last fifteen years. They are populated by recent émigrés, both legal and illegal, from Mexico and Central America. The third *varrio*, Varrio Granos, has been in existence since the early part of this century. Varrio Granos is a mixture of two distinct waves of immigration, early migrant families from Mexico (1900 to 1940s), and more recent immigrants from Mexico (1970s to 1980s).

Originally inhabited by migrant farmworkers and their families, Varrio Granos is now the most "Americanized" of the *varrios*. Many of the adolescents shun the Spanish-language radio stations in favor of the stations that play the "oldies" or contemporary rock 'n' roll music. While many of the adolescents are comfortable speaking both Spanish and English, the adolescents who are unilingual speak English. That is not to say that for the adolescents of Varrio Granos, their ethnic identity as "Mexicans" is not important to them. Many of the unilingual adolescents are embarrassed about their lack of facility in Spanish, and they often sprinkle their conversations liberally with Spanish linguistic tags: "*Sabes que?* This *pinche* car ain't worth shit."

The three *varrios* in Westhills reflect national statistics that indicate that Hispanics in the United States tend to live in highly segregated communities (Orum 1986, 1988). The 1993 census data for Westhills indicate that the median household income in the wealthy, predominantly Anglo residential areas of the city is $50,000. The median household income in Varrio Granos is only $25,000. In Varrio B Street, the median household income falls even further to $17,000 (U.S. Bureau of the Census 1993) More then 60% of the children living in the *varrios* qualify for government nutrition assistance because their families fall below the national poverty line (U.S. Bureau of the Census 1993).[1] In view of the level of poverty within the *varrios*, it is not surprising that the Westhills *varrios* also have some of the highest infant morbidity and mortality rates in the region (San Diego County Offices of Health Services 1993).

The marginal socioeconomic status of the majority of *varrio* residents impacts adolescents in many different ways. For example, most of the adolescents do not have the luxury of making longterm educational or vocational training plans. For many of the *varrio* adolescents, going to college is not an economic option because their income is needed to augment their families' finances. Family obligations, such as caring for younger siblings, also limit many adolescents' participation in after-school activities.

VARRIO GRANOS

Varrio Granos straddles one of the main access roads into the city of Westhills. It is bordered on the north side by overgrown canyons that host a revolving population of homeless people. To the west lies Westhills' downtown area and Westhills High School. The proliferation of fast-food restaurants, auto shops, gas stations, and discount stores advertising easy credit is encroaching upon the area that comprises the *varrio* proper. While the area hosts several fast-food restaurants, *varrio* residents complain that they cannot get pizza delivered after dark because of the potential threat of gang activity. However, while the gang members assert a very visible presence in the *varrio*, most residents go about their daily lives with little fear or apprehension.

The Boys and Girls Club and the Senior Center are located at the southern end of the *varrio*. The disparity between these two buildings reflects the political clout of the large retirement community in Westhills, as well as the socioeconomic gulf that exists between Westhills' older Anglo population and *varrio* residents. The Senior Center is a beautifully landscaped, fully automated, air-conditioned building. Late-model Buick Regals, Oldsmobile sedans, and Cadillac cars fill the parking lot of the Senior Center. In contrast, the Boys and Girls Club is a mason block building that is located on a cracked asphalt lot where the children play soccer and basketball. Despite the fact that these two facilities are directly across the street from each other, there is little interchange between the predominantly Anglo senior citizens and the predominantly Hispanic and African American children at the Boys and Girls Club.

The hub of the *varrio*—a park, two Latino markets, a Spanish-language video store, a beauty parlor, a *tortillaria*, and a travel agency—is located within a three-block radius. The park serves as a central meeting place for the *varrio* residents and gang members. During the summer afternoons and early evenings, children and older residents gather in the park. Girls wearing midriff tops and shorts wander by, sometimes pushing baby strollers. Young boys cruise the neighborhood on their bicycles, often dressed in the characteristic gang-style clothes: white T-shirt and black baggy pants. Harried women, towing several children, hurry past the park on their way to the market or the bus stop. However, by late evening the majority of children and families are gone and the park serves as a gathering place for the local gang members. The gang members whistle greetings to each other and offer catcalls to the girls and young women who wander past the park.

Some of the homes in the *varrio* boast well-attended lawns and gardens; others are littered with rusting cars and trash. The area is a mix of single-family dwellings and small apartment complexes. Many of the utility boxes, telephone poles, fences, and walls in the neighborhood are covered with graffiti from the Latino gang that claims the *varrio* as its territory. A few of the residents valiantly fight the blight of gang graffiti by painting over the graffiti on their walls and fences. Most residents, however, do not.

Vans, station wagons, and 1970-1979 model Chevrolet cars are the most common vehicles seen on the streets of the *varrio*. Several of the *veteranos* (older gang members) have "lowrider" cars that they are renovating. The cars are usually Chevrolets with complex hydraulic systems that enable the driver to raise or lower the car. The cars are elaborately painted and upholstered. The younger homeboys, who cannot afford cars work on their lowrider bicycles. The men and boys who can afford it often compete in lowrider car and bicycle shows.

There is a Catholic church and *capilla* (chapel) located in the *varrio*. The majority of *varrio* residents identify themselves as Catholics. Most residents attend church haphazardly, although baptisms, weddings, and *quinceañeras* are important church and community events. The church also sponsors a Friday night *grupo de juventud* (youth group); however, most of the adolescents and young adults who attend the meetings do not live in the *varrio*.

Residents complain that the character of the *varrio* is changing due to the influx of greater numbers of African American families into the neighborhood. Consequently, racial tensions are beginning to increase. There have been few direct confrontations between Latino gang members and their African American counterparts; however, an undercurrent of hostility is never far from the surface. The summer of 1994, the Latino gang members began a campaign to "take back the park" from the black residents of the *varrio*.

MORENA: It's our *varrio,* man. We can't even go to the park 'cause those niggers are always there. So we're gonna start taking back the park from them. We're all gonna show up and hang by the tables so they can't come.

For the most part, the African American and Latino residents in the area avoid each other.

Many of the local county and city institutions contribute to the segregation of the ethnic/racial populations of Westhills and Varrio Granos. For example, the county-run "alternative" school is also located in the *varrio.* The small one-room school is sandwiched between a Pep Boys Auto Parts store and a nail salon. The school allows students who have been expelled from the comprehensive high schools or junior high schools to fulfill probation requirements by attending class from 8 a.m. until noon each weekday. However, while the school is located in Varrio Granos, Latino adolescents from the *varrio* are usually placed on an independent study program, rather than enrolled in the school. The teacher screens prospective students based on gang affiliation. While members of several of the African American gangs in Westhills tolerate each other, the Latino gang associated with Varrio Granos has instigated a number of violent encounters at the school with both African American students and Latino students from other *varrios.* Consequently, adolescents who are thought to be affiliated or have family ties with the local Latino gang are not admitted at the school because the teacher fears potential conflicts with the other students.

Varrio Granos is the oldest Hispanic neighborhood in the city of Westhills. It has been in existence since the early 1900s when migrant workers and their families lived in the *varrio* and worked in the nearby fields and ranches. There are two origin myths associated with the *varrio*'s unusual name. The first, and the one most residents are familiar with, tells the story of an old woman who used to sell corn hominy on the street corner to the ranch hands and migrant laborers. Thus, the laborers would "go to *granos*" on their free days. The other story relates to the poor conditions of the *varrio* roads before they were paved; the roads were covered with small rocks that resembled corn hominy. The general consensus is, however, that the name and ethnic identity of the *varrio* came into existence sometime in the late 1930s or early 1940s when other ethnic groups began moving into this area of Westhills.

Older community residents remember growing up in the *varrio* almost completely isolated from the Anglo population of Westhills.

MR. MUÑOZ: Living here was like living in a different country, a Third World country. We had dirt roads and outhouses. They didn't put sewer lines in the *varrio* until the military families started to move in the area—that was almost 1940. Even the movie theater was segregated. The Mexicans had to sit on the left side of the theater, always the left side. That didn't start breaking down until World War II. Then when the marines started coming into town, they would all sit together. They had to wear their uniforms in town, and they would all sit on the right side of the theater, no matter what color they were. Then pretty soon everybody was sitting on both sides of the theater.

High school afforded the first opportunity for many of the older *varrio* residents to interact with their Anglo peers. For the earliest residents of Varrio Granos, schooling consisted of attending the Americanization School. The school's mission was to transform Mexican children into proper Americans. This metamorphosis, whereby all Mexican children were to shed their Mexicanness, took place by immersion in an English-only environment. However, a child's facility in English did not necessarily get him or her placed in the other local elementary school.

MRS. MUÑOZ: Even if you spoke English you went there [to the Americanization School]. I say that because I asked my first-grade teacher when we had a party for her several years ago, I asked her, "If the teachers didn't speak Spanish and the students didn't speak English, how did you manage to teach?" She said that there were always a few bilingual kids in the class who would translate for everybody.

The Americanization School did not close its doors until 1954. The older residents of the *varrio* have mixed feelings about the school.

MR. CASTILLO: I missed most of my basic schooling at that school. If I'm watching *Jeopardy* on the TV, I don't know what a vowel is . . . or what's the other one . . . a consonant. . . . I never heard of those things until I grew up.

MR. MUÑOZ: I have good memories of the school, but I know people who don't. They got spanked. When I say spanked, they [teachers] spanked good. I saw a teacher break a wooden pointer—you know, the kind they had with the metal tip. I saw a teacher break that pointer on a girl's leg. The sad thing is we were getting spanked not because we misbehaved but because we were so damned afraid. We didn't understand, and when you're scared you're liable to do anything. Some people, they say we should tear the damn thing down [the school].

Some of the younger *varrio* parents think that the city should reopen the school for the new immigrant children. As one thirty-five-year-old woman told me, "At least that generation learned English. These kids aren't learning anything. They are illiterate in both Spanish and English."

Today the city of Westhills is an integrated community. It incorporates all children, both English speakers and non-English speakers, into its public school system. However, the school system at the elementary level is still segregated, with minority student populations within specific schools ranging anywhere from 37% to 90%. U.S. Bureau of the Census (1993) indicates that there are definitely "white" housing areas that are distinct from the "brown" housing areas in the city—so much so that many of the girls told me that I was their families' first "American" friend.

The city of Westhills is trying to accommodate its growing ethnic and racial diversity. The city sponsors an annual Cinco de Mayo festival that highlights Spanish-language music, Mexican folkloric dancing, and food. It also sponsors a Juneteenth celebration for the African American residents of the community. However, during the summer of 1995, the Juneteenth festival was canceled because of violence between Latino and African American gang members.

Most of the Anglo residents of Westhills assume that all of the adolescents who live in Varrio Granos are intimately bound up with the local gang. While there are families and adolescents who are affiliated with the gang, actual gang members constitute a minority of the population in Varrio Granos. The majority of families that live in Varrio Granos are hardworking and law-abiding, both citizens and noncitizens of the United States. This is not to say, however, that the gang does not impact the lives of the *varrio* residents. The gang represents a glamorous alternative to the drudgery and poverty that many *varrio* adolescents perceive as their prescribed future life in the *varrio*. Consequently, many girls and boys are attracted to the gang, or at least their romantic ideal of the gang. However, most grow out of their fledgling gang membership sometime before their middle to late teens. When I asked the girls why they stopped spending time with the gang, most could not provide any concrete reasons. For the most part, their decisions seem based on a disenchantment with the realities of gang affiliation: "I guess I just had better things to do with my life than go to jail."

GANG HISTORY OF VARRIO GRANOS

Varrio Granos has a long history of gang involvement. Los Sureños Locos, the male gang affiliated with Varrio Granos, claims to have originated in the 1920s. While the tradition of gang affiliation within the *varrio* does have a decades-long history, it is unlikely that the present gang has direct historical ties to the earlier *varrio* "gangs." Most of the pre-1970s gangs affiliated with the *varrio* never passed the incipient stage of gang formation.

In the 1930s a gang called the Black Legion had a short-lived existence.

MR. MUÑOZ: You know the way it is. Three guys get together and they say join us or we'll beat you up. Then they have five guys . . . then seven guys. They beat me up when I was just a little kid. But my dad and my uncle put me in the car, everyone knew who these boys were, and they drove me to the leader's house and showed his mom the mark that he left on my back with their belt buckles. . . . After that, the Black Legion gang disappeared.

In the 1940s the *pachuco* style became popular in Varrio Granos. *Pachuco* is the name given to second-generation Mexican Americans in the 1930s and 1940s who wore zootsuits and spoke a mixture of Spanish and English. Vigil (1988a) identifies *pachucos* as an incipient form of adolescent gang culture. However, although the *pachucos* can be considered a forerunner to the *varrio* youth gangs, the *pachuco* "gangs" never developed into more than social youth groups.

MR. MUÑOZ: It was more a clothing style here than any kind of gang. It was just a group of guys who took a lot of pride in their clothing. They looked sharp. They had shiny watch chains that they wore across their pants. The chains used to be shined from one end to the other—things like that. Then they disappeared, and there wasn't anything until recently with the gangs.

In the 1950s youth "clubs" were popular in the *varrio*. There were two clubs for the neighborhood girls and one for the boys. The youth clubs functioned mainly as social groups. One adult member of the boys' club recalled pulling pranks and engaging in some gang-style activities:

MR. GUERRERO: We hung around in a group . . . stealing hubcaps, drinking wine together, and on Friday nights, we knew there was going to be a fight. . . . We didn't shoot up heroin, didn't do drive-bys. It's much more strenuous and stressful to be a *barrio* teenager now. I understand the power and unity that comes from being in a gang, there's always someone there to back you up. In the 1950's we were the only Mexican barrio. We used to drive down to the USO and flip off the marines, usually *los Tejanos* [Texans]. The Mexican marines, they would follow us and we'd take them to the park where we'd have fifty guys waiting for them. There was a guy who worked for parks and rec, and he integrated us into the community. He set up dances for us, sports, and taught us Robert's rules of order. It was real tough because the guys just wanted to drink beer, and we would try to have these meetings with Robert's rules and spend an hour and a half setting up the meeting arguing that we couldn't drink beer until after. . . . There was a girls' club, but we didn't do much with them. I think we were too insulting to them. We were more interested in getting a reputation for ourselves as a good fighter.

The girls' clubs were less ganglike than the boys'. An adult former member of one of the clubs described their activities:

MRS. MORENO: It was a club for kids not interested in school activities. Mr.— organized the club into parties, dances, fund-raisers. We were in parades—you know, girls in bikinis riding on the cars. We also had picnics. Some of the girls couldn't get along, so we split into two groups. We were rivals but not fighting; it was just competitive. If there was a queen contest, we both had contestants. We had sweaters made. Nowadays if kids did that, they would be a gang. We were just a club. It's so much different now. We were so innocent; we didn't think so at the time of course. We took things very seriously then. I feel so sorry for the kids today. They are really missing out. It was a learning experience, not just fun. We had to learn to have meetings, to write bylaws, to go to city hall to get permission so we could use the park for meetings.

The 1950s girls' clubs were based on more traditionally feminine activities. No one was able to remember how or when the clubs dissolved. Most left the club after high school graduation, although a few girls had to resign their membership because of pregnancy and early marriage. Today there are no such social groups for adolescent girls in Varrio Granos.

It was not until the 1970s that Los Locos adopted its name and claimed Varrio Granos as its territory. Like the girls in Miller's studies (1973), traditionally the female gang members in Varrio Granos were auxiliary members to the male gang. Even as late as the latter part of the 1970s, female gang members acted primarily as gang molls for the male gang members.

MELBA: The homegirls, we hung out together, but we sorta stayed in. There was like fifteen of us. If the guys were gonna do something, then all the girls were going to be at the house they left from, waiting for them to get back. Most of us already started having kids and having families. So basically a lot of us had to stay home. Most of the girls weren't into the fighting. I was, but most weren't. Back then it was mostly sniffing toluene, eating reds, eating acid.

In the early 1980s, the homegirls started becoming more actively involved in gang activities.

HUERA: There was no place for us to go, you know so then everybody started kicking back and going to different towns. There was nothing else to do. It was like, fuck you, there's nothing for us to do. They don't have nothing for the girls to do, and it's good enough for the guys, then it's good enough for the girls. They're not going to let themselves be let out of anything. Who wants to go bowling? There was only five out of the whole clique that was real into it. But there was nothing for us to do, nothing—just follow the guys around. If the guys did the robberies, we went, too. I always drove.

Today the homegirls of Varrio Granos are much more involved in criminal and violent gang activities than previous girl gang members.

INDIA: There was less girls in the gang back then. The girls are more into the gang now. I guess girls are tired of the guys pushing them around and all that. It's hardly never with the homeboys and the homegirls 'cause the girls get together. When you go with the guys, they always want a part of it. Like "I did this and I did that." The girls, we go even.

LD: So you split any money you get with the girls, but you don't share with the guys?

INDIA: No, we don't give it to the guys. Well, it's like sometimes we hang out together, but when it comes to doing things, the homegirls do their own thing and the homeboys do their own thing. Once in a great time, the homeboys, too, and the homegirls are going to do it.

The present-day homegirls of Varrio Granos are also much more autonomous than their predecessors. However, despite the autonomous nature of their specific gang-related activities, the girls measure their success by male standards of respect and often defer to male authority.

METHODOLOGY

The greater part of my fieldwork was conducted from June 1993 through January 1995 in Westhills, California, with a total population of 140,000. I had initially planned to broaden my ethnography by working in all three of the *varrios*. However, hostilities between gangs, their territories delimited by the three different *varrios*, restricted my access. Consequently, I did most of my research in Varrio Granos.

During the initial phase of my research, I concentrated on meeting and interviewing community activists who were involved in both youth-oriented programs and gang intervention programs. It was very difficult for me to explain my interest in the *varrio* to many of these people. As a white woman with little stake in the community and no set status or identity, I was usually greeted with more wariness than friendliness. Eventually, I made arrangements with the principal of

Westhills High School to exchange tutoring services for the freedom to sit in classes and interview students. My affiliation with the high school proved to be a great boon. My status as, *La maestra*, or the tutor, satisfactorily explained my presence to most residents of the *varrio*: "Oh, that's Andrea's tutor. She comes by to help her with her school work." My affiliation with the school also provided me with an opportunity to negotiate the school district's formidable bureaucracy on behalf of the students and their parents. However, because my tutoring obligations were limited, I was able to visit with students in the mornings, at lunch, and after school hours. My roles as tutor, researcher, friend, and confidante were never distinct.

At the beginning, my presence at the school was a source of confusion for both the students and faculty. Because I dressed very casually at school, usually in jeans, T-shirts, and tennis shoes, I was perceived by most of the students as an adult, albeit a strange adult. I did not fit into their perception of an adult because I was not an authority figure and because I protected their confidences. This position of quasi adulthood was at times a difficult role to play. The students would often test my loyalty to them by placing me in awkward positions—for example, by stealing from a teacher's desk while I was in the room or getting me to ditch school with them. Sometimes they confided secrets to me that were difficult to keep. Other times they participated in dangerous behaviors that were difficult to watch. At times I found myself giving advice, both solicited and unsolicited, in what I hoped was a nonparental manner. I tried to temper my advice with phrases such as "I would never tell you what to do, but . . . "

My quasi-adult status also made some of the teachers and administrative staff uncomfortable. Several faculty and staff members thought that I was pursuing a secret agenda and made their hostility to my research project known to me. However, the majority of faculty and staff were very supportive, allowed me to visit their classrooms and meet with their students, and provided me with interview data on their own time.

The majority of the girls involved in this research project are first- and second-generation U.S. citizens. Throughout the research project, I conducted formal and informal interviews with the girls. Sometimes these interviews were conducted with an individual alone, but more often than not, in a small group. Most of the adolescents responded positively to my questions. Rarely did they have an adult listen to them as attentively as I did or take their answers as seriously.

Interview data were either tape-recorded or recorded in hand-written notes. Circumstances often dictated the method. Usually, because of the background noise and the natural ebb and flow of activity, it was more effective to record notes by hand. When I returned home, I would transcribe my hastily scribbled notes onto my computer and fill in the pertinent details of the conversations or social interactions. Of course, when recording conversations by hand, it was not possible to capture entire conversations accurately. Therefore, I would concentrate on conversational snippets that I found particularly revealing or intriguing. I would take care to record these snippets verbatim in my notes while taking abbreviated notes on the other areas of our conversations.

Interviews and most conversations were conducted in English. In instances where Spanish was used by the informants, I have recorded the Spanish phrases in the quotations and provided English translations in parentheses. While the formal interview sessions were very informative, I found that the time I spent hanging out with the girls as their friend and confidante was much more revealing. The fact that my role was not defined exclusively by my status as researcher presented somewhat of a dilemma for me. While I did not hide the fact that I was doing research, most of the adolescents thought that I was only doing research when I had my notebook or tape recorder out. Often, I found myself surreptitiously scribbling in my notebook after concluding a conversation with someone, too embarrassed to take it out during our casual encounter, yet not willing to let the opportunity pass without recording the conversation.

The girls were as curious about me and my lifestyle as I was about them. They were fascinated that a married, twenty-nine-year-old woman would have the freedom to spend her time with teenagers. I sometimes felt that I answered as many questions as I asked during interview sessions.

Throughout the research, I was careful to develop an androgynous identity. I never wore makeup, nor did I wear dresses or skirts to school. While I spent most of my time with girls, I also interviewed boys or accompanied girls and their boyfriends to places. It was important that the girls did not perceive me as a threat to their romantic entanglements. In spite of my intentions, however, I sometimes found myself castigated by girls for spending too much time with a particular boy. For example, after I spent several class sessions tutoring Pablo, Marissa confided to Lourdes that she thought I was trying to "take Pablo away" from her. This created some tension between Marissa and myself, which we eventually resolved.

Because I became a friend, as well as an adult confidante, I was invited to participate in a great deal of their lives. I sat in classes with them, played truant from school with them, and attended their parties and family gatherings. However, I chose not to live in the *varrio*. Instead, I commuted to the neighborhood everyday. Going home to my own space was a necessary emotional respite for me. Sometimes I found the reality of these girls' lives so overwhelmingly depressing that I needed some time away from them and the *varrio*. I also needed to spend time with my adult friends, friends who were not constantly pressuring me to buy beer for them (I never did) or drive them somewhere.

My contacts within the *varrio* grew as the girls I met at Westhills High School introduced me to their friends and families. It was through this type of informal networking that I was able to make contacts with the gang-affiliated girls. My relationship with the Sureñas Locas, the female component of the local gang, however, did not evolve into the same intimate friendship that I developed with the nongang adolescents. While the nongang girls would frequently invite me to join them in their escapades, the gang girls did not. I spent most of my time with the Sureñas Locas in front of India's apartment, conducting interviews or "kicking it" with the rest of the homegirls (gang-affiliated girls). Because of the legal ramifications presented by witnessing illegal activities, I was somewhat relieved to have been excluded from these activities by the homegirls. The fact that I did not participate actively in the gang does bring into question the veracity and accuracy of this account of gang life. For the most part, I assumed that the gang affiliated girls told me the truth. They seemed genuinely interested in accurately sharing their points of view for "my book." So much so that they often argued among themselves about the right answer. Both the gang affiliated girls and the nongang girls were given a draft of this manuscript to review. While there were some points of disagreement (e.g., the gang-affiliated girls did not want me to keep the nongang adolescents' comments in "their" chapter), for the most part they agree that I have written an accurate account of their opinions and lifestyles. However, because I worked with adolescents, some of whom are on probation, I have taken care to protect their identities. All of the names of individuals and places have been changed. In some instances, I have also omitted certain characteristics that I felt might be used to identify particular individuals.

NOTE

1. While the national poverty line is set at $11,890, this number does not reflect the high cost of living in southern California. A more realistic poverty level for a Californian family of four would be closer to $19,882. (Fellmeth, Kalemkiarian, and Reiter 1994).

Chapter 4

The Girls in the "Hood"

The following are brief life histories for seven of the girls that you will meet throughout this book. These girls were some of my most regular adolescent "informants." The girls described themselves as "playing" at being gang members; only two have affiliated with the local gang.

LYDIA

Lydia is one of my favorite people. She is bright, friendly, loyal, and very strong willed. She lives with both of her parents and two younger brothers. The walls of her family's home are covered with photographs of the Camarena children as well as other relatives. Mr. Camarena's soccer trophies are proudly displayed in the living room along with the photo album and video-tape of Lydia's *quinceañera* ceremony. Mr. Camarena works as a machinist for a local company. Mrs. Camarena works on the production line for the same company. All of the food served in Lydia's household is made from scratch. While her mother does most of the cooking, Lydia is also very adept in the kitchen. Bowls of homemade salsa, tortillas, and *frijoles de olla* are almost always found in the family's kitchen.

Both of Lydia's parents were born in Mexico and the family has strong ties to relatives residing both in Mexico and the United States. Relatives are always stopping by to visit, and Lydia's cousins share the duplex that her family rents. While Lydia relishes her close family ties, she also complains that her family members, especially her parents, are too conservative and overprotective.

LYDIA: My dad won't even let me go to the prom. He doesn't want me to date. I can't even bring Carlos over to the house 'cause all my parents do is say bad things about him. So I tell my dad, if you can't be nice to him, I'm just not going to bring him over here to meet you.

LYDIA'S MOTHER: Lisa, you should tell her that her dad acts like that because he's a man and he knows how they are. So he doesn't want you [Lydia] going out with them because he doesn't trust them.

LYDIA: Dad wasn't a man; he was a player. I'm going to the prom anyway. Why should I bring Carlos over if dad is going to yell at him and say no anyway? So I'm not going to ask permission; I'm just going to go.

LYDIA'S MOTHER: See Lisa. She is too wild. She doesn't listen to us, and we just want what's best for her.

While Lydia's "wild" ways at times cause her parents great concern, she is a good kid. As Lydia tells it:

I was into the gang when I was eleven and twelve. It was like a lot of my cousins were into the lifestyle. So I dressed *chola,* and we'd stroll the hood and, you know, get in fights and stuff. But it gets real boring, doing the same stuff all the time. I'm not going to live on welfare like my cousins. My parents are real strict, too, so I just kinda stopped.

Lydia had a difficult transition from junior high school to Westhills High School. Her first year at high school she did not perform well academically. She was almost suspended from high school for coming to class drunk. Her parents never found out about the episode. As Lydia notes, "I guess later I got more serious about school."

While Lydia is not a stellar student, she gets her school-work done. She manages to pass all of her classes while working part-time, although, as she notes, sometimes she just "barely" passes.

ANDREA

Andrea is also the oldest child in her family. When I first met her family, they owned a business in the *varrio.* Her mother ran the business, a small store in the heart of the *varrio.* Her father, a crystal methamphetamine user, spent most of his time with gang members. On almost every occasion that I stopped by the family store, I would find several of the younger male gang members sprawled across the stools in front of the store's counter. Andrea's mother would alternate her time between chasing her two-year-old daughter, serving customers, and trading quips with the teenage boys lounging about the store. Midway through my research project, Andrea, her mother, and younger siblings fled to the local women's shelter after her father attempted to kill her mother. The father eventually entered a drug rehabilitation program. Andrea's mother moved the family out of the *varrio* in order to keep her father away from "bad influences." Unfortunately, the family eventually had to return to the *varrio* for economic reasons.

Andrea is very bright and vivacious. She plans to attend the local community college and eventually become an elementary teacher. Similar to Lydia, she also went through what she calls her "*chola* phase":

It's like my dad is into the gang lifestyle. He grew up in the neighborhood and considers himself a homeboy. My boyfriend is real into the gang. I want to help him, but I don't want to get sucked into the life of my mom. I was into a *chola* phase when I was younger. I only wore black colors and tried to be all hard. I guess I just grew out of it. Besides, my mom said she would disown us kids if we got into the lifestyle and drugs and everything. That sounds real bad, and my mom says she loves us and all, but she would do that. It's real bad to be disowned, and you can't see your family. My aunt is disowned, and it's real sad.

Andrea's mother exerts a very positive influence in her life. She is very supportive of Andrea's education.

My mom's real into education 'cause she dropped out [of school] when she was fifteen to marry my dad. I want to be a teacher. My mom's always telling me to stay in school. She's real into education. She's not like most Mexican moms. She wants me to move out when I'm eighteen and to be on my own. She doesn't want me to have the same life she does, you know, with the troubles with my dad and everything. She says she would rather I date and live with a guy and not get pregnant—she said she would even get me the pills.

However, while Andrea is encouraged to pursue college, her mother often laments that she does not possess any domestic skills.

ANDREA'S MOTHER: Andrea's a good kid. She is willing, and she listens to her mother. She helps me a lot here [family business]. The only thing is, she doesn't help me at home. I tell her her husband's going to be real unhappy because she can't do anything in the house.

LD: I guess she'll just have to get a housekeeper.

ANDREA'S MOTHER: [Laughing] That's what she says—"I don't need to learn to cook. I'll hire me a housekeeper."

ANDREA: Sometimes I do my own laundry. Besides, I know a guy who says he would stay home and do the inside work if his wife did the outside work and got a job, but since he's got the job, she should do all the inside work. That's real liberated thinking, especially for a homeboy. So I'm going to go to college and get a job, and then my husband can do all the inside work. [*We all laugh.*]

While Andrea plans on having a "career," she also plans to have her first child by the time she is twenty-four years old because, as she notes, "I want to have my kids when I'm young enough to relate to them."

MORENA

I met Morena at the alternative school. Morena can be loud and abrasive, but she readily accepted me and became a very enthusiastic supporter of my project. When she found out that I interested in documenting some of the history of the local gang, she invited me home to meet her mother.

Morena comes from a family with a long tradition of gang affiliation. I never met her father; he was in jail but was reputed to have been one of the leaders of the local gang. Morena's mother, Huera, is a lot like her daughter. She can be very abrasive, but she has a good heart. She is also very lonely and isolated. Her family has disowned her because of her drug addiction. Consequently, her teenage daughter and preteen son are her closest companions. She would often call me up and ask me to come to lunch or go shopping with her.

Morena's mother was gracious enough to share her experiences as a former gang member with me in spite of the fact that she was at times embarrassed to share these stories in front of her daughter. She was concerned about her daughter's infatuation with the gang, yet she felt that it was important that Morena be able to take care of herself:

MORENA'S MOTHER: You gotta be ready to protect yourself since there ain't nobody in the world you can really trust to back you up. Sometimes I feel bad she ain't got a real childhood—she's fifteen going on thirty-five. But I don't want her dead; she's gotta learn street smarts.

Morena's mother has been a heroin addict for eighteen years. Before the end of the research project, she had enrolled in a methadone treatment program:

MORENA'S MOTHER: I started using heroin with the marines. I've been a hype for eighteen years. You start at twenty dollars a day . . . then you do what you can to get you smack [heroin], steal, rob, sell yourself. I know a woman who's fifty years old still selling herself. You never see old coke addicts, or old pcp [phencyclidine] addicts, but there's lots of old heroin hypes. I was afraid to tell my kid. When I got out of jail and they gave me my kids back . . . you know, you're afraid your kid ain't gonna like you—that she's gonna look down on you because of what you did because, let me tell you, you lose all respect for yourself with the drug. That's what I tell Morena—it'll take everything away from you.

Morena does not use heroin; however, she does snort and smoke crystal methamphetamine. Morena is also enamored with the gang lifestyle.

MORENA: I hang out mostly with the homeboys—they got more respect, you know. The homegirls, they just hang out like *chismosas* [gossips]. You know, they talk about who fucks who and brag about what they did all the time. I get more respect from the homeboys. They think the homegirls are just there to fuck and talk shit about. The homegirls are just like the guys, you know; they act like guys, like me. But the guys ain't gonna go out with them. You think a guy would go out with me; I mean, I got a boyfriend but he ain't from the hood, you know. See, I get more respect 'cause I don't need the hood, don't need nobody to back me up. The homegirls always have to prove themselves to the *vatos* [homeboys]. The *vatos* hate it. You know, they [homegirls] talk shit, like I kicked so and so's ass, but me, I just do it. I don't care if it's a girl or a guy. I don't go around starting things, but I take care of it when it's started.

Morena attended Westhills High School for two months before she was expelled for threatening a teacher. She attended an alternative school for awhile but was eventually expelled for fighting. Morena then became pregnant after a night of partying with the homeboys. She is currently enrolled in an "independent schooling" program. However, since this type of education requires great amounts of self-motivation, she is not progressing.

CARLA

Carla is a spunky, feisty fourteen-year-old. She had just started her first year of high school when I met her. She is a middle child, in a family with four daughters. Her mother is the sole support for the family because her father, a former gang member, left the family and started a second family with another woman. All of Carla's male cousins are gang members. While Carla spends time with the homeboys, she is not gang affiliated and does not express any desire to join the gang:

CARLA: My cousins, they keep telling me to stay out of the gang. They want something better for me; they already ruined their lives, so they want me to stay out. I'll back up my family, but I won't back up the *varrio*. Besides, being with the homeboys, they got no life. They can get so many girls; some of them have ten babies from different girlfriends, but they ain't gonna do nothing for your future. They're just into getting in trouble, going to jail, or you could have a baby and go to jail. What kind of life is that? My cousins, they can't change their lives. They're too old. They can't get out. . . . You always have to back up somebody, if you got the tatoos and all.

Carla is also the most politically conscious of the girls. In her textile arts class, she cross-stitched a "Brown and Proud" project. She was always challenging me, "Your kind always have money. White people don't care about us. 'Specially us pure-bred Mexicans."

Unfortunately, Carla failed three of her six classes during her first semester of high school. She did not fare much better her second semester of school and eventually quit attending classes. I would often meet Carla and several friends when they were "ditching" school at the donut shop. I drove Carla home on several occasions, but I was never invited in to her house. Carla preferred to keep our relationship hidden from her family. It would be too embarrassing, she once told me, to explain why she was hanging out with a white lady.

MONICA

Fifteen-year-old Monica lives with her mother, two brothers, two sisters, and infant niece in a two-bedroom apartment. The noise and confusion of the crowded apartment are intensified by the rambunctious play of a group of preteen boys that always seemed to be wrestling in the living room and a television set with the volume perennially turned up loudly. Monica's mother works on a production line in a factory. Her father lives in Chicago. One of her brothers is a well-known gang member. Her older sister dropped out of school after her baby was born. I first met Monica in her sophomore English class. While not a gang member herself, she has a reputation for being tough. One of the boys in the class described Monica as someone who "ain't afraid to fight. She'll maddog anybody. She'd even throw down [challenge] a guy."

Monica is a very poor student. She routinely failed her classes, and although she expressed a desire to be a probation officer, she did not apply herself to her schoolwork. However, while "having fun" was her most important priority, she was adamant about not getting pregnant too early: "I seen how hard it is for my sister, and I don't want to have that kind of life."

Monica was working at the indoor swap meet until her mother sent her to Chicago to live with her father. After three months Monica returned home.

MONICA: It was too different there. I guess I just couldn't relate to being in the suburbs. I'm not used to it. I'm more used to things here, in the *varrio*. I just relate to people differently, I guess. I just didn't like it, so I came back.

When she returned, she reenrolled at Westhills High School; however, she began to spend more and more time on the streets with her brothers' friends. She also took chances at work by "hooking her friends up" with items from the swap meet; that is, she would frequently allow her friends to shoplift items.

By August 1995, Monica was eight months pregnant. She was no longer seeing the father of the baby, a local gang member: "The baby's gonna have my name, not his." She still has plans to graduate from Westhills High School; however, she is hoping to enroll in an independent study program and get a part-time job.

MONICA: I want to move out. My mom wants me to stay, but she's pregnant, too, and there's too many people here already. My sister moved out to a government apartment, and me and my friend want to do the same thing. It's only $400 for a two-bedroom apartment. I'm gonna get a part-time job in the afternoons. I don't want to go on welfare. I'm too scared to go on welfare—they check up on you all the time. So me and my friend are gonna split the apartment and baby-sit for each other.

There is a two-year waiting list for the government-subsidized apartment complex where Monica wants to live.

INDIA

India has been an emancipated minor since the age of sixteen. She and her two-year-old daughter live in a one-bedroom apartment with her boyfriend. There are six children in her family. She moved to Westhills from northern California when she was six years old because her mother was "trying to leave problems behind." Her mother and her mother's boyfriend are involved in drug dealing. Her mother was incarcerated for narcotics offenses when I first became acquainted with India. After her mother was released from prison, she moved in with her daughter and granddaughter. Two of India's brothers are very involved with the gang. By the time she was eleven years old, India was spending most of her free time with the gang. She was initiated into the gang when she was fifteen. However, as she notes, "I was jumped in at fifteen, but I'd been a gang member for a long time before that."

One of her brothers and her current boyfriend are very prominent members of the gang. Consequently, India's apartment was a favorite hangout for both the male and female gang members. The apartment itself was very dreary. The only furniture in the apartment consisted of a weathered couch, two folding beach chairs, a bed, and a television set. India's two-year-old daughter did not have many toys. The refrigerator rarely contained more than cheese or milk. However, while the apartment was lacking in amenities, it was always clean. It was also a great place to conduct interviews because it afforded me an opportunity to meet with the gang members who were constantly showing up at the apartment.

LOURDES

Lourdes is the youngest daughter in a family of three girls. The interior of Lourdes's home reflects the importance of their family relationships. The house is festooned with framed photographs of children: cousins, various nieces and nephews, and grandchildren. Her mother, who was born in the *varrio*, is familiar with most of the parents and *veteranos* of the gang members. She is very strict with her daughters and does not want them to associate with the gang members. However, one of her daughters is currently living with one.

LOURDES: I feel sorry for her [the sister]. I tell her she's stupid, you know. When she was at our house, she didn't do any work—she had real nice nails and didn't want to mess them up. Now it's like she's a maid. Every time I see her she's cleaning the apartment or doing the laundry and he treats her real bad. She looks real bad—her nails and her hair. All she does is work.

Lourdes's other sister is married to an abusive husband.

Fifteen-year-old Lourdes has been dating the same boy since she was thirteen years old. They plan to get married as soon as she finishes high school.

LOURDES: He's ugly, but he treats me real good. He really respects me. He gets along real good with my mom. My sisters are jealous 'cause we don't have the same problems they do.

Lourdes's boyfriend has dropped out of high school and is working as a busboy at an upscale Italian restaurant in another city. However, he is studying for his General Equivalency Diploma [G.E.D.]. Lourdes loves children and wants to "have as many babies as he can afford."

Lourdes and all of her sisters are very feminine. They spend a great amount of time getting their nails done, fixing their hair (including dying it auburn) and shopping for clothes. I never saw Lourdes without her makeup on. Whenever we attended lowrider car shows or went dancing or to the amusement parks, Lourdes attracted a swarm of male admirers.

Chapter 5

Machismo and *Femeninidad*: Family Patterns in the Varrio

The stereotype of the Mexican American family is that of the aggressive, sexually promiscuous Chicano male contrasted with the passive and docile Chicana. How much is stereotype; how much is social and behavioral reality? The answer will vary from community to community, house to house, and individual to individual, because analysis of cultural patterns of behavior is complicated by real-life considerations. Culture is not uniform and static. It evolves. It is dynamic and context dependent. This chapter highlights the complex interplay between socio-economic class and culture, emphasizing the relationship between socioeconomic realities and cultural ideals. It is this interplay between cultural values and pragmatic considerations that provides the context from which Chicana adolescents construct their identities and make their behavioral choices.

MACHISMO

Machismo has been called everything from the salvation of *la raza* (Rendon 1972) to a pathologically deviant psychological condition (Madsen 1973). Social science has traditionally argued that *machismo* is a compensation for feelings of emasculation and inferiority (Grebler, Moore, and Guzman 1970; Madsen 1973; Paz 1961; Rubel 1966). The usual argument builds on the stereotype of the Mexican male: the frustrated Chicano male, socially and economically powerless, who aggressively asserts his domination in the only place available to him, at home (Mirandé 1985, 166). In his attempt to assert himself, the *macho* aggressively pursues extramarital affairs and sexual conquests, and demands unquestioning obedience from his family and honor and respect from all others.

Historically, the *macho* has been associated with aggressive sexuality, physical prowess, violence, insensitivity, domination of women, drinking, drug use, fighting, and the constant need to reaffirm and prove his masculinity to others. Some theorists have argued that *machismo* hinders the achievement and acculturation of Mexican Americans, producing families that are passive and dependent on an overly assertive male head of household (Grebler, Moore, and Guzman 1970; Heller 1966; Madsen 1973; Rubel 1966).

The counterpart to the *machismo* male is the passive and docile Chicana, "a child-like, sainted mother whose purity is preserved by her husband" (Grebler, Moore, and Guzman 1970, 363). Historically, the social science models of Chicano family structure have argued that the "cult" of *machismo* and the forced subservience of women to men have kept Mexican American women from becoming independent and dignified (Diaz-Guerrero 1975).

These culturally deterministic social science models assume that all behaviors are rigidly fixed by cultural values. In many instances, these purported gender roles may have been more ideal than real, confounding issues of culture with socioeconomic status (Andrade 1982). Early researchers of Chicano gender roles failed to acknowledge the very real phenomenon of racism, nor did they address socioeconomic factors external to the Mexican American community that may affect behavior. For example, it is possible that in an environment where racism, sexism, and discrimination hinder access to well-paying jobs, it may be an economic necessity for families to completely support the one person most capable of producing an income.

Unfortunately, the culturally deterministic framework has become a popular folk explanation for Chicano behavior even among educated individuals. Teachers and social workers especially used this model when discussing social problems such as teen pregnancy, delinquency, school dropout rates, and domestic violence. During my fieldwork, I constantly came into contact with the "It's their culture" phenomenon. For example, after attending a forum on the issue of domestic violence among Latina women, a social worker made the remark, "There's really not much you can do. It's like these women are programmed to suffer. It's their culture. They don't really want help." This type of model is dangerous, especially in the fields of social work and education, because it places all responsibility for "their" problems on "them," in effect blaming the victims as the cause of their own unhappiness.

In response to the cultural determinism of early social science literature, a form of Chicano-authored literature arose to challenge the historically pejorative view of *machismo*. One of the more vocal proponents, Alfredo Mirandé, criticizes the pathological view of *machismo,* arguing that *machismo* is a "political expression of ethnic identity that transcends gender" (Mirandé 1988, 63). Thus, *machismo* is divorced from conceptions of masculinity and provides a positive symbol of cultural pride and resistance to cultural oppression (Baca-Zinn 1975a; Mirandé 1985, 1988; Rendon 1972).

In effect, Mirandé (1985) redefines *machismo*. He emphasizes *macho* characteristics such as integrity, honor, loyalty, and bravery. He further states that the violence and aggression associated with *machismo* are both an effect of an Anglo-controlled media and a violent response to violent victimization. Unfortunately, Mirandé fails to provide any empirical evidence that Chicanos think, behave, or believe this interpretation of *machismo*.

In a later study (1988), Mirandé attempts to illustrate the diversity and complexity of values associated with *machismo* within the Chicano community. He differentiates between positive and negative conceptions of *machismo*. He argues that the positive conception of *machismo* places the woman on a pedestal, allowing women to wield a great amount of influence within the home (69). However, his study indicates that almost two thirds of the respondents held negative views toward *machismo*, defining the *macho* as an overly aggressive, authoritarian male figure. Of interest is the fact that differences in socioeconomic class had a profound impact on the respondents' views of *machismo*. There appears to be an overwhelming correlation between men of working-class status and the negative conception of *machismo*. In contrast, the men who responded with positive characteristics were classified as "professionals" by Mirandé. It may be that their experiences of discrimination and the lack of social prestige accorded to working-class men by a society that esteems high income may manifest itself in attempts on the part of working-class men to assert themselves in a more aggressive manner.

While Mirandé appropriately calls into question assumptions of *machismo* as a "unitary phenomenon," he fails to conduct any interviews with women in the Chicano communities affiliated with the study. In fact, he does not attempt to discern if *machismo* and/or male dominance is a real phenomenon in these communities at all, a flaw that several Chicana theorists have noted:

In their eagerness to dispute *machismo* and the negative characteristics associated with the trait, critics have tended to neglect the phenomenon of male dominance at the societal, institutional, and interpersonal levels. While the cultural stereotype of *machismo* has been in need of critical analysis, male dominance does exist among Chicanos. (Baca-Zinn 1982, 33)

In contrast to feminist Chicana literature, Mirandé argues that "*machismo* is consistent with equalization of sex roles within the Chicano community" (1985, 165). The conception of *machismo* as a symbol of cultural identity and ethnic pride is problematic for many Chicanas because it romanticizes the role of women, ignoring the disparate amount of influence and authority that exists between men and women within many Chicano households (Pierce 1984).

Horowitz (1983) also argues that the existence of a patriarchal ideal does not weaken the critical position of the Chicana mother. She argues that because it is culturally unacceptable for Chicano men to perform "women's work," the men are dependent on the women; this gives Chicana women significant power (Horowitz 1983, 61). However, this power is tied to the home. Women are always "wives, sisters, and mothers" (70). Census data (U.S. Bureau of the Census, 1990) indicate that 78% of Hispanic women in San Diego County are searching for full-time employment. How is a socioeconomic climate that encourages, even requires, a two-income family structure reconciled with a cultural ideal that links women to the home?

There have been studies that question the universality of a Chicano patriarchal family structure (Baca-Zinn 1978; Cromwell and Cromwell 1978; Hawkes and Taylor 1975; Ybarra 1982). One of the most important variables empowering Mexican American women within the family is her employment outside of the home (Baca-Zinn 1978; Pesquera 1984). When women work, the division of household chores and decision-making power within the family is more egalitarian. However, the type of employment—full-time, part-time, seasonal— may produce different results (Zavella 1987). Women are able to gain greater control over decision making when they are able to attain economic parity with their husbands (Zavella 1987). However, minority women do not get the same "rate of return" on their employment or education as men or white women (Segura 1984). Census data (U.S. Bureau of the Census, 1990) for the county of San Diego indicates that Hispanic female heads of households earn a median income of $12,603, as compared with Hispanic male-heads-of-households who earn $25,456. In comparison, white female heads of households earn $19,528. The majority of Chicanas are employed in occupations classified as "minority" or "female" types of jobs (Segura 1989). Consequently, these women are extremely vulnerable to economic fluctuations. Their ability to become economically independent or achieve parity with their male counterparts is severely restricted.

MACHISMO AND VARRIO GRANOS

In keeping with Mirandé's 1988 study, most of the residents in the working-class neighborhood of Varrio Granos described *machismo* in negative terms. The boys, usually the gang-affiliated boys, described *machismo* in positive terms. At best the boys described *machismo* as acting "tough," someone who could fight and had "respect in the *varrio*." It was interesting that almost all of the girls and women, with the exception of the gang affiliated girls, associated *machismo* with sexism and male violence toward women. In contrast, the men and boys usually associated *machismo* with general aggression, "acting bad or tough." They often talked about *machismo* in terms of their relationships with other boys or men. In contrast, the girls most often talked about *machismo* in terms of how it affected women. It may have been that the boys were not comfortable speaking with me, a woman, about issues of violence toward women.

While the behaviors associated with *machismo* are complex and diverse, most girls decried *machismo* as bad and a *macho* as someone to be avoided. One afternoon, four girls and I met at Morena's house before leaving on a field trip. While we were waiting for everyone to get ready, we started talking, as usual, about boys. The answers of these girls are typical of how most girls in the *varrio* perceived the concept of *machismo*.

LD: So explain to me what *machismo* is.

MYRNA: *Machismo* is when the guys think they're brave. If they're married, they think they can do with the wife anything they want. They can hit her and everything, and she can't say shit.

VERONICA: The man's word is law. That's how *machismo* is.

MYRNA: The wife stays home and has to clean and take care of the kids, and the guy can go out whenever he wants.

LD: Is *machismo* a good thing or a bad thing.

ALL THREE IN UNISON: It's a bad thing.

SYLVIA: *Machismo* is a bad thing. It's power over women in the house, that's what *machismo* is.

VERONICA: The guys think it's like being brave, but it's not. It's a bad thing.

MORENA'S MOTHER: The guys think they're *chingon* [tough] and the *ruca* [girlfriend] ain't got no say so the *vato* [man] comes home drunk and beats the shit out of her. She has to take it. They think the *rucas* are only for cooking and making babies and keeping their mouths shut. *Gabachas* [Anglo women] are more outspoken about that shit; the Chicanas are just starting to talk about it; and in Mexico, the *rucas* don't say nothing.

VERONICA: That's 'cause the women are raised like that.

MORENA'S MOTHER: There're some good things for the *vato*. *Machismo* is protecting your family and going down for each other, but not from the woman's side it ain't good. That's why I never got married. Once they get that paper, they think they own you.

Machismo is not just a cultural symbol; it is a social reality for many women. *Machismo*, in terms of male dominance over women, is a real-life experience for many of the girls in Varrio Granos.

FATHERS AND MOTHERS

Many of the adolescent girls in Varrio Granos had little interaction with their fathers. Sometimes their parents were divorced or had never married at all. Some of the girls contemptuously refer to their missing fathers as "sperm donors." Linda, whose father was in jail, and Carla, whose father had left the family for another woman, both joked that their fathers "had gone fishing" or that they were "on vacation." Fourteen-year-old Carla once confided to me, however, "You need both parents. It's real important. Like my dad don't live with us, and we got lots of troubles 'cause it's only my mom."

The girls who have fathers living in the home describe their relationships with their fathers very differently from the way that they talk about their mothers. Mothers are intimately bound up with the girls' day-to-day lives—sometimes too much so, according to the girls. The girls are most likely to identify their mothers as the most influential person in their lives. Fathers are respected by most girls; however, they are perceived as estranged from their everyday lives.

LOURDES: My dad doesn't really know what's going on with us. I love him and everything, but we're more close with my mom. I don't really talk to my dad much.

LAURA: Dads are real good with kids when they're little, but they don't get along with teenagers. I used to be close with my dad until I went to junior high. Then he stopped talking to me.

BRENDA: I always feel real sorry for my dad when my brother's not home. I think my dad gets lonely when he's gone. You know, 'cause my mom's got us girls, but my dad's got nobody. We mostly talk to my mom. We're real close to each other, the girls in the family, and my dad and brother get left out.

Girls agree that fathers love their children, but they feel that fathers are most affectionate with younger children. It was not unusual to see a father, who all but ignored his teenage daughter, cuddling and playing with a younger child or grandchild. Furthermore, it is perceived as improper for a father to be too close to his teenage children, although many of the girls wistfully commented that they wished their fathers were more understanding. The term most girls use when talking about their fathers is "respect." While the mother wields power over many aspects of the girls' lives, ultimate authority usually rests with the father. If a daughter wants to go somewhere, it is the father to whom the girls go for final permission, although sometimes they have their mothers intercede on their behalf and ask their fathers for them.

Fathers receive more respect from girls than mothers do, but mothers are privy to much more affection and information about their children's lives. For example, mothers and daughters often insist that potential boyfriends meet the father and officially ask permission to "go out" with the daughter. However, if the father denies permission, the mother and daughter sometimes conspire to subvert the father's authority.

LOURDES: My mom covers for me if I want to go to Robert's house. She'll tell my dad that she sent me on an errand or something. But then my mom, she gets mad at me for covering for my sister. You know, she tells me I should tell her, but she don't tell my dad.

This collusion between mother and daughter also helps the mother subvert her husband's authority. Lydia's father was responsible for managing the family's finances. Whenever Lydia's mother was paid, she gave her entire paycheck to her husband.

LYDIA: My dad spends all of my mom's money, and she can't buy nothing for herself unless he says so. It's not right that she works so hard and she can't keep none of the money for herself.

LD: Why doesn't she get her own bank account and put some money in it for herself?

LYDIA: My dad wouldn't allow that. That's not right that she has a different bank account than him. That's what he would say.

Lydia's mother eventually helped open a savings account for Lydia, who was working part-time at a local restaurant. The account was called Lydia's college savings, but it also functioned as a repository for Lydia's mother.

While most of the girls perceive their relationship with their fathers as estranged, there are a few girls who have very affectionate relationships with their fathers. For example, Marissa regularly goes to the gym with her father and feels more comfortable talking with her father than she does with her mother. However, Marissa notes that there are some subjects that are conversationally off-limits, for example, boyfriends: "My dad gets jealous and real mad about stuff like that."

HUSBANDS AND WIVES

All of the girls in the *varrio* assume that they will get married. Most plan an early marriage: "As soon as I finish high school, maybe I'll work a few years." A few girls were already engaged at fifteen years of age. One of the girls, Anamaría, was married during her sophomore year at high school. For some girls, marriage is an escape from their families.

ANAMARÍA: The religion just got to be too much for me. I didn't have no privacy. They were always trying to get me to go to church with them and checking up on me. I couldn't do nothing. I had to come home right after school. I couldn't even go over to a friend's house.

Anamaría married a marine from a nearby military base so that she could move away from the very strict aunt with whom she lived.

While marriage in the church is considered preferable, not all couples get married in a church ceremony: "Sometimes if you been together long enough, they just call you his wife anyway." While many girls expect to be faithful to their husbands after marriage, they know that marriage does not always ensure fidelity. One of the girls told me how her grandmother constantly "covered" for her uncle's infidelities.

Many of the married women of Varrios Granos treat the male ego as something fragile and in need of constant attention. Rosa (Andrea's mother), a thirty-four-year-old mother of three, is married to a man who has a very violent temper. During my fieldwork she was forced to flee with her children to a women's shelter in order to escape from her husband's abuse. However, after she quit working and her husband assumed all of the financial responsibilities for the family, her husband's violence abated.[1]

ROSA: My husband started going out and using drugs before we sold the business. He told me, "You're so good at that [the business] that I'm not needed." In our culture it's a big insult for a man when his wife has to work, but I didn't know that's how he was feeling. The women are supposed to stay home and take care of the family, and the men go out to work. It's like we were competing with each other. Like they think if you work that you want to be better than them. Now I stay at home, and he feels like he deserves to be treated like a husband. Before, I used to lay out his things on the bed for him and make him dinner, and now he thinks he deserves it since he's the only one working.

As Kelly (1990) notes, in many Mexican American households "the tensions between men and women result from contradictions between the intent to fulfill gender definitions and the absence of an economic base necessary for their implementation" (190). Peaceful relations in Rosa's family were achieved only at the price of a significant decrease in family income.

For the most part, husbands are to be respected and obeyed, at least in public. However, in private, wives wield influence. Marissa, one of five daughters, told me that her father wanted to keep having children until he got a son, "But my mom said that's enough." Wives usually told me that their husbands are responsible for making the majority of the family decisions, although their daughters often argue to the contrary, confiding that their mothers are the most influential forces in their lives.

Some of the young married women in the *varrio* feel very strongly about egalitarian marriages. Marilena, a young nineteen-year-old wife of one year, told me that she makes sure that her husband shares in the household responsibilities. She proudly points out that her job at the high school contributes to their family income. Her relationship with her husband is very different from that of her mother's relationship with her father.

MARILENA: I knew that I wasn't going to marry anyone like my dad, that's for sure. My dad is a wanna-be *macho*. He would spend months in Tijuana and spend all the money so that my mom had to work for us. Then he would get violent with my mom. I tell my husband, *We* have laundry to do. I think that's the way it should be if you're married. You should make the decisions together. There are still things I don't like, but I know that my little girls will have it better, and it'll get better and better until it's gone.

Although Marilena does all of the cooking, both she and her husband share financial and household responsibilities and make their family decisions jointly.

The fact that I am married intrigued most of the adolescents and adults in Varrio Granos, especially because my husband rarely accompanied me on my fieldwork excursions. The girls constantly asked me what my husband thought about my work: "What does your husband say when you go out and absorb things [*sic*]?" They were often very concerned about my husband when I went to parties without him, convinced that I had lied to him and sneaked out of the house. Many of them were appalled that I did not carry pictures of him in my wallet. The fact that I kept my family name after marriage also fascinated them, although some of the girls were never quite convinced that it was legal for a woman to retain her maiden name after marriage.

The parents of the girls were usually concerned about two things when they found out about my marital status. First, they were concerned that my husband and I did not have any children. Second, they wanted to make certain that my husband had given me his permission to pursue my work. On one occasion, Lydia's father asked my husband what time he expected me to come home from an evening dance to which I was driving several girls, then nicely suggested that my husband should arrange an appropriate curfew time for me.

My marital status both helped and hindered my research. As a married woman, the girls found it easy to talk to me about sexual matters. It also confirmed my adult status for their parents, making it easier for the girls to obtain permission to spend time with me. However, my behavior was also constantly scrutinized for signs of impropriety, especially with respect to marital fidelity. If I spent too much time interviewing a particular boy, I would often hear about it from the girls.

MACHISMO AND VIOLENCE

Most of the girls in Varrio Granos are familar with someone who had been in contact with the violence of *machismo*. Some of the girls have known this violence intimately.

Susana

Susana is a quiet sixteen-year-old with a shy smile. She is the third youngest child in a family of seven. She is the only daughter, which constitutes a hardship for her mother because there are only two of them to run the household. She and her mother have divided up the chores in the house. The mother does all of the cooking, and Susana does all the cleaning. Three of her five brothers and her father "like to drink a lot" and are "into the gang lifestyle." Her brothers are verbally abusive to both her and her mother, calling them names. "My mom can't say nothing to them [brothers] 'cause you know how they are—they just tell her to shut up and tell her she don't know nothing." One day Susana came to school with a nasty bruise on her cheek. I asked her what happened. She told me that she ran into a door. Later she admitted that one of her brothers had hit her but asked me not to tell anyone about it. Susana wants to be the first person in her family to graduate from high school.

Lucina

Lucina became pregnant right before high school graduation. Before the end of summer, she married her boyfriend. The family, however, does not like her husband, who is abusive. The family is aware of this, and the mother has "a lot of problems with him." Lucina's sister describes her brother-in-law as "real bad and real mean." Like Susana, Lucina also walks into a great number of doors from which she receives various bruises. When she gave birth to their first child, her husband told her that if she cried out during labor and delivery, he would punish her. He told her that crying was an indication that a mother did not love or want her baby. Lucina's family has told her that she can come home whenever she wishes. However, Lucina tells them that she is married now and has to work things out with her husband.

Most of the girls tell me that it is difficult to find a boy or man who does not aspire to acting *macho* with women, especially in front of his friends. However, because the characteristics associated with *machismo* are diverse, not all boys and men are *macho* in the same way. The girls describe some *machos* as "overprotective," while others are "abusive." That is not to say that all men and boys in the *varrio* subscribe to violent behaviors associated with *machismo*. In fact, many of the men and boys had little respect for men who were thought to be "woman beaters." There was, however, a wide diversity of opinion as to what constituted wife beating.

While most girls and women told me that *machismo* is a "bad thing about Mexican culture" and that *macho* men are to be avoided, women's and girls' relationships with *machismo* are often much more subtle and complex. They often collude with men and boys in the construction of *macho* men. For example, one of the most recognizable ways for a boy or man to demonstrate his love and respect for a girl was to act jealous or possessive of her. I often heard girls boast about how jealous their boyfriends were: "My boyfriend won't let me go anywhere without him. He's afraid that other guys will try to scam on me." (This also serves the purpose of affirming a girl's sexual desirability, thus enhancing her prestige.) Often girls told me that they felt "more protected" with their boyfriends than with their parents. Boys and men who do not have some *macho* characteristics—that is, who do not act tough or do not try to keep their *jaina* (girlfriend) in check—are often ridiculed by both girls and boys. Conversely, however, girls who allow themselves to be "put in check" by their boyfriends are also teased by their girlfriends. Love, power, and coercion are intricately intertwined for many of the girls of Varrio Granos.

FEMENINIDAD

Femeninidad, the feminine ideal, is associated with virginity, motherhood, and submissiveness. The stereotype is that of the passive and docile Chicana, "a child-like, sainted mother whose purity is preserved by her husband" (Grebler, Moore, and Guzman 1970, 363). Catholic images of the good woman and the bad woman, the division between Mary and Eve, are intertwined with Chicano cultural ideals of femininity (Fox 1983; Soto 1986). The traditional cultural folk models of Chicano femininity—La Virgin de Guadalupe, La Malinche, and La Llorona— serve to define a dual concept of women: the virginal and virtuous good woman contrasted with the sexually promiscuous bad woman. Good women are chaste, altruistic, and maternal. Bad women are sexual and selfish.

Marianismo, the worship of Mary as the mother of Christ, manifests itself in reverence for virginity and an altruistic model of motherhood. La Virgin de Guadalupe, an apparition of the Virgin Mary, was reported to have appeared to Juan Diego, a poor Aztec boy, on December 12, 1531. She became the protectress, the merciful mother of the oppressed Mexican people. She appeared as a Nahuatl-speaking, brown-skinned madonna, symbol of "motherhood, womanhood, nationhood and peoplehood" for the oppressed (Mirandé 1985, 137). La Virgin represents the positive attributes of femininity, the role of mother as the center of Chicano family and culture.

In contrast, La Malinche and La Llorona are historical and legendary symbols of the *malvada*; they define the bad woman (Soto 1986). La Malinche is a historical figure who lived during the first years of the Spanish conquest of Mexico. She was an Aztec woman who served as guide, interpreter, and mistress to Cortez. Chicana feminists choose to emphasize her positive qualities, for example her intelligence and diplomatic abilities (See Candelaria 1980; Fox 1983; Soto 1986). However, the folkloric tradition of La Malinche is that of a traitor and sexually promiscuous woman. She is a symbol of betrayal. She has come to represent the weak character of women, easily seduced and disloyal. The term *malinchismo* refers to someone who is a traitor or a prostitute (Soto 1986).

La Llorona, the weeping woman, is a legendary example of a woman who has violated the prescribed obligations of feminine behavior, the ideal defined by La Virgin. There are several stories associated with La Llorona. In some, she is an adulterous woman who is killed by her husband and returns as a ghostly apparition, weeping and proclaiming her innocence. Other traditions relate the story of a woman who kills her children in order to exact revenge upon a philandering husband. She returns, a tragic, weeping spirit, looking for her children, eternally suffering.

Soto (1986) and Fox (1983) argue that La Virgin, La Malinche, *and* La Llorona are an integral part of Chicano and Mexican folklore that produces a dualistic ideal of Chicana womanhood. "The message . . . is conform to your role, comply with the feminine imperative, or suffer the consequences" (Fox 1983, 22). This dual role of Chicana womanhood is also evidenced in contemporary Chicano-produced films and television (Cortez 1983; S. Morales 1983). Lawhn (1989) and Lizarraga (1985) also find compelling evidence of this duality in Chicano literature. When women are not classified as *malinchismo*, they are passive and subservient. "Women follow the lead of their men . . . [with] little or no influence over decisions affecting their lives" (S. Morales 1983, 93).[2]

The girls of Varrio Granos are familiar with this dualistic image of femininity. In spite of the rebellion and experimentation usually associated with adolescence, the majority of the young people with whom I worked are very conservative when it comes to gender roles and behavioral expectations regarding femininity and sexuality. They are expected to take responsibility for situations yet not to take control of situations. For example, the girls are adamantly opposed to abortion because "if you can't keep your legs closed, you gotta pay the price." Girls talk about "good" girls and "bad" girls, most often in terms of a girl's sexual availability or, if the girl is a mother, her lack of maternal behavior. While gang girls violate many of the cultural ideals of *femeninidad* and challenge the conventional construction of Chicana adolescent femininity, they still subscribe to a code of maternal conduct predicated on altruism and a form of chastity.

Girls from a variety of ethnic groups are often subjected to ambiguous messages from both peers and adults because behavioral expectations associated with traditional feminine behavior conflict with expectations of adolescence (Hudson 1984). Chicano and Anglo cultural ideals construct feminine behavior as gentle, passive, caring, and virginal. In contrast, adolescence is traditionally characterized by masculine characteristics: a time to sow wild oats, filled with experimentation and adventures. However, while girls are perceived as adolescents—wild, rebellious, and selfish—girls are also expected to behave, or maintain the appearance of behaving, in accordance with traditional values associated with femininity. Both adolescents and adults respond more positively to "feminine" girls.

Even within the school setting, it is very obvious that teachers responded more positively to feminine girls. Anglo or Asian girls who are described as "sweet and sensitive," who do not disrupt the class or question authority, are often pointed out by teachers as model students. At the same time, however, Chicana students are most often described by teachers as passive and unassertive: "Their culture doesn't believe in equal opportunity for women. It's hard to get them to take any kind of leadership role or participate in class." Consequently, girls find themselves struggling at the confluence of different, often contradictory, behavioral expectations.

That is not to say that the girls unproblematically internalize this ideal image of femininity. The girls use various means to assert control over their lives and bodies both inside and outside of school. However, the girls are also subjected to forms of censure that circumscribe many girls' behavior. Cultural ideals (Anglo and Chicano) that construct masculine sexuality as inherently uncontrollable require girls and women to act as moral gatekeepers, freeing the boys and men from the responsibilities of their actions, at least with respect to sexual liaisons, and subordinating girls and women by restricting their behavior.

NOTES

1. While this decision has brought peace and stability to the family, the family's economic situation has become more precarious. The economic situation in Southern California makes it difficult to support a family on one income.

2. It should be noted that these researchers do not investigate the financial constraints associated with producing or publishing Chicano films and literature. It may be that Chicano producers and authors are influenced to reproduce stereotypic Chicano gender roles by external factors, such as the need for Anglo audience appeal.

Chapter 6

Bitches, 'Ho's, and Schoolgirls: Peer Culture and Patterns of Behavior

VERONICA

Fourteen-year-old Veronica had talked about nothing else for weeks, excitedly going over every detail of her upcoming *quinceañera* celebration with her friends. This was her "coming out" party. The preparations involved with her *quinceañera* were so detailed that it had taken her mother, her *madrina*, two aunts, and herself the better part of four months to plan it. She had carefully chosen her fourteen *damas* from her closest girlfriends. Each would be wearing a purple dress as they accompanied her first to the Catholic mass, then to the dinner and reception. The fourteen *chambelanes*, her male escorts, would wear purple cummerbunds to match the dresses of the *damas*. Her mother had chosen her eighteen-year-old cousin to be her *chambelán de honor*, her main escort. He would wear a white tuxedo to match her $600 white gown. One of the local disc jockeys was hired to entertain at the reception, and the Non-Commissioned Officers' club at the military base had been rented to accommodate the 300 friends and family who were expected to attend the event. (Her mother had insisted on holding the reception on the military base as a deterrent to possible gang activity.)

After much anticipation, the long-awaited day finally arrived. As her mother escorted Veronica down the aisle of the church, every head turned to watch them. Veronica looked beautiful. Her aunt, a cosmetician, had arrived early in the morning to help Veronica with her hair and makeup. Her white dress was the stuff of fairy tales. Veronica was so happy that she seemed to float down the aisle to the altar. At the end of the mass, she took her bouquet and laid it at the feet of the Virgin Mary. Her mother brought her a pair of white high heels; Veronica changed from her flat "little girl" shoes into the high heels. Laughingly she climbed into the awaiting limousine with her *damas* and was whisked away to her reception. Celia, who was standing next to me, advised me:

When you're writing your book, if you want to know if a girl is real Mexican or more like American, you gotta ask what kind of party they had. If she's Mexican, she has a *quinceañera*; if she's more American, she has a sweet sixteen party.

Culture is the way in which we define who we are and, just as important, who we are not. For the majority of the Chicano residents of Westhills, their culture is a source of pride, a means of distinguishing between themselves and the other ethnic communities in the city. Cultural traits that may be disparaged by non-Chicanos—speaking Spanish, driving lowrider cars, eating tamales at Christmas—are perceived as positive cultural markers of identity by the residents of Varrio Granos. For the girls of Varrio Granos, the cultural values and norms associated with *femeninidad* and *machismo* are also used to symbolically define the Chicano community of Westhills. Consequently, behavior that falls outside of acceptable cultural norms of *femeninidad* is usually labeled deviant and subject to informal sanctions.

The behavioral norms of *femeninidad*, however, most often legitimate particular courses of actions that further the interests of men and boys to the detriment of those of women and girls. These values and norms are widely shared within the working-class Chicano community of Varrio Granos; however, girls and women are beginning to question the validity of some of these norms. Unfortunately, while many of the adolescent girls recognize the existence of a behavioral double standard, they do not have the resources, cultural or material, to confront it. Their powerlessness is demonstrated by girls' inability to contest labels such as *bitch*, *'ho*, and *schoolgirl*. Both boys and girls use these labels to restrict girls' behaviors.

The criteria for the labels associated with the labels of *bitch*, *'ho*, and *schoolgirl* are at best ambiguous and situational. For example, the girls would admit that sometimes they acted like bitches, especially when they were angry or upset over something. Or they would admit that they sometimes played the part of schoolgirl: "If I have something that I have to get done that night for school, then I'll turn off the phone and stay up all night and do it." However, while girls will admit to temporarily assuming the roles of bitch and schoolgirl, I did not find any girls who would admit to assuming the role of 'ho (whore): "I might be a bitch and a schoolgirl sometimes, but I'm *definitely* not a 'ho. I don't dress like one, and I don't act like one. I'd slap anybody that called me a 'ho."

SCHOOLGIRLS

From the male perspective, schoolgirls are "nice girls." They are the "girls that don't [have sex, take drugs, drink alcohol]." They are the girls that boys want to marry and bring home to their mothers. Most boys want to date schoolgirls because they "know that the girl's always gonna be with him, no matter what." These girls do not cause trouble. They do not exhibit any behavior that might be construed as aggressive in front of their male counterparts, although sometimes they can get quite animated with their girlfriends. These girls are "innocent and *pura* [pure]."

However, the label of schoolgirl or good girl, is much more subtle than the virgin/whore or good/bad girl dichotomy. White virginity is a salient marker of schoolgirl status, girls who are not virgins can also be labeled as schoolgirls. The appearance of virginity and fidelity can also confer schoolgirl status on a girl. As Wilson (1978, 68) notes in her study of working-class girls in Britain, "one-man" girls can also be "good girls." Like the adolescent girls in Wilson's study, among the young Chicanas in the *varrio*, it is socially acceptable, and oftentimes expected, that girls engage in sexual intercourse with their long-term boyfriends. Horowitz (1983) argues that this type of "good girl" status for sexually active girls results from the confluence of three characteristics that define femininity for Chicanas: virginity, deference to the male, and motherhood. Accordingly, girls are caught between the expectation of virginity and deferring to their boyfriend's desire to initiate sexual activity.

Fifteen-year-old Veronica suggests this idea when discussing her older sister's illegitimate baby:

VERONICA: I don't know why everybody was so shocked. She went out with him for five years. You gotta expect that when they been going out so long you know. It doesn't mean that she's a 'ho [whore].

Although Veronica's mother and family were very upset about the pregnancy, Veronica's sister was not disparaged for engaging in sexual intercourse by her peers. Rather, she was praised for "holding out" for such a long time by her sister and peers. "It's hard to wait that long when you really love somebody like she loved him." Love plays an important part in validating a girl's expression of sexuality and protecting her from becoming labeled as sexually promiscuous.

Girls note that there is also a negative side to being a schoolgirl. If a girl is perceived as too smart in school the label can be used in a negative way. A girl who is getting good grades in school, who participates in class, and who receives public praise and attention from her teachers is considered a schoolgirl in the negative sense.

ANA: Everyone asks me, "Are you on the honor roll?" I say, "No." Even though I am. They think, "Oh, if you're on the honor roll, you're a schoolgirl, you're a teacher's pet. . . . Nobody knows that I have a 3.4 GPA [grade-point average].

CLARISA: I think it's a good thing to be a schoolgirl but not too much of one. Sometimes my friends use it like "You're a nerd." If I tell them I have to stay home and do my homework, they tell me, "Oh, you're such a schoolgirl."

In certain situations the label of schoolgirl can act as a form of censure on the overachieving Chicana. The object is to do well in your classes but not to be exceptionally studious. Girls must walk a tightrope between success and failure.

SCHOOLGIRLS AND SCHOOLING

Schoolgirls are appreciated by their teachers because they are so "polite and docile." However, part of the negative connotations of the term *schoolgirl* involve Chicana students' ethnic identity. A schoolgirl in the pejorative sense is a girl who is acting "white."

LOURDES: A lot of Chicanos think that being a Chicano is about acting all tough, ditching [skipping school], dropping out, doing drugs, gang-banging, or anything that goes in that category. . . . People don't want everybody to think you're trying to act white. So you've gotta act Chicano.

Lourdes's comments are made in the context of a school system that provides few Chicano role models and, for the most part, ignores or devalues Chicano culture. One of the ways that stigmatized groups cope with their marginalization is by disparaging what, or who, you can never be. For the Chicano students, stigmatized cultural differences are treated as markers of identity to be maintained in the context of their subordination to Anglo cultural norms.

John Ogbu (1974, 1981, 1987, 1991a, 1991b) has studied this phenomenon among African American students. His model classifies minority students into one of two categories; students are labeled as "voluntary" or "involuntary" minorities. According to Ogbu, African Americans, Native Americans, Chicano, and Puerto Rican ethnic groups are involuntary minorities. Ogbu argues that because these students experience dominant society as discriminatory and hostile, they develop an "oppositional culture" that interprets school rules and skills as a threat to their ethnic identity.

However, acting like a schoolgirl is a much more nuanced behavior than Ogbu's analysis suggests. Ogbu's model is limited because it attempts to explain student academic performance with a single causal explanation (Gibson and Ogbu 1991). Nor does Ogbu address the issue of gender in his model. Although there is a negative aspect to schoolgirl status, it does not carry the same pejorative impact as the male counterpart, schoolboy. A *schoolboy* has purely negative connotations. By bowing to authority, schoolboys are exhibiting feminine behaviors. They are considered unmanly and open to public ridicule. Consequently, the boys go to great lengths to avoid carrying textbooks, notebooks, and any other school accoutrements. Some of the boys hide their notebooks in various nooks and crannies in the classroom and pick them up only after they have entered the class. Other boys palm off their homework assignments to female friends to hold for them. Some boys reject school completely, only showing up to class in order to socialize or not coming to class at all. For Chicana girls, it seems that some of the behaviors prized by the school and labeled as characteristics of schoolgirl behavior—for example demure behavior and deference to authority—conform to behaviors that are prized as proper feminine behavior by both Anglo and Chicano society.

Another limitation of Ogbu's model is that the model is not flexible enough to allow for individual variation. Many of the girls attempt to mitigate their schoolgirl status by displaying a wild side. For example, Carla, who categorizes herself as a schoolgirl, frequently goes on shoplifting excursions and peppers her conversations with swear words.

CARLA: I guess you could say I'm a schoolgirl. See, I got my notebook right here [She laughs, holding up her plastic notebook that she carries rolled up like a poster]. I don't drink, I don't tweak [smoke or snort crystal methamphetamine], and I'm still a virgin. Yeah, I'm a good girl.

Often these girls carry their school notebooks, but on the outside plastic cover, they insert letters and photographs from their prison pen pals. Or they cover their notebooks with gang-style art work. These girls attempt to downplay some aspects of their schoolgirl status among their peers without rejecting the schoolgirl label completely. In this manner they negotiate a middle ground between being a schoolgirl and their ethnic identity.

BITCHES AND 'HO'S

A *bitch* is a complex and confusing label. It can be applied to a girl "with an attitude," someone "who shows it off." Or a bitch can be "someone you got something against because of the way they act." Bitches are usually vocal. They are rarely intimidated and often "talk back" to authority figures and their male peers. However, bitches can also be "tight," girls that spurn the overtures of their male peers. *Bitch* is sometimes used interchangeably with *lesbian*: "She don't like guys; she's a bitch." Other times a bitch is sexually promiscuous: "I hate that bitch. She's always scamming with other people's boyfriends." Perhaps the most salient characteristic of a bitch is her attitude. She is loud, and she never backs down from a fight. Gang-affiliated girls are always called bitches. *Bitch* is sometimes used interchangeably with the label *'ho.*

A *'ho* is the slang term for whore. Someone who "sleeps around, wears skenky [sleazy] clothes and flirts with all the guys, lots of guys." Girls who have this reputation are subjected to verbal abuse, peer rejection, and sexual harassment.[1] Nobody wants to be the friend of a 'ho because your reputation could be put in jeopardy by spending time with a 'ho; 'ho-ness is contagious.

BRENDA: Those kind of girls give other girls a bad name.

MARGIE: If you hang out with a 'ho, they could think you were one, too.

However, being labeled a 'ho does not necessarily mean that the girl is sexually active; oftentimes the label is applied to a girl unjustly or because of the appearance of impropriety.

CARLA: You can get called a 'ho even if they don't know. They just want to call you a 'ho.

PATTY: If you have lots of boyfriends, the other girls will get mad at you and stuff even if you're not doing it [having sex]. They'll say you're a 'ho, and the guys will say more stuff about you. . . . The guys won't put up with that shit from you.

Girls who do not have a steady boyfriend have the greatest risk of getting a reputation as sexually promiscuous and thus being labeled as 'ho's.

LOURDES: One time I came home, and my mom saw me getting out of a car with a bunch of guys in it. She was real mad because it don't look right if you're out with a bunch of guys. But it was okay because I was with my boyfriend, and everyone knows that he's not going to let the other guys get fresh with me.

The fear of getting a "reputation" severely limits a girl's ability to be independent. Girls are placed in a position of depending on a boy to protect their reputation. Having a steady boyfriend serves as protection for a girl's reputation. However, if a girl is thought to be flirting with boys other than her boyfriend, or if she spends time with male friends unaccompanied by her boyfriend, she can run the risk of getting a reputation as sexually promiscuous. Similar to the girls in Lees's (1993) study of British adolescents, the *varrio* girls are most worried about being labeled promiscuous after ending a relationship. Lees argues that the ability of boys to tarnish the reputations of ex-girlfriends acts as a "censure against being unattached" (52). However, girls who are perceived as going from boyfriend to boyfriend in too quick a succession can also be labeled sexually promiscuous. For example, some girls told me that they would never date a homeboy (gang-affiliated boy) because once the homeboy ended the relationship, you were pressured to go out with his friends, and soon all of the homeboys "had abused you." These girls are also labeled as 'ho's, in spite of the fact that they are attached to a boyfriend.

Girls who spend time with groups of guys, like the gang-affiliated girls, are at the greatest risk of being labeled a 'ho. Because boys are perceived as being unable to control their sexual urges, girls are expected to bear the moral responsibility of sexual activity. "All guys want it," so it is the girl's responsibility to say no. A girl who spends time with guys is almost always assumed to be sexually active, as Linda suggests: "If they weren't fucking her, why else would they be with her?" It is interesting to note that girls are almost always blamed for any improper sexual liaisons by both their male and female peers.

[*We watch as one girl and six guys leave together.*]

LINDA: Those guys are gonna pull a train on her, I know it [Where the boys line up and take turns having sex with one girl].

CARLA: She deserves it then. She's stupid.

LINDA: Yeah, a stupid 'ho.

CARLA: Homegirls, they think they're all hard [serious gang members], but they're just there to get fucked by the guys.

In fact, almost everyone, with the exception of the gang girls, referred to the hardcore gang-affiliated girls as 'ho's.

However, whereas girls "gotta have a good reputation to get a guy," boys do not worry about their reputations. For boys, sexual promiscuity is considered a natural attribute.

ROSARIO: In the Mexican culture, for guys, they think getting in trouble is in their nature—you know, they're more mischievous than girls.

PATTY: All guys are like that. They all want to try and take advantage of girls, even if they're married. That's just the way guys are.

PABLO: I know you'll find this hard to believe—everyone does—but I never cheated on any of my girlfriends.

Some girls suggest that boys can get negative reputations in the *varrio* if they are perceived as the "love them and leave them" type. Margie, a bright and attractive sophomore, told me why she broke off her engagement with her boyfriend.

MARGIE: He wanted me to do it [have sex] with him. He told me "Oh, *m'ija* [literally: *mi hija*, 'my daughter' but often used as a term of endearment], I'll be with you always." Then I found out that his old girlfriend had a baby by him, and he left her. I didn't believe him after that 'cause he probably told her the same thing he told me. We were going to get married when I turned sixteen, but now I think it's a good thing we're not together no more.

Margie is more the exception than the norm in terms of assessing boys' reputations. Some girls, though, told me that boys had to be careful of their reputations:

ANDREA: They [boys] have to be careful because some girls won't want to be with them if they're like that. It's one thing to be experienced, but then you can go too far.

Rarely did I see a girl take a boy's sexual reputation into consideration, however, when it came to "going out" with him. Girls often date boys who are known to have fathered illegitimate babies. In these situations, the ex-girlfriend is almost always labeled a "bitch" and is considered the sole cause of the boyfriend's abandonment of her and her baby.

Most of the girls recognize this double standard, but because promiscuity is assumed to be a natural male behavior, they can only complain about the injustice of the double standard.

MAYRA: Reputations are different for a girl because it sticks to you. If you make one little mistake, it's like a scar on you. For guys, it's nothing.

MONICA: It ain't right. If you stand up to them they call you a bitch. If you tell someone about it and report them, then you're *una rata* [a rat], if you give in, you're a 'ho.

IRIS: If we go out with two guys, they call us bitches and 'ho's. When they do it, nothing; they say nothing about it.

The label of 'ho can have serious deleterious impact on a young girl's life. Many girls go to great lengths to avoid the reputation of 'ho.

REPUTATION

As Horowitz (1983) reports in her ethnography of a Chicano community in Chicago, it is very important to most of the girls that they maintain a public image of virginity. Most girls even avoid using tampons because they fear that they will lose their virginity if they do use them. When Arlene told me that she "gave it up" to her boyfriend, she swore me to secrecy: "Please don't tell nobody. I don't want it to get around school." Likewise, when Viviana's boyfriend wanted to know if she was a virgin, she asked me for advice:

VIVIANA: See, this is my problem: I had sex with my ex-boyfriend in the summer, before he moved to Colorado. But I don't know if I should tell Paul because if he thinks I'm not a virgin, then he would want to do it with me, or maybe he would break up with me. Probably he would break up with me 'cause you know how Mexican guys are—they all want to be with a virgin.

Because virginity is so highly prized as a female attribute, rumors and innuendo about a girl's reputation, specifically her sexual promiscuity, are the most powerful tools of censure that both boys and girls use to restrict a girl's behavior.

Girls' behavior is constantly scrutinized for any possibility of sexual impropriety. When a group of junior high school girls were confronted by a man who exposed himself, they were afraid to talk to the school authorities: "I didn't want everyone to think I was looking." While a few girls genuinely do not seem to care about the appearance of impropriety, most girls are afraid of getting a reputation. Consequently, they restrict their own behavior and avoid anything that might present a risk to their reputations. Individual girls took this to different extremes. Most girls avoided groups of boys. Some girls avoided going to dance clubs or any location where boys might be present, unless they had a boyfriend or male family members accompany them. Other girls refused to telephone or initiate conversations with boys or men. Still other girls were so timid that they avoided talking privately with their male teachers.

One young male teacher at Westhills High School became frustrated because, in spite of his numerous efforts to help his students, none of his Chicana students would stay after school for tutoring. He knew that I was working on a project with the girls and wanted to know why they would not come to his tutoring sessions. After speaking with the girls, it turned out that they were afraid that they would be the subject of rumors if they spent too much time with the teacher.

Sometimes the rumors about a girl's reputation are used as a way to limit the aspirations of a particular girl. Girls who are academically gifted, popular, or pretty are often the subject of rumors about their reputation.

LAURA: Even schoolgirls can get a bad reputation. You get it from the things you do after school, who you hang out with—things like that.

The rumors and innuendo function to maintain social equilibrium among the *varrio* girls. Girls censure their peers if they are getting "too big on themselves" or if they are "showing it off." Some of the girls had phone calls made to their homes from other adolescents who would tell family members about the girl's sexual improprieties. Clarisa, one of the brightest students, a straight-"A" student enrolled in college preparation courses, was the subject of several rumors, including an allegation that she engaged in group sex with the homeboys. Her cousin told me that she was "glad that it came out about Clarisa" since her parents were always comparing the two cousins and asking her, "Why can't you be more like your cousin?" The most damaging thing one can do to a girl "is to spread a rumor about her that ain't true." The most damaging of all the rumors is to be labeled a 'ho.

Another part of the reason that many adolescent girls are so conservative about gender roles is the fact that both the high school community and the *varrio* community are small and close-knit. People notice if a girl returns home late and with whom she comes home. Neighbors and family members will also talk about her if they think she is spending too much time with her boyfriend. Parents especially monitor their daughters' behaviors.

PATTY: The guys get to do anything they want. It's different with the guys. My parents let them do anything. But everyone's afraid that the girls are gonna get pregnant, so they have to be more strict with them.

ELENA: We were at a dance, and my dad took the whole family home from the dance early because I was dancing too close to a guy.

Even young adult women are not free of parental supervision.

IRIS: After we bought the house, I stayed in it until we got married. I wouldn't let Jaime stay over even if he slept on the couch. I was afraid that my mom would come over and tell my dad. If my dad heard something like that, he would've canceled the wedding. He would do something like, "Why do you need a wedding if you're already sleeping together?"

For many girls, their behavior is a reflection of their families' reputations.

VIVIANA: My dad cried when they told him that my older sister was pregnant. She isn't married, and he was real upset. He doesn't even want to hold the baby. It's like he thinks everybody's gonna look down on us 'cause of my sister.

MELISSA: My parents don't even let me out of the house. I can't do nothing. They're afraid if I get a boyfriend that I'll get pregnant and embarrass the family.

Most of the girls note that their families employ a much more liberal standard of behavior for their sons.

MAYRA: It's not fair. Parents get more mad if a daughter kisses her boyfriend but they don't care if the sons do it. My dad would *kill* me if he saw me kissing a guy.

SILVÍA: Families, they're real strict with the girls, and with the guys, it's, you know, you're a guy—you can do anything. Even the dads, you know, will be happy 'cause their son is going out with all these girls, but the daughters, it's not the same thing. They overprotect the daughters all the time.

CLARISA: Parents are more hard on girls. My brothers can do anything they want. They go out all the time. Me, I don't get to do nothing.

There is a wide variation in the restrictions families place on their daughters in order to protect their reputations. Some families are very restrictive. At fifteen years old, Arlene is still not allowed to date boys, nor can she have any boys over to her house. (Of course, this did not stop her from sneaking out of her house at night to visit her boyfriend.) Margie and Rosario are allowed to have boyfriends, but they cannot go out on dates without a chaperon. A few of the girls had parents who are even more liberal and place very few restrictions on their daughters except for curfews.

ANDREA: My mom said she thinks it would be better if I lived with a guy and didn't get pregnant than marry him too young. She said she would even get me the pills. She got married when she was fifteen—my dad, too. That's why they have so many troubles.

The girls place their families on a continuum from more Mexican to more American. Families that are perceived as allowing their daughters a great amount of freedom are considered the more American type of families. Families that are considered too restrictive are labeled more Mexican. [2]

There are a few, a very few, girls who do not have any dating restrictions imposed upon them by their families. These girls all risk becoming labeled as 'ho's. The girls that flaunt their freedom are often the butt of jokes and gossip. The girls that escape innuendo are usually more circumspect about their escapades. Girls who are 'ho's are almost universally talked about as coming from bad families. For example, after meeting a young woman who spoke in a very sexually explicit manner, one of the homeboys told me: "She's a 'ho. What do you expect? Her whole family's like that. That's where she learned it from."

Because family reputations are intimately intertwined with the daughter's reputation, the relationship between male family members and the girls is complex. Male family members are charged with guarding a girl's most valuable feminine asset, her virginity. For example, Andrea's father has a reputation as a violent man; this protects her from innuendo.

ANDREA: The homeboys think twice about saying stuff about me. They always respect me because of my dad. But you still can't disrespect them. I'm still careful about what I say to them or how I act in front of them.

Margie is allowed to go out with her boyfriend, but only when her older brother accompanies her. This gives her brother a position of power over her that she resents.

MARGIE: I hate it. It's like he can decide if I get to go or not. Ten minutes before, he just says no. He can change his mind at the last minute, and I can't do nothing about it.

Fathers and brothers are most often the family members responsible for the girl's behavior. When the father of fifteen-year-old Maria caught her skipping school at her boyfriend's house, he made Maria get married in spite of her protest that "nothing happened." Sometimes, however, uncles and cousins also play a role by "keeping the girl from being too wild." When Arlene ran away from home to be with her boyfriend, it was her uncle who found her and brought her back to her family.

Sometimes younger sisters are assigned to act as chaperons for their older siblings. The girls usually collude to circumvent their parents. For example, Celia routinely drops her younger sister off at a friend's house when she goes out with her boyfriend.

While family members attempt to exert control over a girl's behavior, a few of the girls use their sexuality to rebel against their families and resist their ideological construction of femininity as chastity. These girls sneak out of the house at night to go "cruising with guys" or to meet with their boyfriends. Unfortunately, they often pay a high price as a consequence of their actions, most often unplanned pregnancies.

SEXUAL LANGUAGE

In her book *Sugar and Spice*, Sue Lees (1993) documents how the masculine-controlled language of abuse places women in a position of dependence on men. Similar to Lees's findings among British adolescents, the girls with whom I worked have little vocabulary with which to control or censure male behavior, while boys are equipped with a varied and graphic vocabulary with which to censure female behavior. When males control the "linguistic capital" (Bourdieu 1977) of sexist language, this leaves girls a "muted group" (Ardener 1975, 22).

RAÚL: You could call her a bitch, a five-buck special, a main street bitch. You could tell her to go stand on the street corner. If you call a girl a 'ho, that's a good one: a slut, a skenk, a mudduck. You can call them animal names, too.

SYLVÍA: Guys don't say nothing about guys. See, guys get a reputation from girls, but girls get a reputation from guys and girls. You hear girls called all kinds of names, but not the guys.

ANDREA: Lots of guys say things about girls. Like I did this with her you know. . . . I can't think of any for guys. It's a double standard, I guess. Maybe you could compare him to your ex-boyfriend—I read in a magazine that guys don't like that.

In contrast to the work of Holland and Skinner (1987), who argue that women have as many derogatory words for men as men have for women, the girls in the *varrio* have a very limited vocabulary with which to ridicule boys. Furthermore, their vocabulary does not have the same impact as that of the boys' vocabulary; calling a boy an asshole does not have the same impact as calling a girl a 'ho. Whereas a boy can deny the label of "asshole," girls often feel powerless when it comes to counteracting sexual harassment.

ARLENE: You could deny it, I guess, if they called you that ['ho]. But sometimes that just makes it worse. Mostly you just try and ignore it and know that your real friends aren't gonna believe it.

This feeling of powerlessness is compounded by the haphazard enforcement of sexual harassment policies in school. In some instances, accusations of sexual harassment were handled expeditiously by the school administration. However, other times the outcome was less than acceptable. Lupe, a bright, shy sixteen-year-old, left her math class in tears because a group of boys in the class were "saying things about her." Most of the comments they made referred to her breasts. Lupe reported the incident to one of the Latina teaching assistants because the teacher had done nothing to stop the harassment. Lupe was too embarrassed to approach her male teacher about this problem. The teaching assistant brought the very distraught Lupe to one of the school counselors, who listened sympathetically, then sent Lupe back to class. Lupe then resorted to what she felt was her only other option: She stopped going to her math class. Eventually, the boys who were the cause of the harassment quit going to class, and Lupe returned. However, by that time her grades, had suffered.

Julia Stanley conducted a study in which she noted that while she was able to identify 220 words connoting the sexually promiscuous woman, there were only 20 words for a sexually promiscuous male, many of which were not necessarily derogatory terms (cited in Spender 1980, 15). Muriel Schulz (1990) identified 1000 words and phrases that describe women in sexually derogatory ways. She notes that "there is nothing approaching this multitude for describing men" (143). This imbalance in linguistic terms is important because it normalizes the structural imbalances between male and female relationships.

However, it is not just the terms themselves that constitute "sexism." The tone and context in which the terms are used are an integral part of the boys' sexist talk (Wood 1984, 58). As Julian Wood notes, "It is the use of terms . . . combined with the intent to assess the girls in crude and superficial ways that constitutes the element of attempted domination." Boys routinely scrutinize girls' bodies and characteristics and make public remarks about their value.

When I was researching the various terms available for boys and girls to insult each other, one classroom discussion got out of control with boys pointing out specific girls , the one over there—you could call her a frog because she looks like one." I tried to temper the discussion by asking the boys if they would like it if someone did that to them. Their answers are very revealing:

JOE: Guys don't care if girls say something about them. If a girl says something about me, all I have to do is call them a 'ho, and they'll shut up.

JORGE: I wouldn't care. Besides, girls are too scared to make fun of us.

The boys are very cognizant of the power they hold over girls via any implied threat to a girl's reputation. As for the girls, once they become labeled sexually promiscuous, their options are limited.

LD: What could you do if someone started a rumor about your reputation?

SUSANA: I don't know. I guess you can try and explain yourself. It's worse if the guys are saying it. I don't know what you can do. That's never been on me. Nobody's never said nothing about me like that.

LD: What would happen if you went up to them and accused them of lying?

SUSANA: It would get worse if you did that. Like when I was walking with Viviana past a group of the homeboys, and they started saying, "Oh, she's got a fat ass" and "She's got little tits," I got real mad.

LD: What did you do?

SUSANA: Nothing. If you say something to them, you know about down there [she points to her crotch] then it just makes it worse. They say even worse things to you.

There are girls who are willing to take a risk and confront boys when their reputation is at stake:

MARGIE: When I was at the other school, some of the guys started a rumor about me and my cousin. Saying that we were lovers. So on my last day, I found out who was saying it, and I stepped up to him. Told him to say it to my face. My cousin was there, too. The guy said that he never said nothing. That's what I'd do if it happened again—I step right up to them in front of their friends and everything and make him put that on. And the guys are shocked when you do that 'cause they don't expect a girl to step up to them like that.

However, while Margie tells the story about "stepping up" to a guy, it is interesting to note that her male cousin was present when she confronted the boy whom she perceived as the source of the rumors and that she chose the last day of school to make her stand.

The power of male-dominated sexist language is derived from its normalizing function where "power's hold on sex is maintained through language, or rather through the act of discourse that creates, from the very fact that it is articulated, a rule of law" (Foucault 1990, 83). Once a category is identified and given a name, like bitch or 'ho, the category is imbued with the appearance of permanent reality. For both the girls and the boys the categories of bitch, 'ho, and schoolgirl are really real types of people. Whereas male sexual promiscuity and aggression are perceived as a normal and natural part of maleness, female promiscuity and aggression are indications of aberrant females, 'ho's, and bitches. While the girls might question specific instances of someone being labeled as a bitch or a 'ho, they do not question the naturalness of the categories of bitch, 'ho, or schoolgirl. Nor do they question the absence of any similar categories for their male counterparts. *Bitches, 'ho's*, and *schoolgirls* exist because these are words that locate these categories in the real world. Conversely, because these girls lack the vocabulary with which to censure their male peers' behaviors, boys who are sexually promiscuous are "just being boys."

REPUTATION AND EDUCATION

For many girls the fear of getting a bad reputation had a negative impact on their education. The girls with whom I worked limit the amount of time they spend with their male teachers. They often do not seek out special help or tutoring from male teachers, even if they are failing classes, because of fears that "people would talk." This is especially problematic at Westhills High School because the majority of teachers are men, especially in the math and science departments where girls traditionally have the poorest grades.[3]

Sometimes parental concerns about a girl's reputation can impede her access to educational resources. For many girls, school-sponsored field trips are a source of contention between them and their parents. As one high school teacher noted:

When we go on trips, I am very strict. I don't let family members come unless the mother loads them on the bus, especially with "cousins" of the opposite sex. I tell the kids, "Don't mess up my reputation." It's important because a lot of girls can't go out—that's the Mexican way—but they can go on a trip with the club because the parents respect me.

For some parents the school itself is perceived as a threat to a young girl's reputation. After the first semester of ninth grade, fourteen-year-old Patty's parents sent her to Mexico to stay with relatives because "she was getting into boy trouble" at school. It is interesting to note that while some parents are willing to pull their daughters out of school because they are meeting boys, very few parents choose to contest the mandatory sexual education curriculum.

SEXUAL EDUCATION

At the time I conducted my fieldwork the sex-education curriculum was fairly progressive. Topics such as fetal development, birth control methods, masturbation, homosexuality, domestic violence, and rape are all discussed in the classroom. The classes are coeducational. The classes are usually, but not always, fairly balanced in terms of gender, with an equal number of boys and girls in each classroom setting. However, in these classes, also predominantly taught by male teachers, girls rarely make comments or ask questions. This is especially evident during discussions about contraceptives.

Although most of the birth control methods discussed in the classes are designed for use by women, only the male students appear to take an active interest in the birth control methods. During one class, the teacher passed around different forms of birth control for the students to examine. While the boys studied, squeezed, pinched, and pulled the condoms, IUDs (Intrauterine devices), diaphragms, and so on, the girls passed the items with barely a glance. Watching a diaphragm being quickly passed from one girl to the next, I was reminded of the child's game of hot potato. The girls could not get rid of the diaphragm fast enough. After the class, I questioned some of the girls about my perspective of this incident.

SELINA: The girls don't want the guys to look at them and think, "Why is she asking about birth control?"

LD: Why?

SELINA: The guys might think she wants sex if she asks about birth control. She's embarrassed, so she don't say nothing in class.

Most of the girls agree with Selina; girls who ask about birth control or appear too interested in sex education class can be subjected to rumors about them. Unfortunately, this behavior often leaves the girls without the knowledge or means to protect themselves from venereal disease, pregnancy, and AIDS (acquired immunodeficiency syndrome).

However, some girls have a different interpretation about their lack of interest in sex education.

LETY: Girls don't ask about that stuff because it's the guy that's supposed to know about that.

Like Lety, many of the girls deny any responsibility for planning sex and/or providing contraceptives to their boyfriends.

In part, the girls' denial of responsibility rests on the assumption that girls who plan on having sex are 'ho's. However, Chicano cultural norms of behavior that define certain actions as bitchlike or 'holike also affirm Anglo ideals of femininity that define appropriate feminine behavior as behavior that is not too aggressive, too independent, or too sexual. The girls find a great deal of support for their beliefs from outside the Chicano community. For example, television, movies, and popular magazines often depict sexually assertive girls as synonymous with sexually promiscuous girls.

The girls' denial of responsibility also affirms real-world inequities where men earn more money than women and overwhelmingly occupy positions of leadership and authority. Consequently, it seems natural for a girl to depend on her male sexual partner to take responsibility for their sexual encounters.

NOTES

1. Some girls actively engage in behaviors that mark them as 'ho's despite the negative image associated with the label. One social worker suggested that often these girls are victims of sexual molestation: "Sometimes the best way to make sure you are never raped again is to say 'yes' all the time."

2. For many of the recent émigrés from Mexico, the social environment of Westhills is perceived as too liberal and permissive for their daughters. A few parents even refuse to let their daughters attend public high school because they feel that the social environment promotes a potentially dangerous mixing of the sexes.

3. Many of the girls' relationships with their male teachers were also exacerbated by their experiences with authoritarian and intimidating adult men.

Chapter 7

Sex and Love

ARLENE

I first met Arlene at the beginning of her sophomore year in high school. People notice Arlene because of her striking appearance. She has both European and Mayan ancestry that combine to form her unusual features. Arlene is tall, fair skinned, with long, thick brown hair and almond-shaped brown eyes. Because of her clothing style and heavy makeup, I initially thought that she might be a gang member. However, Arlene soon set me straight:

ARLENE: I could be in the gang, but I'm smarter than that. There's only two ways you go when you're in a gang: jail or dead. I know them all [the gang members], and like if you respect them and shit, they're cool with you. Only if you squeal with them do you get problems.

At the time of our acquaintance, Arlene lived in the *varrio* and knew most of the gang members. She had even dated one, in spite of the fact that her parents had forbidden her to have a boyfriend.

Arlene is the oldest child in her family and the only daughter. Her parents, both born and raised in Mexico, are very strict. Arlene was born in Westhills and has spent her entire fifteen years in the United States. She and her parents often argue about what is considered appropriate behavior for good girls. Arlene's parents forbade her to visit with boys or even speak to boys on the phone. Her mother told her that it was improper for girls to approach boys. However, at school, Arlene was known as an incorrigible flirt. In spite of the fact that Arlene's parents had forbidden her to have a boyfriend, she had two, although one of them was "locked up" during most of our acquaintance.

I met Arlene in a college preparatory class; however, she was not a good student. She failed three of her classes the first semester of the school year. Despite the fact that she came to school regularly, she was not planning to go to college. She wanted to be either a fashion designer or a cosmetologist. She often talked about high school graduation in terms of "if I graduate." As with many of her peers, Arlene came to school to socialize. School offered her an opportunity to escape the restrictions placed on her at home.

According to Arlene, her life at home was difficult. Her mother was a strict disciplinarian—so much so that Child Protective Services (CPS) had been called to the home twice during the year. Unfortunately, CPS rarely removes teenage children from the home unless it involves sexual molestation. Consequently, in spite of the bruises on Arlene's legs, she remained at home, although she and her mother were required to attend counseling sessions together.

Arlene and I became good friends. Sometimes we would spend lunch-time together talking and joking. A few times we ditched school with several others, climbing over the wall to spend the day walking around the town. During some of these escapades, Arlene would make arrangements to meet with her current boyfriend. Later she would come to class with hickeys, bruises from her boyfriend's kisses, on her neck. She would pull up her sweatshirt or coat or arrange her hair in order to hide them, but everyone always knew. I would often tease her about them. The thrill, according to Arlene, was not found in getting the hickeys; rather, it was found in hiding the hickeys from her parents. Arlene and her friends would often regale each other at school with stories of close calls, incidents where their parents almost saw the hickeys.

At the time of our first acquaintance, Arlene's current boyfriend was a twenty-year-old man who lived in the rival *varrio*. According to Arlene, he had two jobs, a truck, and a high school diploma: "A big change for me compared to the guys I usually go out with." The boyfriend who was incarcerated in jail was a gang member. She enjoyed the danger associated with having two boyfriends from two different *varrios*.

After several months, Arlene's twenty-year-old boyfriend told her that he wanted her to have his baby.

ARLENE: He told me, "I bet that you have my baby before you graduate."

LD: What did you tell him?

ARLENE: Maybe.

LD: What? Are you crazy?

ARLENE: Well, I think I will. I really like him and I'm kind of stupid. Besides, I want one [a baby] sometimes. And I don't care what people say.

LD: Would he marry you if you got pregnant?

[*Arlene thinks about it*]

MARGIE: If you have to think about it that long, he won't.

ARLENE: I think he would, but I don't know if I would. He would probably, but I don't know about me. They say that your feelings change after you give it up [lose your virginity]. I think that's what would happen to me. I mean, I don't plan to. I haven't given it up yet.

LD: Why would your feelings change?

MARGIE: Because after you give it up, the guys find out and stuff, and you lose your self-respect.

ARLENE: I would feel bad. I wouldn't want to see him no more. I'd be like embarrassed. It would be like he took something from me. If you gave it up, it would be like giving a part of yourself to the guy, and if you think about it, it ain't worth it.

MARGIE: Yeah, Arlene. Think about it. [*Margie turns toward me*] Arlene wants to have a baby. She says if she goes on welfare, she can move out of the house. She knows her parents won't take her back if she's pregnant.

Before the end of the school year, Arlene had admitted that she "gave it up." In spite of my offers to help her get contraception, she did not use any birth control.

Shortly after Arlene became sexually involved with her first boyfriend, her second boyfriend, Tony, was released from jail. Tony was one of the crystal methamphetamine dealers for the local gang. He also had a reputation for being violent and abusive toward his girlfriends. Even a few of the boys noted that "he had no respect for girls." Three days after his release, Arlene stopped coming to school. I found out that she had run away from home and was living with Tony at his family's house. According to Margie, Arlene's parents did not want her back home, "because they think she ain't a virgin now so there's no reason to take care of her. There's nothing to take care of."

Several days later I received a tearful phone call from Arlene. The police had arrested Tony, and she did not have any place to stay. I picked her up and brought her to my house. Together we tried to navigate the Social Services System in order to find out what to do for her. The complexity of the system was overwhelming for both of us. We finally located a temporary teen shelter in the area. The next day we went to the shelter to talk to one of the administrators; however, Arlene decided not to stay with them. She asked me to take her back to the apartment that she shared with Tony and his family.

When I saw where she had been living, I was appalled. The apartment windows were broken, trash was strewn all over the yard, and junked cars filled the back alley. I was incredulous. "Arlene, you want to stay in this shithole instead of going home?" We sat and talked in my car for awhile. I tried to explain to her that you can love someone who is not good for you: "He was arrested for burglary, sexual battery, and attempted rape. Arlene, what does that tell you about him?" At first Arlene insisted that the newspapers and "that bitch" were lying. Arlene countered that she knew that he had problems. She did not plan on spending the rest of her life with him. "Besides, he's been changing his ways." She argued that his family and the homeboys had been good to her. I tried to convince her to go home. She refused.

Almost six months later I received a phone call from Arlene. She was living with an aunt, and she was very pregnant.

LD: So how are things going for you?

ARLENE: I'm getting along better with my mom and all. Now she says something good to me instead of fighting all the time. Mostly it was me, you know. I didn't want to understand her. My dad and me, we don't really talk now. He's real disappointed, and all he talks about is the baby. "Are you going to put his name on the baby? Are you going to write to him?" It's like all he talks about, and I don't want to talk about it. I'm ashamed or something. So when he comes over, I just leave the house.

LD: So what are you going to do about Tony?

ARLENE: I'm not going to waste my time writing to him. It's not worth it. I wasn't even attracted to him. I didn't even like him. Maybe it was because of my mom telling me not to be with him or talk to him. The more my mom told me no, the more interesting he became to me. I don't even know why I was with him. If I had to think who I would give it up to [lose virginity], he would be the last one. I did it on purpose, you know. Probably to get back at my mom. Now I regret it so much. Now it's like I have to graduate. Before I wanted to graduate, I guess, but this has made me think. Oh man, sometimes I cry. I think I should be going out to parties.

LD: Why didn't you use birth control?

ARLENE: Because it wasn't supposed to happen. It was. Then I backed off and started crying. Then he started crying, so I gave in. He wanted me to get pregnant. Now I am, and I regret it.

There is no doubt in my mind that Arlene wanted to become pregnant. For her, as with many adolescent girls, the choice to have sex is complicated by issues of love, coercion, and emancipation.

"TEENAGE" SEX

The trend for girls in the *varrio* is toward early sexual experimentation, but this is not equivalent to sexual liberation. Although some studies indicate that Mexican American adolescent girls initiate sexual activity at an older age than their Anglo peers (Slonim-Nevo 1992), a number of the girls with whom I worked had experienced sexual intercourse. Unfortunately, early sexual experimentation, which may or may not include sexual intercourse, does not afford most girls any sense of control over their sexuality or their sexual encounters. This is due in part to the fact that the majority of teenage girls are sexually involved with older men. Often the reality of "teen sex" involves only one teenager. Teen pregnancy statistics indicate that 74% of fathers involved in teen pregnancies are over the age of eighteen (Alan Guttmacher Institute 1994a). One study conducted by the University of California at San Francisco (Brindis and Jeremy 1988) found that nearly 68% of all men involved in teenage pregnancy were age twenty or older. Even more alarming is the fact that 12% of these men were between twenty-five and twenty-nine years of age. The difference in age between the teen mothers and their adult boyfriends calls into question issues of consent.

As Fine (1988) notes, the line demarcating consent from coercion can be blurry. Even the most consensual sex is tainted by structural and cultural power asymmetries. However, I could never get the girls to agree that there existed a power imbalance between themselves and their twenty-something boyfriends. The girls responded to my arguments by telling me that "girls mature faster than boys." However, it is my contention that many adolescent girls are manipulated by their older boyfriends into having sexual intercourse. When a teenage girl, who may not even have her driver's license yet, dates an adult boyfriend who has a car, money, and the ability to buy alcohol, consensual sex may or may not be occurring within the relationship.

Many of the adolescent girls also have experiences with older men who ardently pursue them. Sometimes the age difference between a girl and her boyfriend is quite dramatic. At one *quinceañera* reception, I was introduced to a twenty-six-year-old man and his girlfriend; his girlfriend was preparing for her graduation from the eighth grade. For the most part, the girls find the attention from these older men exciting and flattering. They like the danger of dating an older man. However, they also recognize that part of their allure is based on their "purity" and aura of innocence. Sixteen-year-old Selena noted that her twenty-five-year-old boyfriend "only wants to go out with me because he thinks he's my first boyfriend."

One night I went with some of the girls and their boyfriends to an underage dancing club. Amidst the sweaty, gyrating teen bodies, there were several older men, who can only be described as predatory, at the club. These men spent their evening stalking teenage girls who came to the club without any male companions. Most of the girls at the club did not know how to handle the men's assertive advances. The adolescent girls, afraid of either hurting the man's feelings or creating an embarrassing scene, often found themselves being mauled on the dance floor. The girls would keep backing away as their older dance partner kept advancing, until the girls had been literally backed into a corner.

Many of the girls refer to sex as a girl letting the boy or man "abuse" her or "take advantage" of her. Margie kept telling me she was afraid that Arlene's boyfriend was going to "abuse her and get her pregnant." A few of the girls were not even certain if they had really had sexual intercourse: "I think I did it, but I'm not sure." Part of the way that the girls talk about sex is an attempt to guard their reputation among their peers. No one wants to be known as a 'ho. Even the sexually active girls are concerned about their reputations; maintaining the public image of a virgin is of paramount importance to most girls.

Many of the girls who confided to me that they were sexually active swore me to secrecy. Some would not even admit their sexual experiences to their best friends. During my entire research project, I only met one girl who openly advertised her sexual liaisons, Marcela. Marcela was an interesting character who commented on boys' penises, made allusions to lesbian vaginal penetration by gesturing with her fingers, and taunted the boys to "get it on" with her. She was considered crude and undesirable by both the girls and boys in the *varrio*.

At school, the girls are constantly assessed by their peers in what Holland and Eisenhart (1990) have called the "sexual auction block." They are exposed to constant peer evaluation of their sexual attractiveness and their sexual availability. On almost any given afternoon, one can see young preteen and teenage girls "strolling" the *varrio* in midriff tops and shorts, their faces adorned with bright red lipstick. Most of the girls reported that they began wearing makeup when they were eleven or twelve years old. While some girls told me that their parents forbade them to use makeup until after their fifteenth birthday, this was rare. When asked why they wore makeup, the girls said that they used it in order to "look good" for the boys. The pressure to transform their little-girl bodies into something desirable to boys and men starts at an early age for many of the girls.[1]

As Nancy Lesko (1988) argues in her study of Catholic school-girls, girls use their bodies as a symbol and locus of identity formation. Most of the *varrio* girls spend a great deal of time and money managing their bodies, making themselves beautiful. Although the gang-affiliated girls' style is decidedly more masculine than their non-gang counterparts, they, too, spend time on their makeup, hair, and clothing. Almost all of the girls bought special shampoos, hair conditioners, hair spray, and gels. These items deplete a great amount of the girls' disposable incomes. What is surprising is that the girls do not see these expenditures as luxury items.

LOURDES: They should have lowriders [a type of custom-style car] for girls, too. But women can't afford them. They cost a lot of money, and we have to buy makeup and hair spray and get our nails done, and that takes a lot of money. So we don't have money for lowriders. It's more expensive to be a girl than to be a guy. That's why guys have more money for lowriders and things.

At both the high school and juvenile hall, the majority of girls wear makeup. My own lack of interest in this area always fostered comments from the girls: "How come you don't ever wear makeup? Is it because you're already married?" For most of the girls in Westhills, beauty is considered to be a girl's main asset, and beauty is almost always equated with appearing sexually desirable to men.[2]

Most of the girls exchange control over their sexuality for control over their sexual attractiveness. Status is measured by "being popular." The most salient measure of this is having a high-status boyfriend or having several boys interested in dating them. Because girls are expected to be sexually attractive but not sexually active, they never admit to planning for sexual intercourse. Consequently, many of the girls feel like they have very little control over their sexual experiences: "The guy just, you know, kinda talks you into it."

MONICA: The guys, they go around and try and get a girl pregnant. They're always telling them, "I love you. I want to have sex with you. I care about you"—like that. And the girls keeps saying no, but the guy keeps telling her and telling her. And come on, if the girl really likes him, she's gonna do something.

Furthermore, when talking about sex, most of the girls reported that they "didn't get anything from it."

LUCINA: It was okay, I guess. It wasn't like I thought it was. You know, like on the TV and movies. It was more like, "Oh, it's over? That's it?"

As one Latina social worker, herself a former unwed teen mother, noted:

Latina girls are not supposed to even enjoy sex. The guys tell you when, where, and position, and the women are supposed to just lay back. The boys are responsible for sex, but they see the girls as responsible for birth control. How are the girls supposed to do this if the guys are calling the shots?

Part of the problem, according to Naomi Wolf, is that girls are not taught that they are sexual beings. "What little girls learn is not the desire for the other, but the desire to be desired (Wolf 1991, 157).

Other than Marcela, I did not meet any other girls who admitted to initiating sex. Sex "just happened." Or sex occurred when a girl "got caught up in the moment." Furthermore, because lack of planning and initiating sex is seen as an indication of a girl's good reputation, birth control is rarely practiced by the girls.

The use of birth control is seen as an admission of planning for sex and an indication of promiscuity; consequently, the girls rarely use any method of birth control. They rationalize this in many different ways. Some girls think that it is more likely that their parents will find out about their sexual activity if they have birth control pills around the house. A few of the girls argue that birth control is against their religion "like abortion. It's like you're killing the baby before it's born."

Some of the girls are afraid that their boyfriends will think less of them if they suggest using birth control.

LOURDES: Girls don't want to get the guys mad, you know. So they don't ask them. And it's mostly the guy's pride, or they say it doesn't feel right and he won't know how it really feels.

The girls are also reluctant to take control of sexual encounters because it is seen as straying into a male sphere of power and control.

Whenever I suggested that they ask their boyfriends to use a condom, they always found the idea outrageously funny. Arlene imitated the Grey Poupon mustard commercial—"Pardon me, do you have any condoms?"—when I suggested using condoms. She followed by saying, "See how stupid that sounds. Beside, it ain't like the guy's going to do it anyway. They always say it doesn't feel good with those things." However, some girls do use contraception.

DAWN: I think I'm too young to have kids. But my boyfriend wants me to have a baby. My mom wants me to have my kids early, too. But I think I'm too young. My boyfriend got mad when I told him I was on the pills. So I told him I'm not taking them no more, but I still am.

Sixteen-year-old Dawn continues to use contraception despite her boyfriend's objections.

Adolescent girls' lack of control over their own sexuality leads to an increased risk of sexually transmitted diseases and pregnancy. For example, teenagers aged fifteen to nineteen have higher rates of gonorrheal infection than sexually active men and women in any other five-year age group from twenty to forty-four years (Alan Guttmacher Institute 1994b). According to the Centers for Disease Control (1994), one out of every fifteen teenage girls in California had a baby in 1993. Extrapolating from the statistics of the University of California at San Francisco study (Brindis and Jeremy 1988), which indicates that 68% of the men involved with teenage girls are twenty years old or older, it looks like many of these girls are "caught" by adult males.

However, some of the boys and men who are fathers genuinely want to be involved with their children. Childbearing can also function as a marker of adult status for teen boys.

JOSÉ: I was kinda hoping things would work out, you know. But they just didn't. I don't know what happened, but now I don't get to see my kid much. Me and Rachel ain't together no more.

Unfortunately, given the poor economic prospects of many of these fathers, they find it difficult to be good fathers. While mothers who are unable to provide for their children economically are still considered good mothers, fathers who fail to provide find it more difficult to sustain their image as good fathers. It is not easy for men to compete with a welfare system that penalizes a two-parent family. Fatherhood at the current minimum wage serves to undermine the father/provider image of the adult male that the boy wants to achieve. Feeling like failures, perhaps perceived as failures by the teen mothers, the fathers often drift away from their children.

LOVE

As Arlene's story indicates, the causes of California's "teen pregnancy problem" revolve around the complex and convoluted issues of consent and coercion often called "love." Love plays an important role in validating a girl's initiation into sexual activity. However, "being in love" is only recognized when it occurs in monogamous heterosexual relationships. In fact, girls who do not conform to this type of romantic relationship are subjected to ostracism and harassment. Girls who have more than one boyfriend are thought to be incapable of being in love. Also, girls who are not heterosexual are not recognized as being in love. Girls who do not conform to the acceptable pattern of monogamous heterosexual relationships can be subjected to emotionally devastating peer harassment. For example, when one student couple openly declared their homosexuality, the two girls were subject to so much harassment that they ran away from home, rather than continue subjecting themselves to the taunts and jeers of their peers. I found the girls' fears of lesbian seduction amazing, given the amount of harassment they find acceptable from male sources.

Being in love is an important aspect to monogamous heterosexual relationships because it is the only means that a girl has to justify sexual intercourse. Among many adolescent populations, love is the means by which good girls are differentiated from bad girls (Lees 1986, 1993; Wilson 1978). However, the girls often confuse love and control.

MARISSA: I hate it when you're in love. It's like the guy's got all this power over you. Like they can make you do anything they want and you do it 'cause you're in love with them.

A boyfriend's possessiveness and jealousy are taken as an indication that "he is really in love" with his girlfriend.

ANA: If the guy really loves you, he's not gonna want you to even talk to another guy. He's gonna be watching you all the time. Keeping you in check, you know. Like if he sees you talking to a guy friend, he's gonna get real jealous and come over and get you.

MARGIE: He was so jealous yesterday that he slapped me in the face. I got real mad. But then he felt real bad. So he got me roses today and told me he was sorry. It's like he can't help it 'cause he's so in love with me that he gets real jealous, and he doesn't want nobody taking advantage of me.

However, having a boyfriend that keeps you "in check" produces both prestige and derision from the female friends of girls. One day in class Lydia's friends started teasing her about how she let her boyfriend control her.

MYRNA: You should ask her [Lydia] about that. Lydia doesn't even play sports anymore because her boyfriend doesn't want her wearing shorts. She lets him tell her what to do. He's got her in check real bad.

Lydia vehemently denied the allegations. She told me that she no longer played soccer on the school team because she had started a job after school. The next day Lydia came to school wearing a pair of shorts.

For some of the girls the power associated with having someone be in love with you does work both ways. Some of the girls would tell me that they kept their boyfriends in check instead of the other way around.

In order to avoid the loss of personal autonomy associated with being in love, a few of the girls limit their romantic involvements and thus protect their freedom to pursue their own interests.

MONICA: A lot of people think I go to parties, I do drugs, I sleep with guys. That's not true. . . . I don't have a boyfriend, so they can't say I'm going out with this guy, this guy, or this guy. I can talk to whoever I want as long as I'm not going out with one person, okay? I could go out on dates or whatever, but I don't want to get too involved with a guy 'cause I like to have fun and I want to go to parties. I like to go out. Having fun is my main thing. They talk about me 'cause they think I should be settled down . . . but I'm not gonna do it.

Of course, this freedom also carries a threat to their reputations as good girls. Girls who go places alone are considered potentially promiscuous. Some of the girls manage this problem by adopting an absentee boyfriend. In this manner the girls are able to ensure their personal autonomy and protect their reputations. Sometimes the boyfriends are in Mexico; usually, however, the absentee boyfriends are locked up. While this does not completely protect a girl from the "sexual auction block," it does give her some protection. The perception of loyalty and faithfulness to an absentee boyfriend brings a girl prestige among both her male and female peers.

However, some girls do not claim absentee boyfriends at all. Fifteen-year-old Monica's parents are divorced. She lives with her mother and three other siblings. Because her mother is often at work, Monica enjoys more freedom than most of the girls in the *varrio*. She often takes weekend trips to Los Angeles with her best girlfriend. When one of the homeboys asked her to be his girlfriend, she refused: "No way. He lives right next door to me. I wouldn't be able to do nothing. He would be checking up on me all the time. I'd rather be by myself—it's more fun." However, among her peers, there was often speculation about Monica's sexual promiscuity. Several girls told me that Monica had a bad reputation among her peers.

Having a good reputation is important because it earns a girl respect. According to the girls, respect is the one sentiment that can subvert the power structure of love. When a boy respects a girl, she does not have to worry that the boy might take advantage of her. As Yesenia suggests, "When a guy respects you, he doesn't *pasa de cabrón contigo* [act like a bastard with you]." Respect is a girl's best defense against potential abuse in a relationship.

The girls' relationships with their boyfriends often take precedence over their same-sex peer networks, although both boyfriends and girlfriends compete with their significant others' same-sex friends for attention.

SELINA: Who you eat lunch with? Mostly it depends on the girl and the guy. It depends mostly on how he is. Because he'll be like, if you want, you can be with your friends or you can be with me, or sometimes he'll come with me. His friends will be like, "Hey, you can't take him away from us." And I'll be like, "Watch me." Like he wanted me to go with his friends at lunch, and I said, "No, it ain't gonna look right, me and a bunch of guys."

MARGIE: When Arlene was with Joe, she put me aside and stopped talking to me. But I never did that with her. I always invited her along with me and my boyfriend. I never put her aside 'cause I knew her longer. We've been best friends for four years. But my boyfriend had to get used to her, you know. I would say, "I'm going with my friends." And he would tell me, "Don't go." So I would say, "I'm going with my friends—you can come if you want to."

The guys would come over with us and leave their friends to hang out with us. The other guys would tease them, "Damn, they got you on a leash" [Laughing].

While both girls and boys try to monopolize their significant others' attention, the boys are most often the winners in this power contest that they call love. Girls are the ones that usually change their after-school activities and friendship networks to spend time with their boyfriends. Modelski (1991) confirms that this is a cross-cultural phenomenon, noting that romance makes it difficult for girls to form their own subculture because boy/girl relationships take precedence over their female friendships.

School and community programs and activities also foster this type of behavior by focusing public attention on male/female relationships. The school cheerleaders are encouraged to put up posters and bake treats for "their" football player every game day. Local gang intervention/prevention programs sponsor basketball and boxing competitions among the "at-risk" male youth, while their girlfriends are encouraged to cheer them on.

Many of the girls harbor a very romantic, idealistic vision of love that is also promoted by the teen magazines, romance novels, and the *telenovelas* (soap operas) with which they are familiar. They usually talk about love as a "happily ever after" relationship. However, they also often temper this idyllic vision of love with more pragmatic considerations.

LYDIA: I really love my boyfriend. He's real good for me. He's the most important person in my life. I feel safe with him. It's like I told him, "I feel more protected with you than with my family." I want to marry him and be with him for the rest of my life. But then he needs to get a job. I told him, "I'm not going to live on welfare for nobody."

Lydia works twenty-plus hours per week at a fast-food restaurant. She is very generous with her money and often gives money to her boyfriend, who does not have a job, so that he can take her out on dates. However, she makes it quite clear that she does not expect to support him forever.

VIOLENCE

The girls often use terms like *abuse* when they are describing a particular girl's sexual relationship with a boy or man: "I'm worried that he's gonna brainwash her and then abuse her." Although the girls often use the term *abuse* synonymously with *sexual intercourse,* they do not always seem to understand the implications of the term fully.

MYRNA: The girls think they're in love, but the guys just leave them with the baby. My friend was a virgin, and the man got her pregnant. I told her, "You lost it now." She should've known better. She shouldn't have been with a married man. Men are like—that they always try to abuse you. There are men that always want to get girls all the time. She should've known better.

In spite of the "abuse" that occurred, girls are far more likely to blame the girl in the relationship for allowing the boy or man to abuse her than they are to blame the boy or man. According to most girls, the girl is responsible for stopping sexual intercourse because "some men can't control themselves." The girls talk about abuse as something men do with impunity. This is not surprising given many of their experiences with sexual abuse.

Many of the girls had some type of intimate experience with sexual molestation. A surprising number reported that they had been physically molested, usually by a male relative. The way that most girls deal with these incidents of molestation reflects their status as young unmarried women (Chesney-Lind 1989, 23). These girls are not able to protect themselves from sexual abuse in the same way that an adult victim or even a male victim is able to. For example, Jessica is a seventeen-year-old mother of two children who was sexually molested by an uncle when she was only thirteen. She told her mother about the incident. However, the uncle continued to frequent Jessica's home. Jessica eventually left home to live with a twenty-six-year-old male friend. This male friend subsequently began a sexual relationship with Jessica.

Because young girls are often kept close to home, the molester is often a relative (DeJong, Hervada, and Emmet 1983). One consequence of the close familial ties between victim and perpetrator is that the abuse lasts for a longer period of time. The girls rarely report these incidents to anyone, including their family members, because they are afraid of "causing problems in the family" or because they do not want the incident to become public knowledge and possibly injure their reputations. Consequently, the molester often sexually abuses the girl with impunity.

I was also often surprised at the level of physical abuse that many girls and women found acceptable within their relationships. FBI crime statistics (Federal Bureau of Investigation 1992a) report that three out of every ten female slaying victims are killed by their husbands or boyfriends. Several of the girls were involved with boys or men who physically assaulted them. While most of the emphasis on research and treatment for domestic violence is oriented toward adult women, NiCarthy (1983) notes:

Battering may be a greater problem among teens than has been recognized. Certain factors associated with battering—a tendency to romantic-addictive love, low impulse control, the female's inability to imagine that she has choices other than to endure punishment—coincides with the situation and characteristics of many adolescents (124).

Even older women are often surprisingly accepting of violence. When violence occurs, they, like their adolescent counterparts, tend to blame the woman for inciting the man.

One afternoon while I was visiting with Rachel in her apartment, one of her friends, Maria, came over. Both women are in their midthirties and sport several tatoos. Rachel is a former gang member and current heroin addict. The women began talking about their relationships with men. Maria, whose "husband" had just moved back in with her after ten years, showed the scar on her forehead where her husband had smashed a drinking glass.

LD: So why are you still with him?

RACHEL: 'Cause she loves him that's why. [*She turns and addresses Maria*] He ain't no woman beater, is he?

MARIA: He beat the shit out of Sarah when he was with her.

RACHEL: Yeah, but look how she acted with him.

MARIA: No, he ain't really no woman beater. He just loses it sometimes when he gets mad, you know. Like last week he tried to strangle me, but he stopped himself. It's like they try to get power over you. It's like a weapon to see how scared they can make you.

RACHEL: I hate it when they try to put fear in you like that.

MARIA: He ain't no woman beater. He just likes to mess with my mind.

A man who has a reputation as a "woman beater" is despised by both men and women in the *varrio*. However, a certain amount of violence is often tolerated as an acceptable male vice and sometimes as a demonstration of the man's passion for his wife or girlfriend.

Adolescent girls encounter a great deal of violence, specifically violence directed toward women, in their everyday lives. Sometimes they have no control over the violence. For example, one male student passed his art project around the room, an etched mirror that said "Trust No Bitch," with the picture of a smoking gun. Other times, however, the girls seem to deliberately seek out situations that pose a threat of violence to them.

At "kickbacks," parties where students skip school and spend the day drinking alcohol, smoking marijuana, and listening to music, young girls are often considered fair game by the older boys. Sometimes the girls are told by the boys that they cannot come to the party unless they are going to "give it up," a euphemism for having sex. Getting a girl drunk and taking her into a back bedroom is considered a sport by the boys. At one party, a junior high student became so drunk that she passed out on the couch. The boys made a sport of dragging her around the floor and slapping her in the face to "bring her to." Her friends eventually put an end to the "game." In spite of the threat to their reputations and physical bodies, there is never a lack of young girls willing to attend these parties; the potential for thrills and adventures associated with an unsupervised party is a powerful enticement to many adolescent girls.

The majority of girls believe that most women who are raped are at least partially responsible for their predicament. I was told things like, "If she didn't dress like a 'ho, she wouldn't be in that situation." One of the teachers invited a guest speaker who passed out a questionnaire asking students to assign blame to individuals in various situations dealing with nonconsensual sex. The exercise involved a scale of one to ten, one representing little or no blame, ten representing complete responsibility for the situation. The majority of girls assigned numbers of seven or eight to women who were victims of rape. They justified their answers with responses like, "She was drinking with a bunch of guys—what did she expect?" or, "She was dressed like a 'ho."

SEXUAL EDUCATION

Almost all of the girls are poorly informed about sex, birth control, and fetal development. This is the norm in spite of the fact that the school district has a mandatory sex education curriculum at both the junior high and high school levels. For some girls, I became their primary source of information about their bodies. I answered questions ranging from "What is a clitoris?" to "How can I tell if I'm pregnant?" The number of myths and misconceptions that the girls have about sex are astonishing. They routinely reference daytime television talk shows when they are discussing "facts" about sexual intercourse and relationships: "I saw on *Ricky Lake* . . . " They would tell me things like, "I heard that if you do it with a condom, that's having sex, but if you don't, that's making love." They talk about their genitals with terms like "coochy" or "down there." Most of the girls do not use tampons because they are afraid that they will lose their virginity or because they think it is "gross" to "touch yourself down there." They conceive of their vaginas as something alien and dirty.

Part of the problem is caused by the structure of the sex education classes; the co-ed classes make many girls uncomfortable asking questions in class. Also the majority of the sex education classes at Westhills High School are taught by male teachers. Many of the girls are reluctant to approach these teachers with questions related to their sexual development.

However, another part of the problem is caused by a recent challenge to the sex education curriculum by fundamentalist Christian parents. Sex education has become a battleground for both the Left and the Right; both groups see education as potentially subversive. The Left perceives education as imposing an anachronistic set of values upon children, whereas the Right tends to see schools as destroying traditional family values.

During the 1993-1994 school year, the recent introduction of a Christian-sponsored "Sex Respect" curriculum in the nearby Northcity School District placed Westhills's curriculum under intense scrutiny. A Christian parents' coalition in Westhills approached the school board with the goal of restructuring the current curriculum to meet their criteria. They argued that the mandatory requirement of sex education classes denies their right to religious privacy. This particular group of parents is currently trying to delegate all sex education to parents. However, as Brumberg (1992) notes, only about 25% of all teens report that they discuss sex with their parents. Furthermore, as one sex education teacher argued:

They [Christian parents] need to drive around our community. Our kids don't come from families where they're going to get information on sex ed. They should come to my class. I've got one girl who was sleeping everyday in my class. It turns out her mom is a prostitute. The kid is waiting up for her every night to make sure she comes home safe, then she's putting her to bed if she's been using [drugs]. What kind of sex education is this kid going to get at home?

Currently, Christian parents in Westhills are fighting to change the sex education curriculum to elective status. They also want all reference to homosexuality removed from the curriculum. In an effort to appease the more conservative parents in the district, the school-based program emphasizes abstinence as the only real form of safe sex. Several teachers routinely emphasize the failure rates of birth control methods during their class lectures. Unfortunately, some of the students interpret this to mean that birth control does not work: "Rubbers don't work most of the time, so why bother using them?"

Sex education does not seem to have much of an impact on a teen's decision as to whether or not to have sexual intercourse. In fact, contrary to what many opponents of sex education argue, adolescents who have been exposed to sex education classes engage in sex at about the same rate as students who have not been exposed to sex education (Zelnik and Kim 1982). However, teens who do attend sex education classes are more likely to use contraceptives than those who do not attend these types of classes (Zelnik and Kim 1982). This is particularly true for Hispanic males (Moran and Corely 1991). Thus, it appears that sex education is an important factor in an adolescent's decision to protect herself from pregnancy and other sexually transmitted diseases (STDs).

This is important because Hispanic women are among the fastest-growing group of HIV (human immunodeficiency virus)-infected people in the United States. While African American and Hispanic women comprise only 20% of women in the United States, they account for 72% of women who have developed AIDS since 1981 (Alan Guttmacher Institute 1994b). Yet Latino teenagers both, male and female, show an alarming lack of awareness about AIDS and HIV; one boy responded to my query, "Oh, is that still around?"

ARACELI: If I loved him, I would sleep with him even if he had AIDS. I would be okay if we both had AIDS together.

Some of them also demonstrate an incredible lack of compassion for each other:

CARLOS: If I had AIDS, I wouldn't want to know. If you have AIDS and you know, you can be charged with murder. So I wouldn't want to know. Shit yeah. If I got AIDS, I don't care if anybody else gets it.

In 1993, San Diego County had 168 reported cases of AIDS in young people aged fourteen to twenty-one years (California Department of Health Services 1993a). According to the Centers for Disease Control (1993), teenage girls have the highest rates of gonorrhea in the nation. Statistics show high infection rates for teenage girls in almost every category of sexually transmitted diseases, including HIV and AIDS infection. However, statistics relating AIDS and other STDs among adolescents are not always reliable because the teen population is among the least likely to have regular physical exams or seek treatment for STD infections. Thus, the increasing rate of STDs among adolescents is very likely to be underreported, which makes the rising numbers of young women infected with STDs even more alarming.

While information about fetal development and familiarity with contraceptive methods are important, the girls told me that they wanted a unit in their sex education curriculum that taught about relationships. The majority of girls are concerned with managing their relationships with boys in such a way that will enable them to protect their reputations and keep the boy's friendship. Many of the sex questions the girls asked me revolved around these types of issues. One frequently asked question was, "How to say no [to sex] without hurting his feelings." This type of information is woefully lacking in the public high school curriculum.

In fact, the school sexual education curriculum includes an incredibly outdated unit on relationships that gives an ambiguous message about gender roles. The unit starts with a section called the "Origin of the Family." Students are told that families are a group of individuals that depend on each other.

TEACHER: Group living is not an accident. It is a necessity, based on survival. The child is dependent upon the mother, the mother dependent upon the father. Look at the handout. At best a mother can gather a few nuts and berries and roots. So she's dependent upon the father to bring in food. Without the father, the child and mother would perish. The children depended on the mother for food and care. The mother depended on the father for food and protection. The male is responsible for getting the bulk of the food and protection and housing. So you can see the roots of male/female roles. These roles are not by choice but out of survival. Usually men got up at the moment of sunlight and were gone, poof, hunting. Women got up and fed the kids. A woman's worth was measured in her ability to bear children. You can't believe how abused women have been because of this. For example, women did not have the right to vote in our country until 1920.

Despite the fact that the teacher talked about the abuse of women, by structuring the family in such a way that the woman is dependent on the man, and the man dependent only on himself, the sex education unit serves to affirm conservative ideas about gender roles, making a girl's lack of control over relationships and sexuality a part of the natural order. This same teacher also told his classes, "Marriage is important to protect women. Women get hurt more easily by sex outside of marriage."

However, when it comes to the unit on female and male reproduction, the sex education classes do a much better job. Many of the sex education classes do a great job of introducing students to the variety of birth control devices available. One teacher routinely invited a speaker from Planned Parenthood to come to his classroom and show the students different methods of contraception, although the value of this information was sometimes undermined by teachers who chose to emphasize the failure rates of contraceptives.

Most of the teachers also address topics like child abuse, sexual molestation, rape, and domestic violence. During one class, the students and I sat in a darkened classroom while the teacher showed a video to introduce the topic of domestic violence. The video, titled *Deck the Halls*, followed a married couple as they prepared to host a Christmas party at their home. During the video, the husband became increasingly upset about losing a promotion to a coworker. As the video couple's friends left their home, the video shows the wife hug and kiss the rival coworker good-bye. The husband flies into a rage and ends up hitting the wife. The students' response to the video was both frightening and enlightening. Most of the students, both boys and girls, felt that the wife deserved the treatment that she received for inappropriately flirting with someone who was not her husband.

The teacher was surprised at the students' response. He tried to get the students to agree that although the wife's behavior may have been inappropriate, she did not deserve to be hit or punched. Many of the students in the class noted that violence was an appropriate way to settle family arguments. Almost 50% of the students in the class raised their hands to acknowledge that they had seen one parent get so angry that he or she had pushed, shoved, or hit the other parent. The next week the teacher invited a spokesperson from the battered women's shelter to give a presentation to his class.

While formal discussions of topics such as domestic violence and rape are an important way to raise students' awareness of these issues, an overemphasis on these topics promulgates the perception that female sexuality is defined by vulnerability and potential victimization (Fine 1988). Often the girls are not provided a forum where they can feel comfortable discussing their sexual desires. The co-ed sexual education classes intimidate them and prevent them from fully participating in discussions about their sexuality. Consequently, their experience of female sexuality is most often discussed in terms of teen pregnancy, date rape, and sexually transmitted diseases.

It is difficult to gauge the impact that sex education classes have on the students. It seems that many adolescent sexual myths survive in spite of the classes.

CARLA: Sex Ed mostly teaches you that having a baby can mess up your life. We already know that. We don't need to go to class for that.

Male sexuality is discussed in terms of both reproductive biology and sexual arousal. However, female sexuality is often oriented primarily toward reproductive information. The sexual education curriculum's focus on birth control, reproductive biology, fetal development, and their links to motherhood perpetuate the notion that childbearing and child rearing are exclusively female pursuits (Ward and Taylor 1994).

Peer culture appears to have much more impact on students' perceptions of sex and gender roles than formal lessons. However, students who attend these classes are at least exposed to information about contraceptives, AIDS, venereal diseases, fetal development, and the physiology of the male and female reproductive systems. Unfortunately, most students are only exposed to this information for one semester, usually in their first year of high school. The information presented in the sex education curriculum may have more positive impact if older students, for whom sexual experimentation is a more frequent occurrence, also attended these classes.

BABIES

Ruth Horowitz (1981,1983) has written on issues of virginity and unwed motherhood among Mexican American adolescents. As discussed in the previous chapter, virginity is the socially expected norm for unmarried girls and women. However, the symbolic importance of virginity does not always ensure sexually chaste behavior. Horowitz argues that an adolescent girl's decision to become sexually active needs to be understood in the context of cultural values. For Chicana girls the decision to have sex is intertwined with cultural values that venerate virginity, male domination, and motherhood (Horowitz 1981, 1983). However, because the norm associated with male sexual behavior is promiscuity and seduction, the girls in Westhills, similar to the girls in Horowitz's study, find it difficult to negotiate the conflict between virginity and "giving in" to their boyfriends. The decision "to do it" or not "to do it" is also complicated by other issues, including a girl's desire for emancipation and adult status, lack of job skills, as well as poor sexual education and a lack of control over her own sexuality. For many unwed teen mothers, having a baby is not the cause of their problems; it is the symptom of society's neglect when it comes to educating adolescent girls.

For the majority of girls in the *varrio*, motherhood is perceived as a sign of adulthood. Babies validate adult status. One new grandmother explained that her daughter, who had recently given birth, would not be attending school because "she's grownup now and has to act like it."

However, while motherhood offers the allure of independence, a chance for the girls to break free from their families, it often has the unintended effect of exacerbating the girls' dependence. The girls most often rely on welfare or their families for economic support. Girls who marry often find themselves living with their husbands' families, creating a situation where they are both economically and socially dependent on their husbands.

Some girls consider motherhood as the only desirable career path available to them: "At least you're doing something important, not like working at Burger King." Their belief in the value of motherhood overlaps with wider society's values that disparage minimum wage jobs and idealize family life.

Some of the girls perceive pregnancy and motherhood as a way to escape their "little girl" status and gain attention.

ANA: When you get pregnant, you get a lot of attention from your boyfriend. He'll be coming up and rubbing your stomach and stuff. And like the adults and stuff respect you more. Sometimes the girls lie about being pregnant to keep their guy. Then they just tell them they had a miscarriage.

Other girls looked forward to being a mother because it is their chance to make decisions independent of their parents: "It's like I can make the rules now."

LOURDES: I asked my mom if she would give me permission to get married. [Fifteen-year-old Lourdes has been dating her boyfriend for two years.] My mom says no unless I was pregnant. So I tell her, "I have to get pregnant to get married, huh?" She says when I'm eighteen I can get married. My mom told me if I get married as a junior or senior [in high school] then I can still live here with them. But she says, "that doesn't mean you can do anything you want to. It's still my house and my rules." That's why most girls want to get married, to get out of the house and so they don't have their parents' rules anymore.

Several volunteers at the local chapter of Planned Parenthood told me they were alarmed at the increasing numbers of young girls who came to them desiring

pregnancy: "You try to counsel these fifteen-year-old girls about the responsibilities of parenthood and all they want to know is how they can get pregnant."
Many of these girls perceive parenthood as a means to emancipate themselves from
their parents. Sabrina told me that she was going to have her Norplant (she agreed
to try Norplant on the advice of her social worker) removed because she wanted to
start her family as soon as her boyfriend was released from jail.

SABRINA: I'm ready to have a baby. I been going out with my boyfriend for two years, and
there's nothing else left to do. This way I can be a mom, you know, and get respect. My
mom's already making baby blankets for me and everything. They think it's a good idea, and
I can settle down into my life, you know.

Sabrina is thirteen years old and currently incarcerated at the Girls Rehabilitation
Facility in Juvenile Hall.

Almost all of the girls are familiar with the welfare benefits associated with Aid
to Families with Dependent Children (AFDC). Some of the girls plan to move out
of their parents' homes after the birth of their babies. For many of the girls,
particularly those who are not legal residents of the United States, unwed
motherhood is the best economic option that society has to offer them. However,
most of these girls have unrealistic expectations about the financial rewards of
parenthood. The girls' visions of financial independence usually turn into long-term
economic dependence. As most soon find out, AFDC benefits ($490 per month) are
not enough to allow them to live on their own. Furthermore, new California
legislation proposes to change the rules for AFDC recipients. The proposed changes
would end welfare benefits to recipients after three years. All welfare recipients
would also be required to work unless they have children under three months of age.
Unwed teenage mothers would also be required to stay in school and to live at home
in order to receive their benefits. This legislation is somewhat misguided because
some of the girls are using pregnancy to try to escape unhealthy or abusive homes.
Given that Child Protective Services offers little aid to adolescents, pregnancy is
often the only means that some girls have of leaving an abusive home.

Most intervention strategies for teens and their families offer few options aside
from family counseling. Teens are rarely removed from their homes unless they are
the victims of sexual molestation. Until Child Protective Services can be restruc-
tured to aid teen children, unwed pregnancy offers one of the few means a teenage
girl has to access social services.

While some girls openly admit to their peers that they are trying to get pregnant,
this is relatively rare. Most girls publicly deny that they are having sexual
intercourse, even if they want to get pregnant. Similar to Arlene, they "accidentally"
get pregnant.

MONICA: Everybody falls into the trap of getting pregnant. A lot of girls are pregnant that
were with their boyfriends. They were so in love with them they didn't really know what they
were doing. They're just in that moment right now, you know. They don't regret the baby.
They just regret all the problems after the baby comes, with the money and everything.

Usually they talk about sex as something that "just happened." Sometimes sexual intercourse between the girl and her boyfriend "just happens" for six or seven months before she "accidentally" gets pregnant.

In the *varrio,* children are talked about as "gifts from God." It is very rare for a girl to choose to abort a fetus. Many of the girls talk about babies as someone who would "belong to me and love me."

OB-GYN PHYSICIAN: Mexican babies do much better than the babies of Anglo or African American teens because of all the extended families, and the fact that the babies are always wanted. For the most part, Mexican babies don't have the same health problems, that is, neglect and abuse, that we see in other teen babies.

Most parents, even those who are upset by their unmarried daughters' pregnancies, welcome the new baby into their homes.

My own status as a married woman without children both intrigued and mystified the girls. They would often ask me why I did not have children. It was a big concern to them because they did not want me to "die alone" without any children to take care of me in my old age. One time when I mentioned the fact that my husband and I might decide not to have children, the girls were appalled.

ARACELI: You don't mean that. Don't say that. That's not right. If you don't have kids, you're going to be lonely when you get old. You've got to have kids.

Many of the girls' parents were also curious as to why I did not have any children after nearly three years of marriage. The general perception was that "American" women were selfish and always wanted to do things such as travel instead of having children.

Families expected young married women to start having children soon after the marriage. Twenty-year-old Iris complained that her family was very upset when she announced that she and her husband were not planning to have children for several years.

IRIS: It's a big deal in my family. They're really upset. I even had to go ask my doctor because my mom kept telling me that using birth control would make me sterile. They don't understand that we need time to get things settled before we have kids. I don't want to have it as hard as they did.

In spite of the fact that Iris is taking classes at the community college and working two part-time jobs, her family expected her to start her family as soon as she was married.

Most of the girls who are not mothers talk about motherhood in idyllic terms. To the girls, motherhood represents unconditional love and, more importantly, self-fulfillment.

BRENDA: I want to get to have my kids when I'm young. You can relate to them better that way. When you're young, then it's more like you're their sister. They still love you like you're the mom, but you can understand them better and go out and do things with them. Having kids is the best thing a woman can do because it's the only thing that guys can't do, you know. It makes you important. It's the best thing you can do for your husband to give him kids. When you have kids, it's like you have something to do with your life.

Most girls dream of getting married, possibly working for a few years, then raising a family with their husband. Lourdes, already engaged at age fifteen, told her boyfriend that she wanted to have as many children as he could afford "because being a mom is the most important thing you can do." Although the girls speak romantically of motherhood, they often contrast this with the particular experiences of their mothers: "My mother has it real hard . . ." The mothers talk about their adolescent daughters as enjoying "the best time in their lives," while their daughters cannot wait until they become mothers.

Unfortunately, some of the teenage mothers that I knew did not always provide consistent parental care to their children. Many of the teen mothers find that the demands of single parenthood, poverty, and adolescent angst are overwhelming. As with other families that fit this profile (Morash and Rucker 1989), some of these teenage mothers are inconsistent and neglectful parents.

In order to address the problems of teen pregnancy, communities need to help girls give themselves permission to control their sexuality. We need to teach girls that there is a difference between sex and love and that sexual assertiveness is not equivalent to sexual promiscuity. Unfortunately, most of the adults and adolescents in Westhills equate sexual liberation with homosexuality and promiscuity. Girls are not getting pregnant because they are using birth control poorly; they are getting pregnant because they are not using birth control at all. Many of the girls who get pregnant are the girls who let sex "just happen." These girls are having unprotected sex for a myriad of reasons, including a desire for adult status, self-fulfillment, lack of sex education, and their desire to be loved and accepted, coupled with their fears of getting caught or tainting their reputations.

TEEN COUNSELOR: Working with pregnant teens you feel like you're sticking your finger in the dike. The problem occurs way before we get them. Why are they getting pregnant? Because there's nothing else for them to do. I gave a class on self-worth and abstinence last week, which is pretty revolutionary considering that I work with teen parents. We talked about how the focus of a relationship changes after you have sex. We also talked about just because you're not a virgin doesn't mean that you have sex with everyone. I had twenty-plus kids in the class, and I handed out information on how to say no. Usually, the kids leave all the information. After the class, I was surprised there were only two pamphlets left behind.

As this counselor's story indicates, girls really want to learn ways to assert control over their bodies and their sexuality.

While teen pregnancy is sometimes inadvertent or the product of a coercive relationship, pregnancy can also be a statement about the powerlessness of female adolescence. As McRobbie (1991) notes, sex is not necessarily a pleasurable activity; rather, it is preliminary to a girl's adult status. For many of the girls, adult life begins after pregnancy and the birth of their first child. Many girls who become pregnant are often scholastic poor achievers who have a realistic sense of the job opportunities that await them in Westhills. Pregnancy thus becomes a way of escaping their scholastic failures and their prospects of a dead-end job. The experiences of their friends and families demonstrate to them that waiting to have children does not necessarily ensure financial security. Furthermore, these girls often live in claustrophobic homes where their freedoms are severely restricted. Consequently, they choose pregnancy as a means of liberating themselves and validating their adult status. For these girls, having a baby has much to offer with little perceived risk.

NOTES

1. Part of this pressure toward becoming sexualized also comes from the media. Much of popular culture presents female bodies from the male perspective, ignoring any representation of female sexual desire (Faludi 1991; Whatley 1994; Wolf 1991). Adolescent girls are constantly bombarded with sexually explicit imagery that publicly displays female bodies. Teen magazines, television, film, and billboards offer up women's bodies for perusal and evaluation on a daily basis. Naomi Wolf has written about the link that popular culture makes between beauty and sexuality (Wolf 1991). Wolf argues that much of current advertising can be classified as "beauty pornography." This media link between sexuality and beauty focuses on female bodies; male bodies are rarely depicted in the same manner.

2. Media, predominantly controlled by the Anglo community, also has a powerful impact on the girls' perceptions of beauty and their ethnicity. Many of the girls associate beauty with Anglo physical features. It is not uncommon to hear girls describe someone as pretty in terms of her "light skin" or green eyes. However, at the same time, girls who try to look and dress "white" are ridiculed: "She should act like her own race." When I began this project, I spent some time during my first summer of research volunteering at the local Boys and Girls Club. I was shocked at the number of African American and Latino children who painted their art projects with blond hair and blue eyes. One little girl who made a black-skinned doll called her "Crispy" and told me that her doll was ugly because she was burned. We have to ask ourselves what kind of self-image we are creating in children when their ideal of beauty is something that they can never achieve. This is especially important for girls because their self-esteem is often closely linked to perceptions of their physical attractiveness.

Chapter 8

Chicanas and Schooling

In the United States, anyone can grow up to be president because success is based on achievement rather than ascription. This is the dominant ideological view of most Americans. In this meritocratic view, public education is supposed to be the means by which all individuals, regardless of ethnic or class background, achieve social mobility. Success is based on an individual's motivation to work hard. Consequently, social inequalities are a result of individual character flaws; a poor person is too lazy or too stupid to get an education and thus achieve financial success.

However, education has also been criticized as a tool by which powerful interest groups selectively transmit skills in order to reproduce the class, gender, and ethnic inequities of the wider social structure (Althusser 1971; Bourdieu and Passeron 1977; Bowles and Gintis 1976; Giroux 1983; Willis 1977, 1981a, 1981b). This theoretical perspective links school organization, course content, and pedagogy to the powerful, thus privileging the interests of the upper classes to the detriment of other social groups. Some feminist scholars have appropriated this theoretical framework to analyze gender relationships within schools (Barret 1980; Deem 1978). Much attention has been oriented toward uncovering the "patriarchal curricula" of schools (Spender and Sarah 1980). Consequently, a vast amount of literature has documented the different treatment that boys and girls receive within education settings (see e.g., Arnot and Weiner 1987; Sadker and Sadker 1994; Weiner and Arnot 1987).

Because specific groups of minority students (African American, Mexican American, Puerto Rican American, Native American) have historically fared poorly under the United States' education system, there has also been a great deal of effort to understand why some minority students perform well in American school settings and others do not. Toward this end, researchers have studied the means by which students cope with the cultural disjunctures between school ideology and the students' own experiences, for example, Gibson's (1987), Matuti-Bianchi's (1986, 1991), Ogbu's (1987, 1991a, 1991b), and Suarez-Orozco's (1991) research comparing different coping strategies of immigrant and nonimmigrant minority students. Ogbu argues that immigrant students perceive "cultural [and] language differences as barriers to overcome in order to achieve their long-range goals" (1991b, 20). In contrast, nonimmigrant minority students "interpret cultural and language differences as markers of identity to be maintained" (26). Thus, while immigrant students may practice accommodation to school rules without feeling threatened by pressures of assimilation (Gibson 1987, Gibson and Ogbu 1991), non-immigrant students often develop an oppositional culture to school that can inhibit academic success.

While I did not work with many immigrant Latino students, the peer culture of nonimmigrant students does not support school success. The ethnic disjunction between school culture, shaped by middle-class, predominantly Anglo teachers and administrators, and the school's Chicano students makes it difficult for many students to retain their ethnic identity and achieve scholastic success. In fact, the most academically successful Chicano students at Westhills High School assumed a "raceless" persona (Fordham 1988; Fordham and Ogbu 1986). Furthermore, many of the Chicano students used their ethnic identity to resist school culture. For example, students would often speak Spanish in the classroom in order to ridicule and criticize their English-speaking teachers.

However, the students with whom I worked did not have a straightforwardly oppositional culture. Their ideas about appropriate feminine behavior and the school's ideals regarding student behavior often overlapped. Also, much of their antischool behavior was not necessarily antilearning behavior. As Holland and Eisenhart (1990) and Gaskell (1985) suggest, most students are pragmatists. They do what is necessary to get by. Students adopt different attitudes toward school that may promote learning without the wholesale endorsement of school. The West Indian girls in Fuller's study (1980) demonstrated high academic achievement and aspirations; however, they did not behave as stereotypical good students. Matuti-Bianchi (1986, 1991) identifies a wide variation in student orientation to school among Mexican American adolescents.

Most of the girls I know can be categorized as neither antischool nor antilearning. However, the majority of girls value school as a social opportunity rather than as an academic one. Most frequently, they complain about specific teachers or classes, not any pervasive feeling of discrimination at school. They find school boring and irrelevant to their lives and resent schoolwork for interfering with the social aspects of school. This type of attitude can be interpreted as a form of opting out of academic competition, a form of resistance to an achievement ideology based on individual competition and the notion of meritocracy (J. Macleod 1987). However, few of the girls appear to question the myth of meritocracy, justifying their poor scholastic performances as a result of laziness or lack of aptitude.

In fact, most of the students I interviewed told me that they planned on going to college. However, statistics indicate that they are far more likely to drop out of school than to enroll in college courses. Only ten Hispanic students at Westhills High School completed the course requirements for entrance into the California university system in 1994 (California Basic Education Data Systems 1994).

So how can we explain this gap between student aspirations and reality? Chicano students' poor scholastic performances must be linked, at least in part, to the failure of the education system to support these students. The girls very rarely complain about institutional racism or sexism within the school organization, that is not to say, however, that these types of discriminations do not have an impact on them. National and local school statistics indicate that the majority of Hispanic students perform extremely poorly in our national education system.

NATIONAL STATISTICS: HISPANIC STUDENTS

Nationally, Hispanic students do not fare well in the public education system. The National Education Goals Panel has adopted six major educational goals as a long-term strategy toward increasing the academic competitiveness of American students. The goals are to be achieved by the year 2000. Hispanic students, however, present a dismal picture for the potential success of these goals.

The first goal of the report states that all children in America will start school ready to learn. Unfortunately, only 20% of Hispanic three- and four-year-old children are currently enrolled in preschool (U.S. Department of Education 1992).

The second goal calls for a national high school graduation rate of 90% by the year 2000. As of 1992, the national Hispanic dropout rate is 35%, consistently higher than the Anglo rate of 9% (U.S. Department of Education 1992). However, within the "Hispanic" category, there exist some surprising disparities. While the dropout rate for Cuban Americans is consistent with that of Anglo students, the Mexican American drop-out rate is more than three times higher than their Cuban counterparts (U.S. Department of Education 1992).

The third and fourth goals of the report project literacy and competency standards in all academic areas. However, national writing scores for Hispanic students are at minimum proficiency levels (U.S. Department of Education 1992). Hispanic students are also more than twice as likely as their Anglo peers to be enrolled in remedial math or no math at all by the eighth grade (U.S. Department of Education 1992).

Goal five states that adult literacy in the United States will be 100%. Approximately 12.5% of the adult Hispanic population has not completed the fifth grade. In comparison, only 2.4% of the total U.S. adult population has not completed fifth grade (U.S. Bureau of the Census 1992).

The final goal of the report indicates that every school in America will be drug and crime free by the year 2000. However, Hispanic students are three times more likely to report the presence of gangs in their school than other students (U.S. Department of Education 1992).

The traditionally poor academic performance of Hispanic students will have long-term effects for the United States. The number of Latino youth in the United States is expected to triple by the year 2020, with nearly one fifth of the new entrants into the labor force projected to be Hispanic by the year 2000 (Hudson Institute 1987). A lack of education for these youths means that they will have limited access to well-paying jobs (U.S. Department of Commerce, Bureau of the Census 1990). Among the Hispanic population, Mexican-origin Hispanics have the highest unemployment rate and the lowest median earnings (U.S. Department of Commerce, Bureau of the Census 1986). The fastest growing poverty group in the United States consists of Hispanic children (U.S. Bureau of the Census 1992).

Demographics alone indicate a great need to address the problems of educating the Hispanic population. Unfortunately, the Hispanic students at Westhills High School do not fare much better than national statistics would predict.

WESTHILLS HIGH SCHOOL

Scene 1

It is nine o'clock on a Wednesday morning, the end of the second period at Westhills High School. The bell rings, and 1800 students, laughing and talking, pour out from their classrooms. They start to meander toward their next classes in small groups, stopping to chat with friends along the way. The male vice principal stands in the middle of the courtyard with a bullhorn and starts calling out, "Tardy sweep. This is a tardy sweep. You have three minutes left to get to class." A few students speed up their pace. Most continue talking with their friends. Again, the vice principal speaks into the bullhorn:

This is a tardy sweep. Teachers are instructed to lock their classroom doors when the second bell rings. Those students not in class will report to the office. This is a tardy sweep. You have two minutes.

Several students straggle past. The vice principal directs his comments directly toward them: "Hurry up, you guys. You have one minute." The second bell rings. Most, but not all, of the teachers shut and lock their classroom doors. Students who do not make it to class before the second bell rings either leave campus by jumping over the wall that surrounds the schoolyard or report to the principal's office.

Scene 2

Thirty-eight students are seated around small tables in groups of four and five. The teacher spends twenty-five minutes giving detailed instructions to the class about their assignment. Instructions are also written on the board in chalk. Most of the students sit in various poses of inattention. The teacher finishes speaking to the class, "Does everybody understand what they're supposed to do? Okay Get to work." The noise in the classroom grows increasingly loud. The students are supposed to be engaged in a group assignment that requires each table to make a poster depicting the critical points of their short-story assignment. From their conversations, it is clear that many of the students have not read the assigned story. In fact, very few of the students groups are actually talking about the assignment. There are fifteen minutes left to the class period, and only one group has begun drawing their poster. The teacher shows me some of the work submitted by her students: "If we can get the kids writing a coherent paragraph by the end of the semester, that would be a lofty goal."

Scene 3

I am sitting in an ESL (English as a Second Language) classroom. The classroom is ghostly quiet. The teacher sits at his desk, drinking coffee and reading the morning newspaper. The students are seated in rows. All of the students have their workbooks open to different pages. Some students are reading and writing in their notebooks. Other students work for a few minutes, then start writing letters to friends, drawing pictures, or doodling. A few students gaze out the classroom windows for the entire period. Several students put their heads down on their desks and sleep. The teacher never looks up from his newspaper. The bell rings, signaling the end of the class. Students get up to leave, the teacher looks up from his paper and tells them in English, "Put your finished work in the tray." The students file out of the classroom, talking to each other in Spanish.

Scene 4

There are twenty-two students in the Advanced Placement history class. The students sit at individual desks, placed along rows in the classroom. The teacher begins a lecture on the causes of the Revolutionary War. However, rather than telling the students which specific social and economic events influenced the Revolutionary War, he asks students to generate their own list using their knowledge of history. The students provide suggestions, which the teacher then writes on the board. The class then discusses the relative merits of each suggestion.

These are scenes drawn from my first several weeks at Westhills High School. I was struck both by the disparity of pedagogical methods found in the different classrooms and by the overwhelming number of students on campus. Students are packed into most classes like sardines. Many teachers are forced to have students stand against the classroom walls or sit on counter-tops because they lack enough chairs and desks to seat them. The large numbers of students contribute to the general lack of discipline in many of the classrooms.

There are two high schools located in the city of Westhills. The residential populations served by the two schools are separated by socioeconomic status and, to a lesser degree, ethnicity. Students attending Westhills High School come from poor, predominantly Hispanic neighborhoods. In contrast, Westhill's second high school was built to accommodate the increasing population growth associated with the many newly constructed housing developments in east Westhills.

Westhills High School is a four-year high school (grades nine through twelve) located in an economically impoverished area of the city. Very few of the teachers and staff live in the area near the school. Almost two thirds of the student population qualifies for the federally subsidized free or reduced lunch program. Most of the teachers tell me that the poverty of their students is an important factor in their students' lack of academic success.

TEACHER: It all comes down to economics. You go down the coast, and the kids don't have to deal with the fact that they can't make rent at the end of the month. I have one girl who wants to drop out of AP [Advanced Placement curriculum] because she has to work and can't do the workload for AP class with her job. Without her job, her family can't make rent. Of course, you don't feel sorry for all of them. Some of them have made real bad choices and caused a lot of their own problems. You've got thirty-five students in your classes, and sometimes you can't worry about the two that have problems. You've still got to give them bad grades if they don't do the homework, and you can't pass them if they don't show up to class.

Teachers regaled me with stories of students who were working forty hours per week to augment their families' incomes. Many students also perform necessary domestic chores, such as child care and cooking. One of the teachers routinely loaned money to a student whose family had trouble paying their rent at the end of each month: "I always get it back after the first of the month. I'd rather do this than have her [the student] drop out of school to work."

In 1994, despite an intensive campaign by school officials and staff, the district voters defeated a school bond issue that would have provided money to Westhills High School for much-needed maintenance and repairs. School administrators, teachers, parents, and students complain that their school is perpetually underfunded and overcrowded.

TEACHER 1: My contract says that I can't have more than twenty-eight kids in a class. I have a classroom with twenty-six chairs and [successive classes with] thirty-eight, thirty-eight, and forty-one students in it. It's not teaching; it's crowd control. I've got them standing against walls until I find some more chairs.

TEACHER 2: We have almost one fourth enriched (college track) classes, and we don't have that many enriched kids in this school. I want to know how many kids are in those classes. I can't teach with forty kids in a class. I'm wondering if we can consolidate the enriched class and add more regular classes. I wish counselors had a better understanding of the whole school and not just use my class as a dumping ground for students who have failed their other classes.

TEACHER 1: That's always the way it is. [*turns to me*] Teachers start the year full of enthusiasm and by the second week, you realize that you are going to do what you can, but you are worn down. Too many kids, not enough support.

Teachers who wish to take students on field trips or require special class materials participate in yearly fund-raising efforts. Students sell candy or cookbooks to friends and family members in order to raise money for their class activities.

Some of the nonelective classrooms do not have enough textbooks to allow students to take the books home with them. Rather, the books stay in class and student "homework" becomes class work. The school is also very technologically poor. The majority of classrooms do not have computers in them. The computer lab on campus is stocked with outdated Apple computers.[1]

The school itself is geographically located between two Hispanic gang territories. Several African American gangs also claim areas near the school campus. In response to a survey that I conducted among the student population, approximately 59% (n=136) of students reported that the major problem at Westhills High School is gang violence. However, while students cited gang violence as the number-one problem within their school, very few reported that they felt threatened at school. As one student wrote on his survey, "If you mind your own business, they don't mess with you."

The school has a minority student population of approximately 72%, and almost 50% of the student population is classified as Hispanic. In contrast, the second high school in Westhills has a minority student population of 55%, only 25% of which are classified as Hispanic. However, the ethnic makeup of the student body is not reflected among the faculty and staff of the Westhills High School. Although approximately 37% of the support staff of the high school are minority (24% Hispanic), less than 15% of the faculty are minority (8.5% Hispanic). The majority of teachers at Westhills High School are white, middle class males.

In addition, there are four high school counselors to serve a student population of more than 1,800. Only one of the four counselors is bilingual, and all of the counselors are white. Many of the Latino students told me that they found it "hard to relate" to the counselors and teachers. The general lack of Chicana role models at the school is problematic since many of the girls in my study found little in school with which they could actively identify. This is not surprising given recent data that suggest Hispanic girls are the students least likely to receive teacher attention (Mckenna and Ortiz 1988; Sadker and Sadker 1994).

TEACHER: I lose so many girls every year to pregnancy and marriage. I think about how much effort I've wasted on this kid.

Teachers who are interested in engaging their Chicana students soon grow discouraged at the apparent lack of results. Thus it becomes a vicious circle: lack of teacher intervention contributing to many Chicana students' increasing alienation from school, Chicana students' alienation from school, discouraging teachers' interventions on their behalf.

Westhills High School has a poor image within the local community. Part of the school's poor reputation is caused by the notorious graduation rate. Numbers indicate that only 292 of the 615 freshmen class of 1990 graduated in 1994, a graduation rate of 47.5%. However, the district reports a dropout rate of 28% (1992-1993). Counselors have indicated to me that there is some discrepancy regarding the tabulation of students who drop out because the ninth-grade population is inflated by "9Rs" (ninth-grade repeats), ninth-grade students who were not promoted to tenth grade. However, while the registrar indicates that the number of 9Rs inflates the ninth-grade numbers by approximately 200 students, statistics do not confirm a corresponding increase in tenth-, eleventh- or twelfth-grade student populations, indicating that the "9Rs" are very likely to drop out of school. Only 65.6% of Hispanic female 1990 freshmen were enrolled in twelfth grade in 1994 (California Basic Education Data Systems 1990-1994). For Hispanic boys, the statistics are even more grim: Only 34.5% of Hispanic male 1990 freshmen were enrolled in twelfth grade in 1994 at Westhills High School (California Basic Education Data Systems 1990-1994).

STAFF: Students can slip right through with all F's, and we carry them until June, then they're gone. They never show up again. . . . We say—it's a terrible thing to say—thank God it's one less headache. They don't necessarily show up as dropouts. They just disappear and don't reenroll.

The district's assessment of the school drop-out rate also fails to accurately track students who leave school during the summer. Nor does the Westhills School District track students who leave school and enroll with independent study programs, some of whom will eventually drop out of these programs. Consequently, it is likely that the school district's reported drop-out rate of 28% underestimates the actual number of student drop-outs.

Ninth grade appears to be the most precarious year for Hispanic students. An exceedingly high number of students do not make it past their first year of high school. At Westhills High, 24.5% of the ninth-grade Hispanic students (eighty-seven students) were listed as drop-outs for the 1993-1994 school year, according to district statistics. In comparison, 9% (sixteen students) of the Caucasian ninth-grade students and only 7% (seven students) of the African American ninth-grade students were noted to have dropped out their first year of high school.

One of the problems facing ninth-grade students, according to the counseling staff, is brought about by the practice of social promotion at the junior high school level. Junior high school students are promoted regardless of attendance and work performance. Consequently, many ninth-grade students do not "buckle down and do the work" expected of them. After the first six weeks of school, the Westhills High School "F List" was published. There were over 350 ninth-grade students with more than 1,300 F's on their progress reports. The counselor who showed me the report noted:

The problem with the dumbing down of our students is so overwhelming. I wouldn't even know where to start. Our F List came out. We had 350 freshmen with over 1,300 F's on it. Where do you start getting a handle on a problem of that size? The answer is programmatic. We've got to change something, but where do we begin? How can you help that many students?

What is even more disconcerting is that of the 292 high school graduates of 1994, only 44 (15%) high school seniors completed course requirements that would enable them to enroll at one of the University of California campuses. Of these 44 students, only 10 (3.5% of graduating seniors) are classified as Hispanic, only 2 (0.7% of graduating seniors) are Hispanic girls.

SEGREGATION AND TRACKING

Westhills High School fits the national profile for Hispanic children, which suggests that Hispanic children attend the most segregated schools in the United States (Donato, Menchaca, and Valencia 1991; Menchaca and Valencia 1990; Orum 1986, 1988). This is troubling, given research that indicates that ethnic isolation and school segregation have been linked to poor academic performance and limited educational opportunities (Donato, Menchaca, and Valencia 1991, Espinosa and Ochoa 1986, Orfield 1988a, 1988b; Valencia 1984).

STUDENT: They call our school the ghetto school.

LD: Who does?

STUDENT: Everyone. They dog [insult] our school because there's a lot of minorities here. They think everybody at this school is a gang member or a drug dealer.

This attitude can also be found among the teachers: "Everyday I come to class, I assume that my students are on drugs and carrying a weapon." This attitude is not common; however, many of the teachers and staff told me that they felt Westhills High School's poor reputation was undeserved: "They're basically good kids. Maybe a little rowdy, but that's what being a teenager is all about."
    However, many of the teachers and administrators placed the responsibility for poor student performance directly on the students and their families.

ADMINISTRATOR: The number-one factor in student academic performance is home environment. That will never change.

Some counselors, teachers, and students attributed their school's poor performance in academics directly to the large Hispanic student population.

TEACHER: A lot of the kids who don't do well in school are the Hispanic kids, especially the ESL kids. One of the big problems is that they disappear in November, and we don't see them again until March. They have to go to Mexico with their families for the holidays. The problem is that the Mexican families don't value education, especially for the girls.

This is an interesting point of view, given the contradictory evidence regarding immigrant and Hispanic native-born student performance. Some researchers have indicated that immigrant students actually perform better than their native-born peers (Matuti-Bianchi 1986, 1991; Ogbu 1991a, 1991b; Romo 1984; Suarez-Orozco 1986). However, other research indicates that immigrant students are more likely to drop out of school (Valencia 1991). The students that I worked with were first, second, and third generation; I was not able to compare their attitudes toward school with that of their immigrant peers. However, it does appear that the peer culture of both groups does not support academic success. This is important because peer culture has been shown to have a strong influence on the retention rates of high school students (Valverde 1987).

Many of the Hispanic students' families rarely intervene in their children's education. While budget considerations and new pedagogical attitudes emphasize greater parental involvement, changing family patterns often work against parental involvement. For example, the parents of many Hispanic students work long hours and often find it difficult to attend school meetings. This is further exacerbated by school counselors who leave school at 3 p.m. Consequently, parents who wish to meet with school officials are only able to do so if they can leave their jobs during the afternoon. Unfortunately, many of the students have parents who work at jobs that make it impossible for them to meet with school counselors, administrators, and teachers. The lack of bilingual counselors also makes it uncomfortable for many of the Spanish-speaking parents to approach the school with their concerns and problems. Also, quite a few of the girls have parents who have never completed high school. The girls told me that while their parents value education, many of their parents feel embarrassed or intimidated about going to the school. Reformers of education who call for increased family involvement in schools (See Clark 1983) fail to address problems and current changes in the structure of family life that inhibit parental involvement (David 1993).

Many parents feel that the school is not doing enough to prepare their children for employment or college. Conversely, the school perceives the parents as uninvolved or unsupportive of their children's education. Unfortunately, many of the Hispanic parents do not have the cultural capital (Bourdieu and Passeron 1977) to help their children navigate through the educational system. Sometimes, students are placed in a position of interpreting school rules and regulations for their non-English-speaking parents, to the detriment of their education. For example, sixteen-year-old Araceli told her mother that she did not need to take any math classes in order to graduate from high school, when in fact the school requires two years of math as a prerequisite to graduation.

Aside from the geographically obvious forms of segregation that occur within and between school districts, within many schools there also exists an even more insidious form of segregation, termed "ability tracking" (Meier and Stewart 1991). This type of segregation is very prevalent at Westhills High School. Hispanic students, both English-speaking and Spanish-speaking students, are overwhelmingly distributed in remedial-level classes.

SAÚL: I was supposed to be in Algebra. There was too many white kids in there, so I told my counselor that it was too hard, and they put me in Math A this semester. That's cool—in that class, it's mostly Mexicans.

Meier and Stewart (1991) argue that tracking constitutes "second generation discrimination" for Hispanic students. They argue that schools use academic grouping and discipline in a discriminatory manner that serves to segregate Hispanic students from their Anglo peers. Students are grouped according to ability;

however, these groupings become permanent education routes for children who have little or no ability to change tracks (Oakes 1985).

Students who are placed in bilingual education classes are often even more disadvantaged than their English-speaking peers, since bilingual classes often employ remedial course content (Meier and Stewart 1991). Such placement tracks these students in nonacademic classes for the duration of their schooling and thus limits their academic future. Furthermore, while research indicates that second-language learning is best accomplished in settings where communicative interaction is encouraged (Chamot and O'Malley 1986; Krashen 1982), much of the ESL curriculum at Westhills High School emphasizes rote learning, memorization, and independent study. Also, because legislation governing bilingual education does not require concomitant bicultural education, bilingual programs are often implemented in such a way as to group students in homogeneous units, thus using language ability to segregate and track students further (Meier and Stewart 1991, 78).

This type of ability tracking has repercussions for students' access to higher education.

TEACHER: This is not a college-prep class. If you think you want to go to college, get your parents to call the school and change this class before Friday.

TEACHER [*talking to me in front of the students*]: You'll notice a stark difference between these kids and first-period kids. The dynamics of putting kids together is very interesting to me. . . . or do you think that intellect might have something to do with it? I think these kids might be more college bound, although they're not supposed to be.

While Hispanic students are attending colleges in increasing numbers, they still lag far behind their Anglo counterparts. The U.S. Department of Education (1992) estimates that only 6% of Hispanic students enroll in college, compared with 76.5% of Anglo students.

The deleterious long-term effects of tracking are also recognized by many of the students:

ANDREA: I want to be a teacher but not a bilingual teacher because those kids are, you know, those kids don't really care. They don't want to learn. You know, they are kind of slow in their classes. My mom didn't allow the school to put me in bilingual classes in kinder-garten. They wanted to, but my mom told them no. But my friend was put in them and now my friend is in all the low classes in school.

As noted by many researchers this type of tracking contributes to the high drop out rate of Hispanic students, since non-academic tracks which emphasize rote learning and limit classroom discussion also have the least holding power for students (Peng and Takai 1983; Brown, Rosen and Hill 1980; Gilmarten 1980).

One of the problems with the tracking system is that many students self-select remedial classes in order to be with their friends. Curriculum choice is also a statement about the student's gender, ethnic group, and class affiliation, as exemplified by Saúl's choice to switch to math tracks in order to be in a class with his "Mexican" cohort. However as Riddell (1992) notes, student agency functions within the constraints of the school-driven channeling of students into specific classes. Counselors at Westhills High School strongly influence student course choice and curriculum tracking:

COUNSELOR: Placement and assessment of a student is based primarily on teacher recommendation. We would love to have someone administer a placement test, but no one is willing to do it. We would like as much information as possible to determine where to place a kid. Sometimes a parent can request a class for their child, but placement is not based on a student's request at all; students have no input into the process.

LD: So why are you taking this class?

STUDENT: I dunno. My counselor put me in it.

While counselors do channel students into different tracks, students may offer little resistance to counselor recommendations. For example, when Azalia complained that her counselor had enrolled her in a class that she had already passed, I suggested that she talk with her counselor about changing her schedule. After meeting with her counselor, Azalia told me that her counselor had refused to change her schedule. Instead, the counselor told Azalia that she would receive science credit for taking the class first semester and elective credit for repeating it second semester. Azalia's response: "It's okay, I don't go to that class much anyway."

As Gaskell (1985) points out, theoretical issues regarding curriculum choice need to address student agency, choice, and consciousness, as well as the constraints placed on them by school organization and social structure. Students are making curriculum decisions, but they do so within the framework of the school organization. Overworked counselors cannot always meet the demands of their jobs. Students who lack a clear idea of their goals are often shuffled into classes simply to get the numbers to work, particularly since such students are often less likely to confront or question an adult teacher's or counselor's decision.

Sometimes students fall through the cracks of the school organization. When Jorge, a graduating senior from El Salvador, tried to apply for college, he was surprised to learn that he lacked high school foreign language credits, compulsory for admission into all California public colleges and universities. Despite the fact that Jorge speaks Spanish at home, the college would not accept his application without two years of high school-level foreign language instruction. His Westhills High School counselor denied all responsibility for failing to enroll Jorge in foreign language classes: "Jorge never told me he wanted to go to college." However, Jorge had been enrolled in college preparatory classes for the last three years of high school. While students should take some responsibility for their own education, it is inappropriate for school administrators and counselors, despite their overwhelming workload (each counselor is responsible for approximately 450 students), to place the entire burden of educational planning on the students or their families.

SEXISM AND RACISM ON CAMPUS

Most students cite peer culture as the locus of the majority of sexist and racist incidents that occurred at school. However, this does not mean that the school organization, faculty, and staff do not affirm these types of prejudicial attitudes. Research indicates that a significant number of teachers have little understanding or tolerance for cultural and racial differences (Brah and Minkas 1985; Mirza 1992). There are several teachers at Westhills High School who demonstrate very insensitive attitudes toward their Hispanic, African American, and Asian students. One African American girl told me that she felt that "Mexican" and "black" boys were discriminated against at school.

RAYLESHA: They see you and they stereotype you. The teachers think you're in a gang just 'cause of the way you dress. It's harder for the black guys and the Mexican guys, especially the Mexican guys. We have this teacher and he's got a bunch of Mexican guys in his class who don't speak English. He doesn't mean to, but I think he gets too frustrated that he takes it out on them. I think they put all those Mexican guys in elective classes 'cause they can't do anything else. Too many teachers don't speak Spanish here, but they [students] should learn to speak English. If they can't speak English, then they aren't American citizens. That's how I feel about it.

Raylesha's prejudice against Spanish-speaking "Mexican" students is affirmed by the teacher's attitude toward his non-English-speaking students.

Several teachers also patronize their Hispanic students in what I found to be an offensive manner. For example, one teacher routinely ended instructions to a group of English-speaking Latino students in the class with comments such as, "Do you guys *comprende* this?"

As noted by Fine (1991), Fordham (1988), and Fordham and Ogbu (1986), schools tend to censure students who have strong political or ethnic identities. This is also true of Westhills High School.

TEACHER: She's a good kid. She's not involved in the gangster image that so many of them are. She's your average, hardworking, middle-class kid. She doesn't seem to hang around the other Hispanic students much. She just doesn't seem to have much in common with them, you know. She's real school oriented.

The Latino students who are the most academically successful at Westhills High School adopt a raceless persona (Fordham 1988).

High-achieving Latino students' raceless images are achieved in a variety of ways. For example, as with many adolescent subcultures (Hebdige 1987), clothing style is one of the more salient markers of group affiliation at Westhills High School. Many of the academically successful Latino students dress in what they call "casual-style" clothing. They avoid wearing the sagging pants, midriff tops, dark colors, and heavy makeup preferred by many other Latina students at the school. In fact, some of these students are so successful that their peers question the student's ethnic affiliation.

CATALINA: In seventh and eighth grade, I wanted to fit in, to be Mexican. So I used to dress *cholo*. But it caused a lot of problems with my mom. Most people don't think it's true that I'm Mexican. But I'm proud to be Mexican, but it doesn't offend me if they think I'm white. They don't think I'm Mexican because I dress casual, not *cholo* style. Sometimes they tell me to prove I'm Mexican and tell me to say something in Spanish. I used to, but now I don't feel like I have to prove myself to them. . . . You know Lydia? She can't decide her identity—she dresses funny. One day she dresses surfer and then she dresses *cholo* style. It's like she doesn't know what her identity is.

Having an identity at school is very important in shaping a student's peer relations. Most of the students form race and ethnically exclusive friendship groups; very rarely do students of different ethnic and racial backgrounds choose to spend their leisure time together.

CINDY: I know there ain't no one way to act for your color, but, please, whatever color you are, please, act it. I know some black girls that are talking valley talk and white girls that are trying to act black. . . . saying, "Girl, you say what, girlfriend?" I want to tell them, "You got it easy—you're white. Why you trying to act black?" Everybody should act their own race.

There are a few students who appropriated a Mexican identity despite the fact that they are not Latino. One Filipina student managed her Mexican identity so well that most of her friends did not know that her parents had immigrated from the Philippines.

Many Latino students are offended if someone identifies them as white. When one of the social science teachers attempted to introduce the concepts of race (what you are born with), culture (what you learn), and nationality (where you live) to a group of students, there was a near mutiny in the classroom on the part of the Chicano students. The Caucasian teacher told several Chicano students that both he and they were members of the same racial category. When he suggested in class to these students that their race was Caucasian, their nationality was American, and their culture was Chicano, the students became very upset with the teacher.

CARLA: The whites always want to claim something that's not white. I don't care what you say. I'm not white. I'm Mexican.

For some weeks after this class, the Chicano students were still discussing, and denying, their racial affiliation among themselves.

Among the Latino students, there is also very little mixing between immigrant students and their first-, second-, and third-generation counterparts. When I tried to encourage several of the students to join the school's MEChA (Movimiento Estudiantial Chicano de Aztlán) club, they declined, saying that the club was "mostly for the ESL students." The students I knew regarded the immigrant students with contempt. This ethnic divide is partly caused by local gang divisions. Most of the immigrant students lived in "B Street" territory. In contrast, most of the first- and second-generation students lived in Varrio Granos. Thus, gang divisions add another element to each group's dislike and avoidance of the other.

Fierce competition for jobs also contributes to the animosity that exists between the two groups. Many of the legal residents of Varrio Granos voted in favor of Proposition 187, a ballot initiative that denies welfare benefits and employment to illegal immigrants. Andrea's father voted for the proposition because he felt that the *mojados* (wetbacks) were unfairly competing with his gardening business by avoiding paying income taxes, which, in turn, allowed them to undercut his prices.

Racism and discrimination also influence gender relationships (Phoenix 1987; Spelman 1988). Class and race issues often shape the intraethnic relationships between men and women. Many of the adolescent boys at Westhills High School are extremely protective of "their" women. Girls who date across ethnic and racial groups are often harassed by their male peers.

While the sexism found in their peer culture powerfully impacts the lives of adolescent girls, traditional male/female relationships are also affirmed by the school in many different ways.

TEACHER: I need four strong boys to carry these books for me.

MELISSA: I'll do it. I'll go.

TEACHER: No, I need boys to do it. They're very heavy.

MELISSA: That's sexist. I can do it.

TEACHER: No, it's not. I just don't want you to hurt yourself.

Conversely, however, girls are often asked to relay messages to the office or other teachers because they are considered to be more reliable than male students.

Sometimes teachers demonstrate blatantly sexist attitudes. I sat in one class while two teachers discussed dividing the students into two separate groups. The male teacher, frustrated over the amount of time it was taking to accomplish the division, loudly stated in front of the class, "Give me all the bimbos. I don't care. Let's just get going on this." In another class, the male math teacher told the students, "Lisa is here to help tutor if you feel comfortable going to a female for help." One male teacher hung a poster of a woman wearing a bikini in his classroom. The poster remained in this teacher's classroom until protests by a substitute teacher forced the administration to take action and have the poster removed.

Westhills High School's sport-oriented culture also affirms sexist attitudes among the student population. With regard to sports, the school is an "active maker of gender" (Kessler, Ashendon, Connell, and Dowsett 1985). The sports-oriented masculine identity emphasized at Westhills High School is based on characteristics such as endurance, intimidation, confrontation, and denigration of femininity. This emphasis on the denigration of femininity in male adolescent culture is not surprising given research that suggests that male supremacy is a key element in the construction of adolescent masculinity (Brake 1980; Willis 1977, 1981b; Wood 1984). What is surprising is that the adult male football coaches particularly encourage this type of masculine identity, using shame and intimidation to motivate their players.

JOE: The coaches yell at you to make you stronger. They call you pansy or girls. It makes you mad and then you can take out your aggression on the field.

COACH: You won't get mad at me, will you?

LD: Why should I get mad?

COACH: Well, whenever a player says, "Coach, I can't block that guy." We say, "Only girls can't; guys do."

Furthermore, the coaches routinely call boys that fail to perform well in practice "wusses," "pansies," and "fags," euphemisms meant to question a boy's sexual orientation and his manhood.

These types of attitudes feed directly into peer relationships that emphasize male superiority to the detriment of adolescent girls. Many girls perceive their appropriate role at school as spectator, cheering for male accomplishments.

ROSARIO: I was thinking about going out for soccer, but the guys don't like it when their girlfriend gets all sweaty. It's better to just watch if you're a girl.

Cheerleaders told me that they were encouraged by their adviser to "adopt" a football player and bake cookies or bring him treats every game day.

This emphasis on sexism and sports-oriented masculinity hurts boys as well as girls. Often the boys get seduced by their star status and consequently fail to perform academically. Michael, captain of the football team and star basketball player, barely managed to graduate from Westhills High School. As of two weeks before graduation, he had still not made any future plans. Michael, at eighteen years old, standing five feet ten inches, still entertains visions of playing for the National Basketball Association despite the fact that he had not been approached by any college teams.

Homophobia is also rampant in the school. Despite the fact that the school has instituted a new sexual harassment policy, students who call each other names such as *fag*, *homo*, or *lesbo* are very rarely reprimanded by teachers or staff. Two lesbian students chose to leave school rather than endure the taunts of their peers. Furthermore, this type of attitude is not limited to the students. Several members of the school staff and faculty also demonstrate severely homophobic attitudes. When a staff member started rumors that a particular teacher was lesbian, the administration was unable to quell the rumors effectively. Some of the faculty, staff, and students are openly hostile toward this teacher. Several teachers refuse to work with this woman on committee projects, and one staff member was fired, then later reinstated because of the incident.

The demographic profile of the school's teaching staff also affirms students' sexist attitudes. The following conversation occurred during an interview session with three ninth-grade girls.

LD: Are the teachers different than in junior high?

All three: Yeah.

LINDA: I got almost all guys. They have more guy teachers in this school 'cause they're stricter. In elementary school there's more girls. Women teachers here are for the textile arts and home ec and stuff like that.

SONYA: I have one for English and PE [physical education] too.

LINDA: Oh, yeah, PE, too. Women teachers can teach PE.

However, even where the school district attempted to diversify the school's administrative staff, student perceptions limit the impact. When the school introduced its new female principal, many students had difficulty believing that she was in fact the principal. Most students refer to the male vice principal as the person in charge of the school. This is partly a reflection of school policy that defers most disciplinary problems to the vice principals for handling. However, even among the two vice principals, there is a gender division. According to the students, the female vice principal is someone who can intercede on your behalf, whereas the male vice principal is perceived as the school enforcer.

STUDENT ATTITUDES AND CLASSROOM INTERACTION

At the beginning of the school year, I conducted an anonymous survey of high school students to assess their attitudes toward school. Out of the 136 students who returned the survey, approximately 48.5% of the respondents were girls, and 67% of the respondents identified themselves as Latino or part Latino (e.g., Latino/Anglo). The majority of the students who took the survey (82%) were in their ninth- or tenth-grade year at school. The survey was administered during class in several different classroom settings, including one college preparatory class. Some 68% of the students reported that they liked school. They did not present much in the way of any collective critique of school or the school organization. Students cited gang violence (59%) as the most pressing problem at Westhills High School. Drugs (15%), poor student attitudes (4%), lack of money (3%), poor teachers, graffiti, and bad neighborhoods composed the rest of their complaints. When asked directly about the school staff and faculty, the students complained about specific teachers or specific classes.

Students most frequently complained that school is boring and irrelevant to their lives. As one male student noted about his literature class, "What's the point in learning this? It ain't gonna get me a job." Ninth-grade students also complained about the "dumb" words they had to learn on their weekly vocabulary lists. Students are given weekly vocabulary lists that include words such as *avarice* and *disperse*. However, the student essays and written survey material that I reviewed indicate that most of the students cannot spell words such as *kitchen* or *brought*, nor do they know the difference between *their, there*, and *they're*.

The second most frequent litany of complaints that I heard from students during interview sessions focuses on specific teachers, "Mr.— is so boring. All he does is talk at you," or, "Mrs.— is really mean. You can't say nothing in her class."

VERONICA: I would change everything about this school. The teachers don't teach nothing. They don't care. You sit in the classes—don't you think they're boring? The teachers don't do nothing.

The students seem to object most often to the modes of discourse used by teachers (Strong 1993) (i.e., lectures and rote learning drills) and the inflexibility of the curriculum. For the most part, students are not encouraged to create their own meanings or to deconstruct "objective" knowledge. However, to be fair to the teaching staff, many of the students are not engaged in school. For the most part, the students adhere to the form of schooling, yet do not engage the content. Students are more concerned with turning in homework than understanding the lesson. They routinely copy from each other or hastily scribble an assignment the morning before it is due. In one instance, Linda enrolled in the same class her sister had taken the year before. Linda used her sister's notebook of assignments from the class and simply erased her sister's name from worksheets or copied the work over and handed it to the teacher.

Teachers and curriculum also privilege form over substance. For example, according to the manner in which Westhills High School implements Math A, a California State curriculum alternative to Algebra 1, teachers are not required to test student knowledge. According to the Math A teachers from Westhills High School, students play math games in order to build self-esteem and raise the students' interest in math. Class work includes games such as "To Build It." Students are assigned a set of colored blocks, then they are given a set of directions on how to place the colored blocks in relation to each other. Students turn in their completed assignments at the end of class. Homework is not part of the curriculum. In response to my query, teachers agreed that students who pass Math A are unable to do even basic math, for example, balancing a checkbook. The key to passing Math A is to turn in work at the end of the period. There are no tests or exams in the class. The only way to fail Math A is to fail to attend class. Thus, students who pass Math A more than likely cannot balance a budget or calculate interest on a loan.

The Math A curriculum is an extreme example of form-based curricula. However, even in many of the other classes, teaching methods emphasize form at the expense of content. One science teacher required that her students color code their lecture notes and turn them in for credit. The students did not understand the purpose of coloring their notes—"To make them look nice for the teacher, I guess." Other teachers dictate class notes to the students, word by word, including punctuation. Some teachers write out the class notes on the chalkboard and give students time to copy them during class. Students are then encouraged to go home and memorize the notes for exams.

This type of teaching methodology limits meaningful discussion. For the most part, critical analysis is not encouraged on the part of the students. During one classroom assignment, student groups were asked to make a list of leadership qualities and then identify individuals who best exemplified their list of characteristics. After presenting their list of characteristics and identifying Martin Luther King as an example of a historical leader, one group of students gave a presentation arguing that present-day leaders do not exist because "nobody cares about unity anymore. There are too many crazy people out there. Everybody's too selfish." Rather than engage these students in a discussion about their perceptions of a current leadership crisis, the teacher became visibly angry at this group of students and demanded that they redo their project and this time follow the directions by identifying an appropriate leader. In this way, students are "silenced" (Fine 1991) into compliance, and meaningful critique is limited.

This silencing is very apparent when it comes to discussion of controversial issues. Rather than use controversy to stimulate classroom discussion, knowledge is presented by the teacher in a manner that is flat and prepackaged. In one classroom, when students broached the subject of the abortion debate, the teacher became visibly agitated. Instead of allowing students to explore the reasons and rationalizations presented by each side of the debate, the teacher squelched all discussion.

TEACHER: We don't need to start a discussion on that. Some people are for abortion and some are against it. Let's just leave it at that.

This lack of interactive learning impacts both the students' and teachers' perceptions of classroom dynamics. Students complain that the teachers "don't teach." Teachers complain that students just want to be "spoon fed" information.

For most students, peer interaction takes precedence over everything else at school—so much so that socializing and academic work often come into direct competition in the classroom setting. Talking among themselves is a favorite classroom activity for the students. For many of the Latino students, their peer group is not very supportive of academic pursuits. For example, becoming labeled as a "schoolgirl" or "schoolboy" usually had very negative connotations.

Students most often cite "passing" as their primary academic goal. However, a grade of "D" will earn a student credit toward graduation. Consequently, most students interpret this to mean that a "D" grade is passing. Thus, many students put forth a minimum of effort in their classes.

In one sophomore English class, the students routinely failed to do the assigned homework. Each week the teacher became more frustrated as she realized that the students were not reading any of the assigned material. In order to stimulate the students, the teacher resorted to playing an audio recording of the novel that they were studying. However, even this was only partially successful. Many students tuned out during the recorded reading of the novel. Finally, in desperation, the teacher rented a movie adaptation of the novel and showed it during class.

STUDENT GOALS AND SCHOOL ORGANIZATION

Most of the Latina girls at Westhills High School received ambiguous messages from school, family, and the media about their future roles as adult women.

ANDREA: My mom's always saying to me, "You won't get a husband because you won't learn how to cook." I don't do anything in the house.

LD: You need to go to college so you can hire a housekeeper.

ANDREA: That's what my mom keeps telling me—"Do you want to support Octavio like I been supporting your dad? You need to get a good education so you can get your own job, a good job."

Many girls feel torn between their desire for a good job and their desire to be a good wife and mother to their future husband and children. As with other adolescent girls (Gibson 1988; Goldstein 1986; Riddel 1992; Weis 1990), the majority of Chicana students endorse both conventional gender roles and a belief in equal opportunity for women. They value school education as a means toward achieving economic independence, yet most of them do not plan on pursuing careers. Of the students who express a desire to go to college, most are not enrolled in college preparatory classes, and even fewer have taken the PSAT (Preliminary Scholastic Aptitude Test) or SAT (Scholastic Aptitude Test) college entrance exams.

Many of the students that I spoke with cannot detail any specific future goals for themselves. The students who do have goals either harbor unrealistic goals or do not have any idea how to achieve these goals. Most of the girls who envision a future career for themselves aspire to traditionally female occupations, usually in child care or elementary education. The majority of girls plan on working for a few years, then staying home with their children: "I want to have a big family, so I only want a job for now. I'm not interested in a career."

LOURDES: People want to get married. They want to get out of the house and have kids, you know, start their life right away after high school. Mostly the girls talk about getting married.

As with many working-class adolescent girls, the girls at Westhills High School tend to emphasize their future domestic role (McRobbie 1991; Valli 1986). However, many of the girls are aware, at least at some level, that the domestic ideal, a two-parent household where the husband works and the wife stays at home, is not the experiential norm.

LD: Do you think it's more important for guys or girls to graduate, or is it the same?

LINDA. I think it's the guys.

CARLA: I think it's the girls.

LINDA: It's the guys because they can get the jobs so you don't have to work.

CARLA: But if they leave, what can you do? 'Cause the guys, they can work in construction; a girl can't because it's too hard for them.

LINDA: They need office jobs.

CARLA: Yeah, they need office jobs, so girls have to get a diploma.

LINDA: If I graduate, if I get that far and everything. . . . I always wanted to be a vet. I always liked animals and everything.

LD: You're not sure you're going to graduate?

LINDA: Whatever happens, happens.[2]

Girls still overwhelmingly consider office jobs the ideal job for women. Carla notes that construction work is too hard for girls. However, she also recognizes that a woman needs to be economically self-sufficient.[3] Most of the girls have mothers who work, usually at low-status service sector jobs with poor pay. Given their perceptions of potential job prospects, it is no wonder that the girls choose to emphasize their future roles as wives and mothers, rather than as workers.

As Valenzuela (1993) and Ogbu (1974, 1981) have noted, students' perceptions of their potential job opportunities influence their orientation toward school. While the link between employment opportunities and educational aspirations is less clear for girls than for boys (McRobbie 1991; Valli 1986), most of the girls have a fairly realistic assessment of the financial value of a high school diploma in the current labor market.

MONICA: I can get the same job without graduating from school. You don't need a diploma to work at Burger King; all you need is a green card or Social Security number.

The limited material resources available in the *varrio* make the decision to conform to cultural values that emphasize motherhood appealing to many girls. The girls are aware that the labor market offers very few well-paid opportunities for women who do not have a college degree.

Several of the girls also noted that job opportunities are also often based as much on personal appearance as aptitude.

AZALIA: You gotta look pretty. That's how you get the job.

LD: What job?

AZALIA: Any job. They're not gonna hire somebody who isn't pretty.

This perception is not without foundation, especially for girls (Cockburn 1991; Valli 1986). Valli's research (1986) on girls' transitions from school to employment indicates that appearance plays an important role in determining the type of jobs for which girls are considered employable.

Westhills High School does offer career and college counseling to its students. However, the school is caught between encouraging the somewhat unrealistic goals of its students and providing information requested by the students. For example, many of the girls indicate that they are interested in pursuing jobs as either models or fashion designers. Consequently, the school's career counselor sponsored a variety of speakers from both modeling and fashion schools. Arlene, Margie, and Yesenia all attended a presentation by the Fashion Institute of Design and Merchandizing. None of them know how to sew, although they all express an interest in becoming fashion designers.

While the school's career counselor tries to interest girls in nontraditional career choices, she has difficulties recruiting girls to these types of presentations. Home Depot developed a corporate partnership with the school and offered classes in wallpaper hanging and tile setting to the students. However, while the school bulletins encourage girls to become involved in these ventures, they rarely do so. Peer and family pressure keep them from attending: "That kind of work is for the guys. I would be embarrassed to go there. They would make fun of you if you went. Besides, my dad says that's not a good job for a woman—too many guys around."

However, while nontraditional career choices are emphasized by the career counselor, at times efforts toward engaging students in nontraditional job opportunities do little to affirm students' own efforts toward this end. During the year, the school sponsored a group of students to attend a nontraditional job fair in downtown San Diego. However, among the pipe-fitting, bricklaying, and military displays were booths sponsored by Maric College, specializing in careers such as receptionist, medical assistant, and nurse's aid, and two colleges of fashion design.

Many high schools, in their efforts to engage the students and cut costs, allow proprietary schools access to their student population. These proprietary schools often offer to provide free presentations to high school classes in exchange for an opportunity to speak about their schools. The presentations run the gamut from "How to Dress for Success" to "Successful Job Interview Techniques." However, often the presentations are thinly disguised recruiting opportunities.

During one presentation by a proprietary school specializing in fashion, the glamorous school representative told a fascinated group of adolescent girls:

Wouldn't you just love to have a job where all you have to do is shop, girls? It sounds much more fun than the boring jobs like accounting, doesn't it? Our goal is to make you a professional in two years.

The speaker next presented details about her school's new associate's degree in retail.

SPEAKER: We have a new program that offers an AA [Associate of Arts] degree in retail. Companies are real excited about our new two-year program because they can offer our students more money. And you don't have to take courses that have nothing to do with fashion like at other colleges.

The school representative then mentioned names of several high-profile clothing and department stores, such as Charlotte Russe and Nordstroms: "So, girls, wouldn't you just love to work there and shop all the time?" Then she mentioned that people who have M.B.A.s are competing directly with graduates from her particular fashion college. According to the speaker, the girls could expect to earn $20,000 to $25,000 annual salary after graduating from fashion college.

The impact of these types of proprietary schools on the working-class Latino students is exacerbated by the fact that the majority of students do not differentiate between four-year universities, two-year community colleges, and proprietary schools. Most students refer to all of these postsecondary institutions as "college." Students often choose which "college" to attend based on the decisions of their friends.

Unfortunately, the advertising methods employed by many of the proprietary schools often confuse students into making poorly informed decisions. When eighteen-year-old Catalina received a brochure from Maric College advising her that she had been accepted to the school, she approached me to find out if that meant that she *had* to go to that particular school. Catalina was concerned because she was hoping to go to school somewhere else. When I asked her if she had sent any money to Maric College or signed any papers, she replied that she had not even talked to representatives from the college. Catalina eventually opted to attend community college, partly for financial reasons. Her parents were unable to pay for Catalina's enrollment into a proprietary school because they were making payments on a loan for her brother who had enrolled at another proprietary school several years earlier. Unfortunately, her brother's school had declared bankruptcy before her brother had finished the program; her parents were left paying the loan while her brother looked for employment.

Some of the Chicana girls at Westhills High School can be characterized as goal oriented. They conceive of school as something that one has to finish in order to achieve a better life. Andrea has plans to go to college to study for her teaching credential. Leticia is not sure about her career goals, but she definitely plans on attending the local community college. While both of these girls look toward attending college, neither of them is an A or a B student.

The two girls are participating in a special school program, Achievement Via Individual Determination (AVID). The program orients "underrepresented" (defined by socioeconomic status and ethnicity) students toward college by offering tutors and special instruction that enables these students to enroll in college preparatory classes at the high school level. The program also provides money for field trips to college campuses and provides tutorial material to enhance AVID students' preparations for their college entrance exams.

As with many of the high-achieving students, both male and female, Leticia and Andrea have very Jeffersonian notions of achievement. Students who do well in school, according to them, work hard. Students who perform poorly in school, they characterize as lazy.

LETICIA: If you want it more, you're going to get to school and get the job. If you don't, you're lazy. Then you're poor—like you're on welfare, like that. Some people make an effort to make themselves better.

ANDREA: Yeah, people make choices. If you're gonna have a baby at a young age, you're set up to live on minimum wage.

LETICIA: I'm going to work my butt off. I'm going to college 'cause I want money. You just don't get something 'cause you think you deserve it.

LD: Is that why you guys have stayed in school?

LETICIA: I'm here 'cause I want a better life. I don't want to just spend my life working at McDonald's. I want to be able to buy a nice car and clothes and things.

ANDREA: I want to prove to my family, especially my aunt. She doesn't even think I'm going to graduate. My mom tells me to ignore her.

LETICIA: It's like some of them think, like the gang members, they don't know anybody in school. They don't think it can make your life better. They don't have people telling them, encouraging them to go. They haven't been on any field trips [to college campuses].

LD: So you think this class is helpful because you go on field trips, and it encourages you to go to college?

LETICIA: Not really. It's myself. If you want to do it, you can. Just like my mom says, it's 'cause of her always yelling to get me up for school. But it's not her yelling; it's myself.

ANDREA: Yeah. If you didn't want to go to school, you're not going to go even if your mom gets you up . . . but for some people, they aren't successful because they have to be taking care of things at home, taking care of other little kids or parents or other things more serious to worry about.

LETICIA: Some people just don't want to. I feel sorry for people like that. They can have the chance if they try, but they haven't seen the chance or they don't want it. Like my cousin, she's seventeen and she thinks it's too late for her to go back to school.

Both Leticia and Andrea made the decision to stay in school based on their perceptions of future educational and job opportunities, their need for self-respect, and their desire for peer and family approbation. In spite of the fact that both of these girls see education as a means of taking control of their lives, they are also cognizant of the obstacles that confront their peers, such as pressing family obligations, lack of educational awareness, and peer pressure. Thus, while they articulate a belief in the school achievement ideology, at some level they are also aware that the field of academic competition is not level.

While both Leticia and Andrea are academically oriented, they also maintain an affiliation with their Chicano peers. This makes it difficult for them. Leticia does not get good grades, nor does she apply herself in her classes. Contrary to her statement that she "works her butt off," Leticia is more interested in obtaining the latest clothing fashions than studying for exams. However, relative to many of her peers who have very little interest in school, she does spend more time on homework.

Leticia perceives school as something that will enable her to find a well-paying job. Thus, it could be argued that she conforms to the school's ideology that hard work produces monetary rewards. However, she makes maintaining her appearance a priority at school. She once confided to me that she skipped school on days that she did not like her particular clothing outfit. She always comes to school fashionably attired. She constantly fixes her makeup and hair during her classes. She also refuses to wear her prescription glasses because they make her look like a "nerd." Thus, while she professes a desire to go to college and conform to school norms, her actions often contradict school norms and values related to academic achievement, conforming, instead, to norms and values (both school and peer) that emphasize the link between appearance and femininity.

Andrea is also caught at the interstices of two cultural frameworks. She is encouraged by both the school and her mother to pursue her education. However, her mother also often laments that fact that Andrea will not be able to find a husband if she doesn't take an interest in domestic skills. Andrea has decided that she wants a career as a teacher, but she wants to work with elementary schools because she loves children. She has also decided that she is going to have her own child when she is twenty-four years old, even if she is not married, because she wants to be young enough "to relate" to her children.

Both of these girls perceive school success as a means toward achieving control over their lives. However, while they conform to school ideology, they do so in a way that also subverts it by conforming to values of femininity that emphasize appearance and motherhood.

While students like Leticia and Andrea perceive school as a means of asserting control over their lives, other students drop out of school for the same reason (Fine 1991; J. Macleod 1987; Ogbu 1974, 1981; Willis 1977, 1981a). For some girls, leaving school is as much a strategy for asserting control over their lives as choosing to stay in school and pursue a college education. For these girls, choosing to leave school can be a means of escaping academic failure. They are in effect opting out of school in order to pursue success within a different set of norms and values.

PAYASA: It [the decision to leave school] didn't matter anyway. I would've flunked out if I stayed in [school].

Most girls who drop out of school report that they had very dismal academic records prior to leaving school. Many female dropouts become pregnant. For these girls, the respect and approbation they receive from pursuing the valued role of mother more than makes up for their lack of academic success.

The option to pursue a domestic role makes the link between school resistance and economic opportunities more tenuous for girls than for boys. Are these girls opting out of a school system in which they cannot fully compete, or are they conforming to a construction of femininity that privileges the domestic role over an economic one? The question is not an easy one to resolve because not all forms of resistance are clearly linked to school, and their choices are often constrained by the limited options and resources, cultural and material, available to them.

SCHOOL RESISTANCE

Students who do stay in school resist school authority in a myriad of ways. While boys most often confront authority figures directly, or publicly disrupt classes, girls usually resist school authority by failing to pay attention in the classroom. Girls frequently write letters to their friends under the guise of note-taking during class lectures. They also put on makeup or style their hair during class. Sometimes they ignore a teacher's directions or comments, even when the comments are directed specifically toward them. Girls who do not pay attention in class are expressing a disdain for school. However, they are also expressing their femininity to their peers.

This feminine style of resistance is also somewhat congruent with the school's expectations of model student behavior. Whereas the school encourages student behavior that does not question school authority, many Chicana girls exaggerate this model as their primary mode of resisting school. These girls do not simply acquiesce to school authority; they often exhibit extremely passive behavior such as failing to perform schoolwork or failing to respond to their teachers. Because both peer culture and school ideology construct femininity as nonassertive, girls who act out in class are considered to be aberrations by both their teachers and peers. Rowdy behavior inside the classroom is less likely to be tolerated if it is demonstrated by girls. So girls are less likely to act out or confront their teachers or peers, limiting the oppositional content of their resistance.

In contrast, many boys find that the masculine sports-oriented culture of the school combined with a peer ideology of *machismo* conflicts with the school's expectations of model student behavior. Hispanic boys tend to exaggerate the competitiveness and confrontation found in the school's male culture as a means of achieving peer approval. Consequently, boys are more likely to be expelled for disrupting class or confronting school authorities than are girls. This may help explain the disparity between the consistently higher drop-out rates of Hispanic male students at Westhills High School when compared to their female peers.

Not all girls, however, resist school in the form of exaggerated passivity. As noted by Lesko (1988), Griffin (1987), and McRobbie (1978), some girls use overt sexuality to disrupt their classes. Carla routinely tried to embarrass her young male social studies teacher by asking him sexual questions: "Are you a virgin?" However, this type of sexualized behavior is censured by both school authorities and peer culture. The school rules forbid "inappropriate" clothing, including midriff tops and blouses that expose underclothing. Peers threaten girls with the label of sexual promiscuity if their behavior becomes too overtly sexual.

Truancy is also another means by which both boys and girls assert control over their personal space and time at school (Weis 1990; Willis 1977, 1981b). Rather than directly confronting school authority, students often ditch class in order to pursue social activities. Sometimes flyers advertising kickbacks, parties held during school hours, would be passed out at school among the students. These parties could get quite wild; alcohol and drugs were almost always present, usually provided by an older sibling or friend.

In some respects, attending a ditching party or kickback is as much a rebellion against cultural (Anglo and Chicano) constructions of femininity as school authority. Girls who attend these parties shed their demure image for one that is wild and daring. They often deliberately engage in behaviors deemed inappropriate for girls or women, such as public drunkenness, drug use, and excessive flirting and petting.

CARLOS: It don't look right for girls to get drunk. It's okay for the guys, but the girls—it's like they're trying to act all wild. I don't know why they come to the kickbacks. I guess they just want to be wild, you know, like the guys.

Similar to the boys, the girls drink alcohol in order to get drunk. However, they are cognizant of the fact that they face risks that their male counterparts do not.

LOURDES: I keep telling Veronica that she's gonna get a bad reputation from going to all those parties. It's real bad if a girl gets a reputation like that. She's too wild. She says she can take care of herself, but you know how the guys are. She's gonna end up in trouble.

VERONICA: I only go with my friends. We watch out for each other. It's just mainly for fun. You know, to do stuff you're not supposed to.[4]

As Lourdes notes, girls who regularly attend these parties risk becoming labeled as sexually promiscuous.

Whenever I attended the kickback parties, the girls treated me as an on-call chaperon. When the girls felt threatened by aggressive male attention, they would come and sit by me until they felt that they had regained control of the situation. The boys were not overly fond of my role as unsolicited chaperon, and eventually they stopped including me in their parties. Therefore, toward the end of my research, I found myself excluded from these kickbacks because, while girls often participated in these parties, they rarely hosted them.

Girls rarely resist school in a collective, confrontational manner. However, some girls demonstrate a more masculine form of resistance. Gang-affiliated girls adopt a mode of school resistance that closely resembles the working-class lads in Willis's (1977, 1981b) ethnography of British adolescents.

MORENA: I walked into class, and the teacher tells me to get out of my class. I told her right off, "Fuck you, bitch. . . . " I went to my counselor to get transferred out of that class, and they wouldn't do it. I told them, "Take me out of that class or I'm leaving school." My counselor said, "Go ahead. Try to leave school. You can't." I said, "Watch me." And I did—I got expelled. I hated that class and I hated that school.

Gang-affiliated girls participate in a more confrontational style of resistance, which often results in their expulsion from school. However, gang girls are not simply resisting school authority. As Giroux (1983) notes:

[S]tudents may violate school rules, but the logic that informs such behavior may be rooted in forms of ideological hegemony such as racism and sexism. Moreover, the source of such hegemony often originates outside of the school. Under such circumstances, schools become social sites where oppositional behavior is simply played out, emerging less as a critique of schooling than as an expression of dominant ideology. (285-286)

Gang-affiliated girls also use their gang membership to resist both the powerlessness associated with cultural constructions of adolescent femininity (Anglo and Chicano), as well as school norms and values. Their resistance, however, is best understood as conformity to the gang's hypermasculine ethos. However, while gang-affiliated girls attempt to align themselves with the masculine power associated with gang membership, they are also constrained by the gang's cultural values, which emphasize masculinity to the detriment of women.

SCHOOLING AND CHICANA ADOLESCENTS

There are four factors that contribute to the dismal scholastic achievements of Westhills's Chicana students: school, society, community, and the individual student. Within the school setting, boys and girls, Anglo and non-Anglo students often receive different treatment, leaving Chicana students marginalized. The curriculum and lack of Latina role models increase Chicana students' alienation from school. The school administration and faculty also fail to demonstrate enough flexibility to accommodate the needs of their Hispanic student population. Students and their parents are often overwhelmed by the bureaucracy and administrative details required to manage a student's education. Historical practices that deny Chicanas access to good jobs and economic security also increase the disjuncture between school ideology and their own experiences, making it difficult for Chicana students to stay in school or pursue higher education. The Chicano community in which they are immersed also conspires against their ability to achieve academic success because scholastic success is often equated with "acting white" and denying one's ethnic heritage. Last, the individual student also participates in her own scholastic failure by making inconsistent, impetuous, and immature decisions, a characteristic of most young people regardless of ethnic group affiliation.

NOTES

1. However, at the end of the school year the school was awarded a grant that procured funding for a new computer lab and an Internet project called the "Global Classroom." Unfortunately, the project was implemented after I left the campus. However, the Global Classroom is currently open to only sixty students from the campus.

2. Both Linda and Carla dropped out of Westhills High School before the end of their tenth-grade year.

3. Carla and her sisters were being raised by her mother and grandmother after her father left home. They did not receive any financial support from her father.

4. Veronica became pregnant before the end of the tenth grade.

Chapter 9

Girls and Gangs

Social science and public policy have historically ignored female gang members and issues related to female juvenile delinquency (Campbell 1984; Leonard 1982). Female participation in gangs has been neglected by researchers for several reasons. First, gangs are predominantly a male phenomenon. Law enforcement personnel estimate that only 5% to 10% of all gang members are female. However, this estimate is very conservative and probably underreports female gang membership (Pennel, Evans, Melton, and Hinson 1994). Second, male gang members have traditionally dominated the more high-profile/high-risk gang activities. In contrast, female gang members were relegated to the roles of "gang moll" or "den mother" (Harris 1988; Murphy 1978). However, this is changing. Girls are increasing their participation in the actual gang activities.

While the literature on gangs is overwhelmingly male oriented, there has been some limited research on female gang participation (Campbell 1984; Harris 1988; Taylor 1993). Unfortunately, however, most gang research addresses female delinquency and gang membership from the perspective of male gang members (Cohen 1955; Jankowski 1991; Padilla 1992; Miller 1958; Whyte 1955). Consequently, while there exists a great deal of research that investigates the relationship between gangs and their socioeconomic environments (Cloward and Ohlin 1960; Jankowski 1991; J. Moore 1985; Padilla 1992; Thrasher 1927; Whyte 1955), there has been little research that investigates both the cultural and gendered aspects of gang affiliation (Vigil 1988b).

DEFINING GANGS

In California the law enforcement agencies use four criteria to define a gang: (1) a group has a name or identified leadership, (2) members claim a territory or a criminal enterprise, (3) members associate on a continual basis, and (4) members engage in delinquent or criminal activity. The definition of a gang and gang membership has significant impact for both public policy and the public's perception of gang-related violence. Miller (1980) has argued that police departments may broaden or restrict the definition of gangs in order to further their own agendas. For example, the way that a "gang" is defined also determines the extent of the "gang problem" within a community. The public's perception of the gang problem, then, impacts on the amount of funding and number of officers allocated to the local law enforcement departments, as well as funding for social services and gang intervention programs.

Gangs have been consistently defined as a problem associated with male adolescents. While the majority of gang members are male, female gang members have a significant impact both directly and indirectly on gang subcultures. Their role in gangs has not been addressed by social services and gang intervention programs. Whereas gangs have been defined as a male problem by governmental agencies, teen pregnancy has been defined as a female problem. Almost all gang intervention/prevention programs are male centered: midnight basketball, boxing tournaments, lowrider art shows, and so on. In contrast, girls receive prenatal counseling and AFDC.

Definitions of gang membership may also have a deleterious impact on the gang members themselves. Horowitz (1990) notes that defining a gang as illegal shifts attention away from the "complex and problematic relationships" between gang members and legal institutions (45). Zatz (1985) notes that the label of gang member generally correlates with more stringent treatment of individuals within the juvenile justice system, including more severe treatment and harsher penalties than their non-gang-affiliated counterparts.

The way that a community chooses to define gangs also impacts gang statistics. For example, variation in record keeping and documentation across local law enforcement agencies skews statistical information. Curry, Ball, and Fox (1994), cited in Pennel et al. (1994, 19), found that some police departments did not classify female offenders as gang members. Thus the involvement of female gang members may be underreported in national statistical surveys. Furthermore, some departments define a gang-related homicide as a homicide involving two or more gang members, while other departments have a more stringent definition (Maxon and Klein 1990). There are no national guidelines to define what constitutes a "gang-related" crime. Consequently, if a gang member kills a rival over a drug deal because of a personal grievance, the homicide may not be categorized as gang related.

Researchers, law enforcement personnel, and gang members recognize a variation in levels of involvement with the gang. Most gang experts differentiate between hard-core, associate, peripheral, and "wannabe" (want to be) gang members. Hard-core, those who most seriously embrace the gang lifestyle, and associate, those who spend time with the gang on a semiregular basis, are the only gang members that are officially documented by local San Diego police departments. Local intervention agencies focus most of their attention on the peripheral members, individuals who live in gang neighborhoods and are friendly with gang members, and the wannabe's. However, as one agency worker noted, "unless we can offer them a better deal [than the gangs], and we can't, we lose them." The gang members also differentiate between members who are "real down for the hood" (protective of the neighborhood), those that "just kick it with us" (socialize or party), and wannabe's.

GANGS IN CALIFORNIA

Gang Profiles

At this time California's gangs are primarily divided along ethnic and racial lines. This is changing. Gangs are becoming more ethnically and racially diverse, but there still exists a great deal of tension and distrust between racially and ethnically segregated gang populations. While general profiles of gangs can be drawn along ethnic and racial lines, it should be noted, however, that even within ethnic and racial groups, there can exist a great deal of diversity.

Hispanic Gangs

In California, the Hispanic gangs, primarily of Mexican ethnic origin, constitute the majority of the gang population. The Department of Justice estimates that there are approximately 95,000 Hispanic gang members in California. This is not surprising given the population demographics of the state. Hispanic children comprise 31% of the population under eighteen years of age in California. They also comprise the largest group of California children living on incomes that fall below the national poverty line (Fellmeth, Kelemkiarian, and Reiter 1994).

The forerunner of the Hispanic gang derived from the Mexican tradition of the *palomilla*, the grouping of young boys and men who spent recreation time together. When Mexican families began migrating to the Untied States they often grouped together for protection, continuing the tradition. Later, during the famous zoot-suit riots of the 1940s, the *pachuco* "gangs" came into prominence.[1] By the late 1960s Hispanic street gang members formed two rival prison gangs, the Mexican Mafia who represent southern California, and the Nuestra Familia from northern California. The geographical dividing line between these two organized crime groups is Bakersfield, California. Local street gangs, although not necessarily members of either prison gang, align themselves along the north/south divide. Thus the name of the girl gang with which I worked, Las Sureñas Locas (The Crazy Southern Girls) indicates their affiliation with the Mexican Mafia. San Diego gang members often refer to themselves as *sureños,* and many have family ties to the Mexican Mafia.

Hispanic gangs can be categorized generally as "traditional" gangs (Olson-Raymer, Jefferson, and Ortega 1989). That is, they are often linked to a particular neighborhood for several generations and are very protective of their neighborhood territory. Hispanic gangs are polydrug users. They usually characterize their involvement in narcotics trafficking as less important than demonstrating gang loyalty and protecting the neighborhood from rival gangs, although most of the heroin, crystal methamphetamine, and marijuana trafficking in the state of

California is controlled by Hispanic gang members with connections to the Mexican Mafia (Marynik, Vickery, Jones, Murry, and Luca 1993).

African American Gangs

The best known of the Californian African American gangs are the Crips and their rivals the Bloods or Piru's. Law enforcement personnel report that these two gangs originated in south central Los Angeles and Compton during the 1960s (Marynik et al. 1993). They were composed of male adolescents who bonded together for protection from rival gangs. However, throughout the 1970s both Crip- and Blood-affiliated gangs spread across the state, each "set" claiming a territory. These sets, although they claim affiliation with either Crips or Bloods, are very diverse (Marynik et al. 1993).

Most sets can be categorized as instrumental gangs, motivated by economics (Olson-Raymer, Jefferson, and Ortega 1989). They are particularly associated with narcotics trafficking. African American gangs control most of the crack cocaine trade in California, although they are also involved in the distribution of PCP and marijuana. It was the introduction of crack cocaine in 1983 that greatly increased both the profit and violence associated with the narcotics trafficking of these gangs. The Department of Justice estimates that there are approximately 65,000 African American gang members in California (California Department of Justice 1993).

Asian Gangs

Local San Diego law enforcement officials note that Asian gangs are the newest and fastest-growing gangs in California. They began to emerge in the 1970s and are known for preying on their own ethnic communities (Marynik et al. 1993). Their hallmark is the "home invasion" robbery. Because many Asian refugees keep cash and valuables in their homes and are wary of police intervention, the gang members are able to commit many of these robberies with relative impunity. Some Asian gangs have been linked to organized crime syndicates; most notable are the Wo Hop To Triad and the Wa Ching (Marynik et al. 1993). Some Asian gangs are also heavily involved in narcotics trafficking.

According to statistics from the Department of Justice, there are about 15,000 Asian gang members in California (California Department of Justice 1993). However, the cultures of these gangs are very diverse. For example, Vietnamese gangs do not claim a territory; they often have gangs made up of members from various locations. In contrast, Laotian and Cambodian gangs are more like "traditional" gangs, which claim and defend a territory.

Anglo Gangs

There are approximately 5000 Anglo gang members in California (California Department of Justice 1993). These gangs originally evolved from motorcycle gangs such as the Hell's Angels. (Outlaw motorcycle gangs are considered to be organized crime groups by the California Department of Justice and are not considered street gangs.) The most violent of these gangs are the "skinheads." These gangs are involved in hate crimes against ethnic and racial minority groups. Some of these gangs have begun to affiliate themselves with other white supremacist groups, for example the White Aryan Resistance and the Ku Klux Klan (Marynik et al. 1993).

CALIFORNIA'S RESPONSE TO GANGS

California's Department of Justice (1993) estimates that the state of California has approximately 175,000 to 200,000 gang members and predicts that these numbers will increase by another 50,000 to 75,000 members by the year 2000. These figures indicate an increase in gang membership of 230% to 280% since 1982. However, the office of the California attorney general cautions that these figures are only estimates since there does not exist a statewide system that can measure the number of gang-affiliated youth accurately. The attorney general's office also predicts that the projected increase in gang membership will bring about an increase in gang violence and an increase in female participation in gang activities and will foster a new level of sophistication and organization for many of California's gangs.

The increase in gang membership has spurred the state of California to become "proactive" in stemming gang-related violence. San Diego's Department of Justice has implemented new policies in an attempt to prevent the "Los Angelization" of their gang problem.[2]

Many gangs engage in common types of behavior. For example, many gang members have street names, wear "colors" (clothing colors designating their gang affiliation), have gang-related tattoos, and flash hand signals to identify their gang affiliation. Because even the most diverse gangs engage in common practices, California police departments use a list of five characteristics to identify gang members regardless of their particular gang affiliation. In order to be "documented" as a gang member by the police department, an individual must meet three of the following five criteria:

1. Self-admission of gang membership
2. Tattoos, identifying gang membership
3. Gang-style clothing
4. Continuous association with known gang members
5. Arrested with a known gang member

When gang members meet these criteria, they are "documented" by police, placed in the local department's gang file, and eventually added to the Gang Reporting Evaluation and Tracking (GREAT) system. GREAT is a computer data-base that enables law enforcement to track gang members from different counties. The computer can print out a photograph, criminal history, and list of the gang member's identifying marks and nicknames. In December 1993, aspects of the police "documenting" procedures, specifically the detainment and photographing of suspected gang members, were deemed illegal by a California 4th District Court of Appeal. The court argued that these procedures constituted "too significant an intrusion of the individual liberties to be justified" ("Court Rules" 1993). However, police in Westhills still continue to stop, photograph, and conduct field interviews of neighborhood adolescents.

In order to better address the problem of gang-related crime, the Department of Justice has also made changes in the way that gang members are prosecuted. They have developed a special gang prosecution unit that works closely with the local police departments—the Jurisdiction Unified for Drug and Gang Enforcement (JUDGE) unit. As part of the JUDGE unit, the prosecuting attorney will arrive at the crime scene as it is reported to the police, before the crime is officially assigned to the district attorney's office.

The JUDGE unit prosecutes gang-related crimes "vertically." Whereas most criminal cases are prosecuted by a team of attorneys who become involved in the process at different stages (i.e., horizontal prosecution), the JUDGE unit assigns only one attorney to each case. This attorney follows the case from beginning to end. Thus, instead of meeting and working with as many as eight different attorneys, victims and witnesses are able to establish a relationship with one attorney. This is particularly important in gang-related cases because many times both the victims and witnesses are reluctant to testify. Working with one attorney enables the victims and witnesses to develop a relationship of trust with the attorney and thus makes it more likely that they will testify.

Until 1975 the emphasis within the California juvenile justice system was to provide discipline and guidance for wayward youth. However, in the 1970s a new "get tough" policy was instituted within the juvenile justice system. Since 1977, sentencing of juveniles has become more punitive in orientation. Juveniles are locked up more frequently and for longer amounts of time. This has increased incarceration rates for youthful offenders. For example, Federal Bureau of Investigation (FBI) statistics show that in 1979 approximately 16.5% of all juveniles arrested were incarcerated; however, by 1991 the incarceration rate had risen to 28% (1992a).

In 1977, California passed a law (Penal Code 707b) allowing children sixteen years or older to be tried as adults for murder, armed robbery, and voluntary manslaughter. Currently, there are twenty-four different offenses for which a juvenile can be prosecuted as an adult. On January 1, 1995, the California legislature passed a bill that allows juveniles as young as fourteen years old to be prosecuted as adults.

In the state of California, juvenile offenders often serve more time than their adult counterparts (California Department of Corrections 1993). Adults convicted of murder in California can expect to serve forty-one months of prison time. Juveniles convicted of this same crime will serve sixty months at the California Youth Authority (CYA). The average amount of time that an adult inmate serves in a California prison is sixteen months. In contrast, the average stay for a juvenile offender at CYA is approximately twenty-six months at a cost of more than $66,000. Juvenile offenders can also be required to serve time until they are twenty-five years old.

California's juvenile incarceration rates have increased in part because the character of juvenile crime has changed. Juveniles today are more likely than their predecessors to commit violent crimes. For example, a regional crime report by San Diego's Association of Governments' (SANDAG) indicates that 23% of all 1992 juvenile arrests were for violent crimes, an increase of 10% over the last five years. The percentage of felony arrests (42.2%) is higher for juveniles than for any other age group. Homicide has become the number-one cause of death for California juveniles age fifteen to nineteen years (65 to 75% are killed by a gun). This is due in part to the upsurge in gangs. A Department of Justice survey of California law enforcement agencies indicated that 100% of those surveyed predicted an increasing escalation in gang-related violence (California Department of Justice 1993). According to the district attorney's office: "[O]ne percent or less of the population is responsible for 30-40% of the crime. If you take away the gangs, you'll see a big decrease in crime." However, a study by Curry and Spergel (1992) indicates that contrary to anecdotal evidence, delinquency is not always linked to gang affiliation.[3]

While gang membership is still viewed as an adolescent activity, perceptions are changing. Gang members range in age from eight years to thirty years of age. Trends suggest that gang members are affiliating earlier and staying active longer (Pennel et al. 1994). This is due partly to a lack of economic opportunities for older gang members, which impedes their ability to mature out of the gang lifestyle.

The public's perception of violence related to gang activities has fueled new legislation specifically oriented toward gang members, most notably the "Gang Mom" Law and the "Drive-by" Law. The California Supreme Court (1993) upheld the state's ability to file criminal charges against parents who contribute to their children's delinquency. The maximum penalty for these "Gang Moms" is one year in jail and a $2,500 fine. However, most parents convicted by this law have only been required to attend mandatory parenting classes by the courts.

In 1994 California legislated new mandatory sentences for any person convicted of murder that was committed by shooting a gun from a car with intent to kill. This law has become known as the "drive-by law." It was specifically intended to combat one of the most dangerous activities that gang members engage in: the drive-by shooting. The new law defines a drive-by shooting as first-degree murder, as opposed to voluntary manslaughter. Persons convicted in a drive-by killing will receive a mandatory twenty-five years to life prison term or the death penalty.

THE GANGS OF WESTHILLS

The community of Westhills is especially vulnerable to gang formation because residential patterns in the city combine the cultural heterogeneity of San Diego's population with isolated low-income, high-density ethnic communities. Cities with these characteristics produce increased support for ethnic separatism and alienation from conventional society and its institutions (Jankowski 1986). Geographically isolated neighborhoods reinforce a sense of ethnic solidarity, as well as rivalry with other ethnic groups (Vigil 1988a).

In 1983 Westhills had five recognized gangs. However, when crack cocaine exploded on the local drug scene, Westhills became a center for distribution of the drug, and the number of gangs in the city has increased dramatically. Today, Westhills has between twelve and fifteen documented gangs. (This does not include tagging crews, groups of youths who spray paint graffiti in the city.) This increase in gangs is due partly to an influx of Los Angeles gang members into Westhills.

The city is geographically situated along the corridor of the West Coast's narcotics trade, midway between Mexico and Los Angeles. Furthermore, the city provides a very lucrative cocaine market, sometimes commanding prices that are two to four times higher than those found in Los Angeles. The increased drug trade in Westhills has escalated the level of violence and intergang fighting. This drug-related violence has been further exacerbated by the geographic proximity of U.S. military bases, which affords gang members access to high-powered weapons. For example, local police have reported confiscating light antitank weapons from local gang members. The influx of drugs and violence into the community is further complicated by lack of employment and recreational opportunities (Olson-Raymer, Jefferson, and Ortega et al. 1989).

Westhills gangs, like most other city gangs, are ethnically and racially divided. Currently, the city has approximately thirteen documented gangs: three Hispanic gangs, two Samoan gangs, seven African American gangs, and one multicultural gang. (The multicultural gang is composed of middle-class wannabe gang members. Many law enforcement personnel and local gang members do not consider it a "real" gang.) Gang membership rarely transcends ethnicity and race, although that does occur. For example, the "Mexican" gang with which I worked had two African American members. However, both boys were raised on the "Mexican side of the neighborhood," and both spoke Spanish. One of the other "Mexican" gangs had several Samoan members as well.

The local media in Westhills capitalizes on the public's fear and fascination with gangs by reporting sensational drive-by shootings and other gang-related stories. When the high school excluded several gang members from participating in the school's graduation ceremony because of their gang activities, the local newspaper ran the story on its front page. In contrast, the graduating valedictorian, a non-gang-affiliated Latino adolescent awarded a four-year scholarship to Harvard, was not mentioned in the newspaper's coverage of the graduation ceremony. Most of the adolescent residents of Varrio Granos are cognizant of the media's biased reporting:

CARLA: The news says where I live is not safe; there's drive-bys every night in my neighborhood. They exaggerate it. It's more dangerous in town. It's not really dangerous over here. The gang members, they don't do nothing, if you don't mess with them, and they don't steal in their own area.

MR. CASTILLO: The newspapers never help anyway. The only time this community gets in the paper is when there is a shooting. We never get in because of something good happening in the community.

The news media, in cooperation with the local police department, no longer publishes the names of the gangs in their articles. However, the gang members often find themselves cited as sources in the newspaper accounts of gang-related crimes, and many of them have scrapbooks detailing their gang's activities.

In the past the news media has largely ignored female gang members detailing instead the more flamboyant behavior of their male counterparts. When I began this project, there was almost no mention of female gang members in the media. However, recently there has been an increased interest in girls and gangs. Homegirls and experts in the field of female crime are now frequent guests on the afternoon television and radio talk shows. A full-length movie (*Mi Vida Loca*) on female gang members was recently shown in movie theaters, and several newspapers have published articles detailing the lives of female gang members.

Gang Intervention and Prevention

The community of Westhills, like many other communities in the United States, has tried several strategies to curb gang-related violence and crime. Since the late 1980s several different gang programs have been tested by the community, including gang suppression by local law enforcement, gang prevention and education of community children, intervention programs directed toward adolescents, and mobilization of residents in conjunction with community-based law enforcement. Some of these experiments have failed miserably; others have had mixed results.

In the summer of 1991, the Westhills' Police Department began the first in a series of "gang sweeps." Local police officers descended on the *varrio* as a unit and proceeded to round up and arrest all suspected gang members. While the police counted the success of their tactics in the numbers of gang members detained, the overall impact of the sweeps was largely negative. Local residents were further alienated by what they perceived as the capricious actions of the police. This was especially damaging, given that employment statistics from Westhills Police Department indicate that the racial/ethnic makeup of the police department was approximately 81% Anglo police officers at the time of the sweeps. Neighborhood residents complained that nongang members were also picked up in the gang sweeps, then "documented" by the police department as gang members (see also Huff 1990).

The Westhills Police Department, recognizing that the long-term impact of the sweeps damaged community/police relations, recently changed to a community-based police strategy. Officers are now assigned to a neighborhood where they are encouraged to walk or bicycle their beat. School Resource Officers (SROs) are assigned to the community's public schools in order to increase the gang awareness of teachers, administrators, and students and to provide a police presence on the school campuses.

The police department has also opened several community centers. The centers provide supervised recreation for young children and support groups for the parents. These centers are staffed by community volunteers and police officers. The hope is that this type of police presence will help build a coalition between law-abiding residents and the police department.

The summer that I began my project (1993) the local police department implemented a new community-based police program, called NETWork (Neighborhood Enhancement TeamWork). NETWork police officers are each assigned to a particular community within Westhills. The officers then patrol their designated areas on foot or bicycle. The goal of the program is to gain the trust and cooperation of the community as well as to bring together city officials and community residents. To date, the new program has met with limited success. City officials, community residents, and local law enforcement have mixed reviews concerning the new policy.

Gang prevention programs in Westhills have been plagued with financial mismanagement. The summer of 1994, the community lost a $1.5 million federal grant because it was unable to forge a coalition between local gang prevention/intervention agencies. Other federally sponsored programs have also been targeted for review of their questionable fiscal management. For example, Hire-a-Youth, a program that helps at-risk youth find summer employment, spent $6.4 million in federal money to employ 4,300 youth at minimum wage for four-, six-, or eight-week increments; this program has come under scrutiny for its financial practices (Powell 1993).

Most of Westhills's gang prevention programs are oriented toward young children. As one social worker noted, "We want to catch them before they make the decision to join [a gang]." The programs can be divided into two categories: education and recreation. The YWCA and the local police department have put together several gang education programs. Representatives of these programs travel to the different elementary schools in the area. The intent of these programs is to show children the negative side of gang affiliation. Some of the programs are perceived as ineffective by my teenage informants.

JOSÉ: Sure, maybe like DARE helps when you're a kid. But when you get to junior high, you know what's up. It's like you know you're not gonna die if you smoke weed. I was graduated from DARE and look at me. Ha Ha. It's a dumb program.

For example, DARE (Drug and Alcohol Resistance Education) was unanimously ridiculed by high school adolescents. However, police officers argue that the efficacy of the program lies in teaching children how to recognize and overcome peer pressure.

The community programs that receive the most funding are the programs that offer recreational alternatives to children in gang neighborhoods. In Varrio Granos there are an amazing number of these programs, most of which are located within two miles of each other. Some of these programs are administered by professional agencies, for example, the YMCA or the Boys and Girls Clubs of America. Other programs have been coordinated by concerned residents. Each of these local programs offers essentially the same type of activities and adult supervised recreation, arts/crafts, games, cup-stacking, soccer, and so on.

The adult leaders of these agencies continuously squabble with each other. Money is the major point of contention among the varying groups and agencies.

Because all of the groups are competing for the same source of money, Community Block Development Grants (CBDG), there exist a great deal of competition and animosity between the agencies. I heard it mentioned several times by city council members that the agencies were "more territorial than the gangs."

For the most part, all the gang prevention programs target young elementary-age children. While some groups attempt to recruit teens to their programs, most are not very successful. However, two community-sponsored programs, boxing and twilight basketball, are successful in terms of recruiting community funding and adolescent males. One community group has also received funding to sponsor lowrider car shows and Chicano art-work.

However, because the gangs have been identified as a male phenomenon, there are no intervention programs specifically oriented toward gang-affiliated girls and women. While statistics may justify a male-centered gang intervention program, they do not tell the whole story. Males are more likely to commit the high-profile crimes, but gang-affiliated girls have higher rates of delinquency and substance abuse than their nongang male counterparts (Fagan 1990).

Community-sponsored intervention programs in Westhills at best ignore girls and at worst denigrate girls and women. Girls are encouraged to attend boxing, basketball, and lowrider shows as spectators. Girls watch as their boyfriends, brothers, and male friends take center ring, while they sit on the sidelines. At the lowrider shows and art exhibits, the sexism is even more blatant. Men and boys exhibit their customized bicycles and cars, many of which have pictures of women with bared breasts painted on them.

Some of the agencies recognize the growing problem of delinquency among girls, but they perceive programming for girls as something difficult.

YMCA: Right now distribution is about 60% boys, which is amazing to me. When I grew up, only boys got in trouble. Now we have a lot of at-risk girls. I guess women are really liberated now. They can get in as much trouble as boys.

BOYS AND GIRLS CLUB: It's hard to do girls' programming. With the boys, it's easy—you just throw them a basketball. But the girls don't know what they want. I ask them, and they can't tell me what they want.

One of the directors for the Boys and Girls Clubs was trying to introduce programming for adolescent girls, including a jazzercise class.

Only in terms of job training do girls receive equal attention. Job Corps actively recruits girls from the *varrio* for its training and education programs, as does the summer job program "Hire-a-Youth." However, community perception of the Job Corps representative's outreach efforts is interesting:

JOB CORPS REPRESENTATIVE: When I placed an ad in the paper, they asked me, "Why only girls?" They said that they felt uncomfortable placing an ad for only women. So I let them use my number for both, and I refer the boys to the male coordinator.

Job Corps places 84% of its graduates in jobs or school (Conly, Kelly, Mahanna, and Warner 1993). Unfortunately, many of the girls entering Job Corps–offered training programs want to learn traditionally female jobs, which are also traditionally low-paying jobs. The top job choices for girls are certified nursing assistant, secretarial/clerical, and child care certification (personal communication Job Corps Representative, 1994).

Programs for Girls

Child Protective Services will remove young children and some teens from their homes and place them in protective custody from their parents. However, for teens, the services they offer are appallingly inadequate. Because of understaffing and inadequate funding, CPS is forced to perform a type of triage with troubled young lives.

CPS: The problem with the system is that families can't access social work services unless they molest, beat their kids, use drugs, don't feed their kids, or break the law. There's nothing out there until they're bad enough to get into the system. We can't reach families that we could actually help, the ones on the verge. We can't prevent. Options for adolescents are real limited. The funding is limited and case loads are too much. The belief is that a teen can run away, a four-year-old can't. So if it's a molest situation, yes, CPS responds. If its a slap mark or a bruise, well, we look at the priors. In a molest situation the kid has a right to be removed from the home, but we don't tell the kids that because they will all claim to be molested.

Girls that are removed from the home are usually placed in one of several temporary teen shelters. However, adolescent girls are hard to place in homes, especially in the case of molestation victims. Because it is often difficult to find permanent homes for adolescent girls, in practice many of the temporary shelters cannot meet their legal requirements for outplacement. Consequently, these shelters often become semipermanent homes for these girls. At one temporary shelter where the girls were legally required to be placed outside of the shelter after two months, I met two girls who had been at the shelter for more than a year.

While shelters do not always offer the best situation for most adolescents, sometimes placement can be even more disruptive to their young lives. Fourteen-year-old Sharon and her eleven-year-old sister had been removed from their mother's home because of sexual abuse. Sharon's mother was Mexican American; her father was Inuit. Sharon's sister was fathered by a different man. A tribal council in the state of Alaska determined that Sharon would have to be placed with an Inuit family. Sharon's only other family, her sister, was not allowed to accompany her. So Sharon packed up all her belongings in a green garbage bag and left to go live with a family in Alaska, alone.

Although the community of Westhills is guilty of slighting girls in terms of gang intervention programs, the community does support varying prenatal and teen pregnancy programs. Currently, Westhills has one of the highest teen pregnancy rates in all of San Diego County (California Department of Health Services 1993a, 1993b). However the city is trying to address this problem by hosting many teen pregnancy and teen parent support services, including WICS (Women, Infants, and Children), prenatal outreach, GAIN (Greater Avenues for Independence), Planned Parenthood, and SanDAP (San Diego Adolescent Pregnancy and Parenting Program). These programs provide vouchers for everything from formula (WICS) to day care (GAIN). Many agencies also offer free parenting classes and group counseling. A few programs are now experimenting with teen father groups. However, many of these agencies find themselves limited by funding and bureaucracy.

SanDAP is a local agency funded by the state of California and fiscally managed by the board of education. The agency offers individual and group counseling for teens. It is one of only two "family life" programs that are involved with the school district. Counselors routinely conduct home visits and check on the emotional and physical welfare of both the infant and the teen parent. While most of their cases involve young unmarried mothers, they also counsel teen fathers. However, the counselors often lament the fact that their efforts are frustrated by political constraints.

SANDAP: Having two bosses sometimes causes problems. For example, the person that put this together at the state level must have been a "Right to Lifer." We're not allowed to talk about abortions at all. If a teen approaches us and asks for information or referral, we are required to terminate the conversation immediately. We also aren't allowed to talk about birth control in a one-to-one situation. If the girl wants to talk about birth control, we have to find another party and bring them into the room. It's tough to talk about AIDS when you can't mention condoms. So of course we work around the limitations. We've tried to get into the comprehensive high schools, but they wouldn't let us in. It's politics, etcetera, like in Lakeview—they're in denial that they have a teen pregnancy problem. They've got a posse passing disease, etcetera, around and passing girls around, but they don't think they have a problem.

Political constraints on their services are often reinforced by lack of funding. Currently, the organization employs eleven full-time counselors to service the entire county of San Diego. Consequently, the program has a current waiting list of 400 to 500 adolescents.

Other programs have also become entangled in misguided rules and regulations. Westhills High School began a subsidized child care center on the campus. The center is funded by the school district, but only two high school students were able to place their children at the center. The first priority of the program is allegedly directed toward teen mothers, but the regulations prohibit most of them from participating in the program. Eligibility rules state that a parent who wants to place her or his infant at the facility cannot receive AFDC and must be working. Thus, most high school students are unable to qualify for the subsidized child care. Instead of helping teen parents stay in school, the center serves as a site for gaining "field experience" for students enrolled in the high school's "Child Development" classes.

There is one program, Adelante Mujeres, that specifically targets Latina adolescents and women. This program, however, fails to do any outreach in the *varrio*. Nor would they defer the entrance fee for low-income girls to attend the conference that they sponsored on employment opportunities, despite my telephone calls. While the newspapers report that the 1994 employment conference hosted by the group was a success, for the girls in the *varrio* who did not attend, the conference was a failure.

REVIEW OF THE RESEARCH LITERATURE

Female gangs share some characteristics with their male counterparts, although there are differences between male and female gangs. For example, female gangs are usually offshoots of the neighborhood male gang. Female gangs usually have fewer members than their male counterparts and tend to have a higher turnover in gang membership due to pregnancy and motherhood. Girl gangs are also less likely than their male counterparts to use coercion or intimidation to recruit members.

As with their male counterparts, however, there are cultural differences between female gangs. Taylor's (1993) study of African American female gangs suggests that these girls are much more independent than Hispanic female gang members:

While male dominance is shared by both groups [Hispanic and African American], African-American females in Detroit have moved into more serious modes of independence and operation. . . . The influence of drug commerce has played a key role in black female emancipation (23).

Thus, issues of cultural differences must also be addressed by researchers who study female gang members.

Few of the early gang and delinquency theorists attempt to address the issue of female delinquency in their work. When they do mention female delinquency [Thrasher devoted 1 page out of 600 pages to the girl gang members], it is almost always discussed from the male gang members' perspective. Anne Campbell's (1984) review of early gang literature notes:

Girls. . . are seen in relatively few roles: as agents provocateurs, generating wars and feuds between otherwise peaceful male clubs; as fallen women; and as cat fighters. But the overwhelming impression. . . is of gang girls as Sex Objects. (14)

In early studies, female delinquency was seen as a measure of male sexual prowess or as a threat to the unity of the male gang. For the most part, the girls' attitudes and problems are not analyzed.

Most gang researchers assume that gang culture is specifically male and that most female offenses are confined to sexual delinquency (see Cohen 1955). While it is true that males are disproportionately involved in crime, early theorists could not adequately explain why females were less likely to become involved in criminal activities, nor their motivations for engaging in delinquent behavior when they did participate in these activities (Leonard 1982).

However, the advent of the women's movement brought with it a new awareness of women's issues, including women and crime. More recent literature attempts to interject women into gang and delinquency theories. One of the most sensational "woman-centered" crime theories is found in Freda Adler's book *Sisters in Crime* (1975). Adler (1974) posits a direct relationship between women's liberation and female criminal behavior. She argues that as women become liberated and move into traditionally male occupations with their attendant socioeconomic pressures, we should expect a concurrent move into traditionally male-dominated illegal activities. Her argument is a revision of Cloward and Ohlin's (1960) opportunity structure.

Adler has been criticized by Leonard (1982) and Giordano and Cernkovich (1979) for her oversimplified definition of *liberation*. They argue that Adler mistakenly equates liberation with masculine behavior. Giordano and Cernkovich go on to argue that Adler's definition of liberation as "an individually held set of values and beliefs" cannot accommodate the multidimensional character of gender roles. Women can have conflicting attitudes, both traditional and liberal, about gender roles. This value conflict is something that I found to be prevalent among the girls of Varrio Granos. The girls that I knew subscribed to some of the traditional values associated with femininity while rejecting others. Long and Vigil (1980) have also noted this type of value ambivalence among other Mexican American girls. Because of this, the extent of the impact of the women's movement on female delinquency is debatable.

Other theorists have reworked older theories on delinquency and criminology in order to understand the specifics of female crime. Some theorists linked differential expectations for male and female social roles (Hoffman-Bustamante 1973) or differences in the extent and type of social control exerted on male and female adolescents (Hagan, Simpson, and Gillis 1979) to explain the disparity between male and female rates of delinquency.

While Freda Adler suggests a large increase in female crime linked to the women's liberation movement, Rita Simon and Sandra Baxter (1989) use opportunity theory to support findings that suggest that female criminal activities have failed to increase as dramatically as predicted by Adler. Simon and Baxter examine the Interpol statistics on female crime from thirty-one different countries. The study examines the relationship between female participation in the labor force and female criminal offenses. They found that there was a positive correlation between the two variables: Countries that had higher rates of female participation in the labor force also had an increased number of female criminals. However, they concluded that this correlation is less than would be predicted by Cloward and Ohlin's (1960) opportunity theory. Their work indicates a need for further research to explore the relationship between gender roles and female criminal activities.

Simon (1975) also examines the role of the criminal justice system and its impact on female criminality. Her analysis of incarceration and conviction rates of male and female offenders suggests that women are more likely than their male counterparts to be treated leniently (see also Chesney-Lind 1981). Her findings suggest that sexism in the criminal justice system forces men toward careers in criminality and women away from it. Anecdotal evidence from my own research confirms Simon's findings that female delinquents are treated more leniently by the courts. Simon concludes that the women's movement may eventually have an impact on female delinquency, but only if the sexist policies and attitudes of the criminal justice system are changed. If this happens, according to Simon, we may see an increase in the number of female criminals.

Another attempt to link liberation and delinquency was published by Hagan, Simpson, and Gillis (1987). In their article the researchers elaborate on their earlier study (1979) in which they argue that female adolescents are less likely to engage in criminal behavior because they are subject to more "informal" social control than their male counterparts. They define *informal control* as control exerted by a "patriarchal" family and kinship group, which they contrast with the formal social control exerted by governmental and legal institutions. The new study argues that daughters whose mothers work, especially in high-status jobs, are more likely to be involved in delinquent activity. They build their argument on the assumption that mothers who work in high- status occupations have "egalitarian" families, which in turn exert less "patriarchal" control over their daughters' activities.

Chesney-Lind (1989) has criticized this argument as "a not too subtle variation on the earlier 'liberation' hypotheses. Now the mother's liberation causes the daughter's crime" (20). Among other methodological problems with the Hagan, Simpson, and Gillis article, Chesney-Lind cites their lack of evidence. While the number of female-headed households and women's participation in the work-force have increased dramatically, female delinquency rates, both self-reported and official crime statistics, have remained relatively stable (Chilton and Datesman 1987).

In contrast to earlier theoretical models and their emphasis on macrolevel analysis, social science research during the 1980s and 1990s begins to focus on the individual gang member. Departing from their predecessors, anthropologists, most notably James Diego Vigil, introduce issues of cultural values and variations into theoretical models of delinquency and gang affiliation. These theorists merge cultural, structural, and psychological perspectives to explain gang formation. Gang members are often talked about as individuals "betwixt and between," searching for a place to belong. James Diego Vigil (1988a) develops a concept of "multiple marginalities" to explain gang affiliation.

Multiple marginality encompasses the consequences of barrio life, low socio-economic status, street socialization and enculturation, and problematic development of self identity. The gang features arise from a web of ecological, socio-economic, cultural, and psychological factors. The use of this concept . . . will help avoid the difficulties stemming from single cause examinations of previous gang studies. (9)

Vigil's gang members perceive themselves to be both culturally and economically marginal to conventional society. Harris's (1988) study of Chicana gangs also talks about the gang members as caught between the worlds and cultures of adult and child, Chicano and Anglo.

Some theorists report that gang members are seemingly unaware of Anglo middle-class norms and values (Harris 1988). Others argue that gangs evolved in communities that are overly sensitive to Anglo values (H. Moore 1988) or that gang members are integrated into a complex relationship with conventional society (Jankowski 1991).

The literature reveals a great deal of variation among gang cultures and research perspectives. While most recent theorists acknowledge the marginal status of gang members, some emphasize the instrumental aspects of gang membership, arguing that gang membership is a rational decision based on limited opportunities and discrimination (Jankowski 1991). Other researchers stress the expressive elements of gang affiliation (Vigil 1988b). For example, the gang members in studies conducted by both Joan Moore and Diego Vigil talk about being pushed into gang affiliation by both structural and psychological factors.

Horowitz (1990) argues that the contrast between these two perspectives may be reconciled at the level of individual experiences: "Some people experience their lives as being pushed and buffeted about by factors beyond their control, while others experience their lives more as a series of choices" (48). There may also be gender differences. Jankowski's research offers an exclusively male perspective on delinquency that may explain the emphasis on the instrumental aspects of gang culture. The homegirls in Varrio Granos stressed the expressive aspects of gang affiliation. Most of them said that they joined the gang to "feel love and caring." That is not to say, however, that they do not rationally evaluate their choice of delinquent behavior. They often screen potential victims carefully and balance the consequences of their actions against the potential benefits.

Despite the efflorescence of research on gangs, and new research on female gang affiliation, the majority of the research still represents an overwhelmingly male perspective. This has serious impact on female delinquents because of the influence that social science research and the media exert on the allocation of public resources and gang intervention programs. For example, in the community of Westhills, the majority of local gang prevention/intervention programs are oriented toward male gang members. The city regularly funds gang intervention programs such as boxing competitions and twilight basketball. However, the city does not have any locally funded programs that specifically target gang intervention for adolescent girls in the community.

HOMEGIRLS: THE MALE PERSPECTIVE

Jankowski (1991) has written a well-regarded comparative analysis of gang organization that spans the ethnic and geographic diversity of gangs from New York to Los Angeles. However, his analysis of women gang members is reminiscent of gang research from the 1950s. Jankowski states that among (presumably male) gang members, women are considered a form of property (146). Gang members have a right, according to Jankowski, to "trade women" without the consent of the woman involved. How do the women feel about this? Jankowski states:

The one aspect they [women] felt most comfortable with was being treated like servants, charged with the duty of providing men with whatever they wanted. While the role of servant only applied to the man with whom the woman was sexually involved, it nonetheless established the women as the property of men. (146)

In fact, according to Jankowski, one of the major motivating factors for joining gangs is to gain access to a sexual pool of women. However, because women appear so rarely in Jankowski's ethnography, it is difficult to determine if his evidence is taken from male informants, who might be tempted to exaggerate their tough-guy image and sexual prowess, or if this evidence has been verified from his observations of female gang members' behaviors. It is possible that Jankowski's failure to incorporate women into his ethnography meaningfully might be a result of his gender; male ethnographers may have limited access to female informants in a gang context.

Another recent gang ethnography by Felix Padilla (1992) acknowledges the limitations of a male researcher attempting to ascertain female gang behavior. He notes that his book is "a book about a male gang" (7). However, he argues that the "ethnic entrepreneurship" of the gang's drug business does not involve women. According to his informants, while the male gang members are at work, they are not allowed to be disturbed by their girlfriends. Girls (we do not know if they are gang members or not) appear in Padilla's ethnography only in their capacity as girlfriends.

In contrast, Anne Campbell (1984), writing from the perspective of female gang members, demonstrates that girl gang members are as interested as boys in achieving status in their same-sex groups. Moreover, young women are now using traditional male arenas, for example, fighting, to assert status. Another female ethnographer, Mary Harris (1988), also documents female gang members vying with each other to achieve prestige for "acting wild and being bad" (136).

What does this gulf between the two divergent ethnographic descriptions of female gang members suggest? Perhaps the diversity is a reflection of a contested area of gender relations? It is possible that for the gangs studied by Jankowski and Padilla that women's roles within gang subculture have not changed yet? Different gangs do exhibit different cultural values and orientations, which can also change over time. This is a phenomenon I have documented in Varrio Granos; the female gang members today participate much more actively than their predecessors of the 1970s and 1980s. J. Moore (1991) also documents a great variation among the roles of women in the two Los Angeles gangs associated with her study. However, while Jankowski assumes that subordination to men is completely unproblematic for women, this is not the case for the female gang members in the Varrio Granos.

My work with female gang members suggests that the girls do not subscribe to the notion of women as property. My research supports the assertion made by Campbell and Harris that female gang members are actively seeking status among both their male and female peers by using traditionally male arenas of competition. However, the homegirls also use some traditionally female arenas of status acquisition, such as motherhood, to gain prestige among their peers.

NOTES

1. *Pachucos* were groups of boys and men identified by their distinctive clothing style. They have been suggested as a precursor to contemporary gang cultures by several researchers, among them Vigil (1988) and J. Moore (1985).

2. Statistics comparing the extent of gangs in Los Angeles and San Diego indicate that San Diego's gangs have not reached the critical level of Los Angeles. Whereas San Diego law enforcement estimates that one out of every fourteen adolescents is involved in gangs, the city of Los Angeles estimates that one out of every four adolescents is involved in gangs. The Department of Justice registers approximately 15,000 gang assaults and 320 gang-related homicides per year in the county of Los Angeles. In contrast, the county of San Diego registers 330 assaults and 22 gang-related homicides (Department of Justice, personal communication 1993).

3. This same study did note differences between Hispanic and African American gang members. Whereas nongang delinquency was relatively rare among Hispanic adolescents, it was more common among African American adolescents.

Chapter 10

LAS SUREÑAS LOCAS: The Homegirls of Varrio Granos

As the research indicates, female gangs must be understood in the context of a complex interplay between economic, social, and cultural environments. Gangs flourish in areas where specific structural, psychological, and cultural factors operate to encourage gang affiliation and activities. Adolescents may choose to subscribe to the gang lifestyle for diverse personal reasons: desire for peer recognition, companionship and acceptance, rebellion against parental control, or anger and frustration directed toward school or authority figures. Most of the girl gang members cited "family problems" as the reason they joined the gang. Many had been left to fend for themselves at a very young age by abusive or negligent parents.

Some of the homegirls grew up in "*cholo* families" (J. Moore 1990; Moore and Devitt 1989), families where their parents and other relatives were intimately involved in gang activities. Morena's mother is a former gang member and practicing heroin addict. India's mother was just recently released from prison for narcotics trafficking. Both of these girls experienced the influence of the gang lifestyle intimately as they were growing up. Their affiliation with the gang was a natural progression of their life at home.

It is interesting to note that the girls who have family members affiliated with the gang are less prone to high-risk, potentially self-destructive behavior than their peers who come from conventional homes. It seems that their familial ties to gang-affiliated parents, brothers, sisters, and cousins constrain their delinquent behavior. Because their families are also intimately involved in the gang, they are able to monitor the homegirl's behavior more closely. Although part of gang norms involve participation in a street-based culture that emphasizes delinquency, there is an ideology of gender differences that also pervades gang culture. Families, especially brothers, uncles, and male cousins, and boyfriends restrain gang-affiliated girls' behavior. Also, gang-affiliated family members provide a sense of control or "backup" for the gang-affiliated girl. As noted by Moore and Devitt (1989) in their study of heroin-addicted women, homegirls who are raised in *cholo* families are less male dependent than their more conventionally raised counterparts.

The homegirls almost unanimously cite family problems as their motivation for choosing the gang lifestyle; however, these issues are often related to the social, economic, and political elements of their environment. Children growing up in Varrio Granos experience the effects of poverty, racism, and sexism. The unemployment rate in the *varrio* is two times larger than the unemployment rate for the entire city of Westhills and nearly sixteen times higher than in the more affluent, predominantly Anglo American enclaves of the city (U.S. Bureau of the Census 1993). Many of the *varrio* residents who are employed work at jobs that offer little room for advancement.

This type of chronic unemployment or underemployment can produce stressful family situations that may lead to child neglect or abuse, or alcoholism and drug abuse, on the part of both parent and child. Economic poverty can also contribute to a corrosion of traditional values, undermining the parents' authority (Vigil 1988a). Adolescents who do not find emotional support and success within the family or community find a substitute family of peers within the gang. They also find an arena where they can achieve, a place where they are respected as an important and worthwhile person.

Children growing up in the *varrio* often suffer from ambivalent gender and cultural identities. This is especially true for the girls, who often receive very contradictory cues about what constitutes acceptable feminine behavior. On the one hand, girls are expected to do well at school by their peers but not to be "too smart." They are expected to be sexually attractive but not sexually active. This ambiguity is further complicated by the "betwixt and between" cultural experiences of these girls.

Girls who do not subscribe to behaviors associated with *femeninidad*, who express interest in having careers, are considered by their peers to be acting "white." These girls risk alienation from their peers with only moderate chances of being accepted by their Anglo peers. In contrast, gang girls also do not conform to the norms and values of *femeninidad*, but they are not considered to be acting white; rather, they are resisting both Anglo middle-class norms and *femeninidad* by conforming to gang culture. They do not risk becoming labeled *pochas* or *gabachas* (Anglo) because the form that their rebellion takes is provided within Chicano cultural tradition.

Dominant social institutions also play a role in the discrimination and alienation of *varrio* adolescents. For example, the public school system often adversely contributes to adolescents' alienation and insecurities. In an effort to protect the nongang students, the school district has initiated a zero-tolerance policy for gang activities on campus. Any student found participating in "gang activity," which includes fighting, "mad-dogging" (threatening), flashing hand signals, and so on, is immediately suspended or expelled from school. Consequently, for even the peripheral and wannabe gang members, school is a hostile place. Most hard-core gang members are not enrolled in school; the few who do attend school are not academically successful. Only two of the seven girls who comprised the core membership of the gang attended school, and they went to school only haphazardly.

Part of the problem resides with school administrators and faculty who are insensitive to the distinct social and cultural environment of the *varrio*. The local high school situated between two of Westhills's *varrios* was referred to by some teachers as the "ghetto school." I heard one teacher remark that he felt like he worked in "taco land." Teachers routinely assumed that many non-gang-affiliated students of Mexican ethnic origin were gang members. However, for many students, dressing and talking like a gang member are often less a declaration of gang membership than an indication of ethnic solidarity. Assuming gang-style clothing and speech patterns often functioned as a means by which Chicano students distinguished themselves from their nonChicano peers.

Also, district policies that send students to different schools often put students in rival gang territory and in danger of violence. When Celia's family moved, she was expected to enroll in a different high school. However, because of her family's gang affiliation (her father and three brothers are very well known gang members) she was threatened with violence from the homegirls at the new school. At first, Celia's mother drove her to Westhills's High School. Unfortunately, Celia's mother, a crystal methamphetamine addict, eventually found the burden of driving Celia to school too overwhelming. Celia, at fourteen years of age, is now an unofficial high school dropout. She has not been classified as a dropout because she still intermittently attends classes; however, she did not pass a single class during the academic year.

Despite administrators' efforts to provide a gang-free, neutral environment, schools are unable to provide a crime-free area for the students who do attend. Students on many San Diego school campuses are often harassed by dropouts or older gang members, and school officials have limited authority in these situations. The local high school in Westhills built an eight-foot-high masonry wall around the school in order to protect the students from gunfire and other gang-related violence. Campus security guards told me that their most time-consuming duty was keeping nonstudents off campus. Westhills High School even employed a uniformed police officer to monitor the campus several days a week. Fights both on campus and off campus are frequent, especially between the two rival Latino gangs that attended the school.

In general, *varrio* adolescents develop a sense of alienation that is coupled with poor economic mobility, police harassment, and a perception of antiChicano sentiment. All of these social characteristics of the *varrio* combine to promote the development of gangs. For troubled youth, the normative guidelines of the gang provide both personal recognition and a sense of belonging. The gang replaces social institutions like school or the family, which do not address the emotional and instrumental needs of these girls.

JOINING THE GANG

Before girls officially become gang members, they usually adopt the stylized visual markers that identify the gang. For the most part, female gang members dress much like their male counterparts. They wear large baggy pants or jeans, black flat shoes, and either T-shirts or long-sleeved Pendleton shirts.[1] Their hair is worn long and straight, sometimes dyed an auburn color. When the girls "dress down," they spray their bangs straight up from their foreheads. The girls also wear very heavy makeup around their eyes and lips. They make what they called their "raccoon eyes" by outlining their eyes with black eyeliner and heavy mascara.

DIABLA: To me, makeup is warpaint. It's like a symbol of war. You want to get hit up. You want to fight to get respect.

This stylized appearance visibly marks a young woman's identity as a gang member or a wannabe. However, because gang culture has become fashionable among adolescents, many non-gang-affiliated girls in the *varrio* adopt some form of the gang's clothing or makeup style.

Fashion is an integral part of the gang scene. The style of clothes that an adolescent wears dictates the terms of her personal interaction with others. Clothing functions as a cultural "sign" (Barthes 1967, 41). Adolescents often use clothing to express solidarity with a particular group or difference from others. For the homegirls, their masculine clothing style upsets notions of appropriate feminine behavior, distinguishing them from other Chicanas, as well as from their Asian, Anglo, and African American counterparts. An adolescent who is wearing gang-style clothing can expect to be "hit up," that is, asked to identify her gang affiliation. Even going to the local mall can be a dangerous event for a girl who is dressed in gang-style clothing. Linda, a gang wannabe who lives in Varrio Granos and dresses gang style, told me about a weekend visit to the Westhills shopping mall.

LINDA: I was just sitting there, and this girl came up to me and said, "Where you from?" I told her, "I ain't from nowhere." The girl asked me, "Then who do you kick it with [spend time with]?" I told her no one. Then she asked me, "Who are your friends?" I told her Las Sureñas Locas. We just started talking and shit—nothing happened. But if I would have started saying shit about her neighborhood, fucking with her, then something would have happened; If you don't back up the neighborhood, they ain't gonna do nothing to you. I hate the mall. Everyone's looking for a fight. Fights and shit happen all the time there.

However, contrary to what Linda reports, sometimes an adolescent, even if she does not claim affiliation with a particular gang, can be victimized by the homegirls. Maria lives in the territory of the rival gang in Varrio Mojado. She is a softspoken young girl who does not affect gang-style dress. However, she has had trouble with the gang members of Varrio Granos.

MARIA: I never go there [Varrio Granos]. When I do, the gang members' girls and the homeboys will say stuff to me. I tell them I'm not from anywhere, but they know me, so they know I live in the other *varrio*. It doesn't matter if you're from there or not; it's what they think. They make you from somewhere. If they think you're a homegirl, then they'll fight you.

For the homegirls of the *varrio*, being "from somewhere" is synonymous with claiming gang affiliation. Whether or not a person will be threatened either physically or verbally depends on the gang member's mood: "Somedays it's like, you know, we're bored. So we jump people for fun."

The seven homegirls that comprise the core group of Las Sureñas Locas are proud of their reputations as aggressive fighters. Toughness and the ability to act crazy are prized behaviors among the homegirls of Varrio Granos. The girls never backed down from a perceived threat or insult. The most violent and aggressive of the homegirls, Payasa, earned the greatest respect from the other homegirls.

When I met with them to conduct interviews they regularly boasted of their exploits, which included jumping and robbing young military men and Mexican migrant laborers as well as other homegirls.

INDIA: One time there was three marines and we were looking for our homeboys, but they weren't nowhere. So we went up on our own and asked them for a dollar. When he took his wallet out, and we saw all that money, we said, "Bingo." We went on our own and drove back, nine of us homegirls, and we pretended we had guns and knives and we had bottles, and he ended up giving us his wallet—his whole wallet not just the money. We threw bottles at them—not really at them, just at their feet. Then we ran away. After, we got drugs and partied. It was just like a fun thing, you know.

PAYASA: You know how they said in the papers how the homegirls had weapons and attacked illegals? What the newspapers said, it's not fair. They weren't raised over here. It's not like that. We don't all have guns, but if we really need one, we can get one. Yeah, it was true that we did attack those aliens several times; and on two of them, we used guns but it was just like a plaything to us, just to mess with them.

The homegirls are very selective when it comes to choosing potential victims. Their choice of undocumented immigrants (they call them "border brothers" or illegals) or marines is not haphazard. These two groups of people offer the girls the potential for a big payoff with little threat of retaliation. The girls told me that both the undocumented immigrants and the marines are less likely to report the crime to police than "regular people." The illegal immigrants are afraid of the INS (Immigration and Naturalization Service), and the marines are afraid of ridicule.

Unlike their male counterparts, Las Sureñas Locas do not actively recruit gang members. While the older male gang members often pressure younger boys to demonstrate that they are "down for the *varrio*" and "school" the younger boys in the gang lifestyle, the female gang members join through much more informal methods. Usually the wannabes begin by meeting and partying with friends who are gang members. Eventually, they increase the amount of time they spend with the gang members and begin to participate more actively with the gang. They demonstrate their desire to belong to the gang by "backing up the hood" during confrontations.

One day Patty, a thirteen-year-old gang wannabe, excitedly approached the neighborhood gang members, showing off the bruises on her face and arms. She had been involved in a fight with rival homegirls from Northcity: "I backed up the *varrio,* man. They wailed on me and they were fat, fucking bitches, but I backed up the hood." Patty, however, never did become a gang member. Her parents sent her to Mexico to live with her grandmother because she was spending too much time with the homeboys.

To be accepted as a member of Las Sureñas Locas a girl has to prove that she is worthy of the gang. A gang member is expected to be loyal and to conform to the norms of the gang. The norms of gangs can vary; some gangs emphasize violence and aggression; others may stress drug use and partying (Moore and Vigil 1989). Contrary to Horowitz's (1983) assertion that among Chicano gangs aggression is only associated with masculinity, the homegirls of Varrio Granos value aggressive behavior. Participation in gang activities, such as fights, that demonstrate loyalty to the gang are means by which members of Las Sureñas Locas achieve personal recognition and status. Over and over again, I heard the phrase that girls had to show that they "were down for the *varrio.*" This included claiming gang affiliation even in threatening situations:

PAYASA: Yeah, you gotta hang just like in the hood, even if there's fifteen homegirls hitting you up.

INDIA: After you're in [the gang], everybody gets to know where you're from.

PAYASA: And if some other gang hits you up and you don't claim the *varrio* and you renk out and we find out. . .

INDIA: 'Cause we always find out. Somehow, some way, we always find out that.

PAYASA: And we get them—either they kill you, or we kill you. You gotta be down for it, you know what I mean?

Girls who fail to remain loyal to the gang suffer serious reprisals. One of the girls, Lazy, earned a reputation as a "buster," someone who has failed to remain loyal to her gang, and either switches her gang allegiance or denies her gang allegiance.

GIGGLES: She don't know how to respect herself, so we're gonna teach her respect. She won't come around. She knows that we're gonna jump her. . . but she only comes with her mom, and we don't disrespect moms.

Las Sureñas Locas were primed to beat up Lazy should she ever attempt to come back to the *varrio* alone.

In order to become a full-fledged member of a gang, girls are usually jumped in, although some girls who have been "raised in the gang lifestyle" were not jumped in. The "jumping-in" ceremony consists of physically beating the initiate. In preparation for the ceremony, like any fight, the girls remove their jewelry and braid their hair in order to minimize injuries to themselves. A group of the homegirls form a circle around the initiate. After they are given the signal, they begin to hit and punch her. While all the girls agreed that the purpose of the ceremony was to allow the girl to prove that she was tough enough to justify inclusion in the group, there was some disagreement about what the initiate's role was supposed to be in the ceremony.

INDIA: It's like she's standing there, and it's like four or five girls are around her, like in a half circle, and they start throwing [punches].

PAYASA: If she don't hit, then she's not from the *varrio*.

INDIA: No, that ain't true. She don't have to hit to get in. Look at Lazy.

PAYASA: And look who got out . . .

INDIA: You get qualified by hitting, but if that person don't hit, they let them get up again and give them another chance.

The jumping-in ceremony is a rite of passage for the girls. After the member is accepted into the gang, she is given a personal nickname, her gang identity. The nicknames usually reflect the personality or physical characteristics of the gang member: Tiny, Giggles, India (Indian), Payasa (Clown), Lazy, Clumsy, Wicked, Diabla (Devil), Morena (Brown-one).

The primary age for core gang activity is between thirteen and eighteen years of age. Unlike their male counterparts, most girls "matured out" of gang membership in their late teens.

MONICA: Girls mature faster. They got to worry about the kids and the bills, and the homegirls end up taking care of the homeboys.

Older gang members often provide support for the younger homegirls, such as letting them stay in their apartments, hiding them from the police, and feeding and clothing them.

Sometimes gang affiliation can start much earlier; children are often introduced to the gang lifestyle by siblings and parents. It is not unusual to see toddlers wearing gang-style clothing. Pregnant Morena planned to have her baby's picture printed in *Teen Angels*, a magazine featuring gang-style art. I even met one two-year-old boy whose father had tattooed the gang's name on his arm. The children who grow up in the gang will more than likely never be jumped in because they have always been considered a gang member.

To further demonstrate their loyalty to the gang, the girls adorn themselves with tattoos. The tattoos, done in blue or black ink with the aid of homemade tattoo machines, are a visible, permanent mark of their gang affiliation. The most popular places to have tattoos are on the wrists and ankles, although quite a few of the girls had tattoos on their necks, forearms, shoulders, and faces. The tattoos varied from a triangular pattern of three small dots (signifying *la vida loca*, the crazy life) to the gang member's street name or the name and initials of the *varrio* and gang. Some of the girls had their boyfriends' names or initials tattooed, but this was fairly rare because, as Tiny told me, "You can't trust no man, so why put them on when they ain't gonna be around." The girls who were mothers often had their children's names tattooed on themselves, as did some of the homeboys.

The homeboys' tattoos are much more elaborate than the girls' tattoos. Several of the homeboys had large tattoos of the Virgin de Guadalupe on their backs. Oftentimes the Virgin Mary was depicted next to tattoos of naked women or with a stylized spelling of the gang's name. Homeboys also often tattooed their mothers' names on their chests or backs.

The girls also engage in graffiti, a type of territorial tattoo (Vigil 1988a). Graffiti is used to challenge other gangs, mark territory, and achieve personal aggrandizement. Sometimes graffiti is used by the homegirls to incite or tease their male counterparts. For example, Clumsy spent a great amount of time crossing out the graffiti "tag" of her homeboy who shared the same name, Clumsy, and replacing it with her own tag.

While the homegirls engaged in some graffiti the "tagging crews," groups of adolescents primarily con's freeway underpasses, they easily distinguished be-tween the graffiti styles of the gang members and the taggers, though I was less able to do so.

MAY: For the most part, taggers are still different from the gangs. They both do graffiti but different styles. If there's some gang member under the overpass, we walk by and go in a different direction. You can be into tagging if you're a gang member, but mostly we leave them alone and they mostly leave us alone. Except the Mexican girls. They will start anything with anybody. If you're in their neighborhood and they don't know you, they'll hit you up and jump you.

However, as the gang culture becomes more pervasive, even the tagging crews are evolving gang-type group dynamics.

ANA: See these two crews [*points to two different sets of stylized initials spray painted on the concrete overpass*]? They're enemies. They're taggers, but they are getting to be like real gangs. At first it was just tagging . . . but they defend what they put up on the walls, like if you cross it out, they're gonna fight . . . Before you would just paint and stuff; now you have to get jumped in like a real gang.

Like the gangs, tagging crews relish dangerous behavior. The more dangerous the tag, the more popular you get. The girls pointed out graffiti on freeway medians as an example of an impressive tagging location. In contrast to the tagging crews who base their affiliation on graffiti—many of their members carried small sketch-books with them in which they outlined designs for their graffiti "pieces"—some members of Las Sureñas Locas deplored the activity, because it "messes up the neighborhood and makes us look bad."

Like most female gangs, Las Sureñas Locas is smaller than its male counterpart. Traditionally, female gang cohorts consist of ten to twenty members, while male gangs may number in the hundreds. Partly because of their small numbers, the girls do not have the same distinct age sets, or *klikas,* of the male gangs. The homeboys of Varrio Granos could identify three distinct age groups: the pee-wees, the teenagers, and the *veteranos.* The homegirls' gang structure is much more fluid. The girls could identify *veteranas,* some as old as midforties, but younger girls and the older adolescents mix freely. Oftentimes the homes of the *veteranas* function as flop houses for the gang members, especially if their children are involved in the gang.

Rachel, former gang member and current heroin addict, is a grandmother at the age of thirty-four. Three of her four children are gang members, two of whom were locked up in a CYA (California Youth Authority) facility the entire time of our acquaintance. Every time that I visited her apartment, there were several gang members hanging out, sleeping on her couch, or raiding her refrigerator. One time I ran into Li'l Chato ironing his Pendletons at her house. She often complained about the influx of teenage gang members but told me there was really nothing she could do about it: "Even if I moved to Idaho, they would find me." Rachel served as a type of surrogate mother for the homeboys. She would often help them hide from the police, for whom she had nothing but contempt.

GANG ACTIVITIES

Many of the girls' gang activities revolve around territorial disputes, although to a lesser extent than their male counterparts. Gang violence is used by both girls and boys to defend the honor of the gang or to avenge an insult to the gang or a specific gang member.

GIGGLES: It's more like you get respect if somebody says shit to you—you gotta step up to them. If you show weakness, they take advantage of you.

However, while the boys describe themselves as "warriors" or "soldiers" who "protect" the neighborhood, girls are less likely to do so. The girls are more likely to talk about their escapades such as stealing cars and committing robberies as something they do "just for fun" or "to get respect."

Most gang researchers report a code of gang fighting that prohibits male gang members from fighting with female gang members (Harris 1988; Horowitz 1983). Male gang members most often corroborate this: "There ain't no men against women. We don't commit crimes against women and children." However, the members of Las Sureñas Locas are involved in quite a few male/female fights.

LD: Do you and your homegirls get into fights with the girls from Varrio B Street?

INDIA: Actually, we got into a fight with the guys from Varrio B Street.

LD: Really? I thought the girls fought the girls and the guys fought the guys?

INDIA: Well, that's the way it was, but I think we're the first *varrio* that got into a fight with guys.

LD: How did it happen?

INDIA: By the K-Mart. One car with guys pulled over, and we got into it [fighting]. One of my homegirls ended up taking their car, and she burned it. She sold the parts from it and burned it and rolled it in the canyon. We told the homeboys, "You guys ain't doing nothing. We're taking care of business, and you guys are just kickin' it."

PAYASA: Yeah, I got hit by so many guys. But I don't care. It don't hurt. It's just like getting hit by a girl.

Although they deny it when asked directly if they gang-bang (participate in gang activities) to impress the homeboys, the homegirls seem to be competing directly with the homeboys for respect. The girls often told me that they were better than the homeboys. At times, it did seem that the girls were more active than their male counterparts. Some of the social workers confided to me that they thought the homegirls were more dangerous than the homeboys: "Someone with a point to prove is far more likely to blow your head off than someone who already has a reputation in the neighborhood."

This competition with the local homeboys sets the tone for the activities of Las Sureñas Locas. However autonomous their activities, the neighborhood homeboys dictate the standards for achieving prestige, which include participation in high-risk activities. For example, one of the best ways for a homegirl to achieve respect in the neighborhood is to fight or "step up to" the male members of rival gangs.

Fighting male gang members does carry more risks than fighting with girls. Sixteen-year-old Payasa was involved in a fight with a female gang member in Los Angeles; she sustained some bruises but was not badly injured. However, when the girl's boyfriend found Payasa, he beat her so severely that she had to spend several weeks in the hospital. Payasa always shrugs off the risks of gang life. She often told me, "Everybody's gotta die sometime."

When they do fight, the homegirls use a wide variety of weapons, everything from fists and fingernails to knives and bottles. While some of the girls have been involved in drive-by shootings, "not just for the hell of it, only for revenge," most of the girls do not use guns. The girls insist, however, that they can get a gun whenever they want one. However, during another interview session, India and Payasa lamented the fact that the homeboys had taken their twenty-two-caliber rifle away from them.

The girls are often used by the boys to smuggle guns into parties or to hide them from the police. The girls would stick the guns inside the waistband of their pants in order to take advantage of the male security guards' and police officers' inability to search girls.

There is an interesting difference between the homegirls and the homeboys when it comes to fighting. The boys almost always describe the goal of fighting as gaining power over their rivals or protecting the neighborhood. In contrast, the girls describe fighting as a means of proving gang solidarity.

INDIA: When we fight another hood, people are there for you, and you know they care. The ones that ain't there, you know they don't care. The ones that care for you, and they're always gonna be there for you.

LD: That's really interesting. The guys don't say that.

GIGGLES: That's not really the words of the guys but I know that's how they feel sometimes.

Although gaining respect is important for the homegirls, they place far less emphasis on competition and status achievement among themselves than the homeboys do among their male cohort. While competition often defines their relationships with the homeboys, the girls seem to be more interested in fostering familylike relationships among themselves. The girls told me that while there were many reasons that girls joined gangs, including family involvement in gangs and a quest for popularity, most girls joined the gang because they wanted "to feel love and caring." That is not to say that bickering and feuding among the homegirls does not exist. There were often several girls in Las Sureñas Locas who did not get along with each other at any one time; Payasa often complained that she had to act as mediator between the homegirls who were feuding among themselves.

Although all the homegirls know each other, there are small groups of "best friends" or especially "close friends" with whom the girls spend the majority of their free time. However, the gang-affiliated girls have much more extensive friendship networks than the nongang girls. These friendship networks include boys, as well as older men and women, most of whom are associated with the gang in some way. In contrast, the nongang girls' friendship networks are more likely to be limited to same-sex groups, a single boyfriend, and family members.

Familylike loyalty to the gang is of paramount importance to Las Sureñas Locas. The homegirls, like their male counterparts, expect each other to uphold a code of silence that prevents any of them from cooperating with outsiders, especially the police, even against rival gang members. During my research an article in the local newspaper reported a story about a young girl who was raped by several gang members. This girl refused to reveal the names of her attackers to the police. I asked the homegirls what they thought about this, and they all agreed that they would have acted in a similar fashion, preferring to let their "homeboys take care of it."

However, when I told the girls that some of the girl gang members in Juvenile Hall had told me that they would set up other girls to be raped by their homeboys, the members of Las Sureñas Locas were appalled. Several of the homeboys who overheard our conversation came up to me and angrily demanded to know the name of the person who was "saying shit like that about our *varrio*." All of them, both the homeboys and homegirls, vehemently denied ever employing these kinds of tactics in their gang fighting. The boys found the idea particularly insulting: "That's bullshit. We don't need to rape some girl so we can get laid."

DRUGS

Drug use also plays a major part of gang activities, although none of the homegirls are drug dealers. Most of the drugs in the *varrio* are distributed by individual entrepreneurs, the "Mexican cowboys," mostly older men with connections to the Mexican Mafia.

Like most Chicano gangs, the homegirls of Varrio Granos are polydrug users. Most of the money the girls make from their other gang activities, such as stealing car stereos and robbing people, is used to buy drugs. Often the homegirls do not have to pay for their drugs, however, because the homeboys are usually willing to trade drugs for sex or at least the promise of sex.

GIGGLES: It's easier for girls to get drugs than guys. Even when you're walking by, you meet some guy and he says, "Hey, you do drugs? I got some. Wanna come with me?" You know, like that. And you play up to them.

INDIA: Well, you know it's like when you're out there you know how the guys try to pick you up and they try to give you everything free just so you could be with them. Yeah, I would like tell them I would be with them, but it wouldn't never get to that point.

MORENA: My mom is a heroin user . . . back then, heroin was the biggest thing, but people don't use it no more. Now it's crystal. I started using when I was eleven years old. You like it. . . .The homeboys like it because it makes you crazy, stronger; you don't feel anything, but it speeds you up so you can stay up and party. . . . Me, I never pay for none of my drugs. Homegirls hardly never pay. . . . It's about favors. . . . It goes back and forth.

Some of the older homeboys, late teens to midtwenties, would use drugs to lure young neighborhood girls to their parties. Porky, a grossly overweight drug dealer, had a reputation in the neighborhood for supplying thirteen- and fourteen-year-old girls with drugs, then having sex with them. It was the young girls, not Porky, who earned the contempt of the neighborhood homegirls. The homegirls criticized the girls who fell prey to Porky's sexual advances as "getting what they deserved for being stupid" or "trying to act too big."

The drugs most frequently used by the homegirls are marijuana, crystal methamphetamine, and alcohol. A few of the girls smoked shermans (cigarettes dipped in PCP) or *primos* (marijuana laced with crack cocaine). Although incidence of heroin use is growing in San Diego County (California Department of Health Services 1993b), in Varrio Granos most of the younger homeboys and homegirls avoid the drug. By far the most preferred drug is crystal methamphetamine:

JAIME: Everybody knows once you shoot up, you're fucked for life. You see people on the street and everything. But crystal's different. It makes you get real wired so you can do your job better.

Drugs are the allure that keeps many of the older gang members involved in the gang lifestyle. The *veteranas* who are still involved in the gang lifestyle are mostly heroin or crystal methamphetamine addicts and use their gang connections to supply their habits. However, as the addicted gang member's need for drugs increases, her commitment to the gang decreases. Some addicted *veteranas* eventually became ostracized from their own neighborhood.

MORENA: Like Crazy L., she used to be a real *firme jaina*. You know, *firme* for the *varrio*. But she's into the drugs now. She don't care about nothing—not her kids, not nothing but getting her drugs. The drugs they messed her up. She's crazy—like all fucked up in the head, you know. I heard she even shoots PCP in her neck.

Crazy L. has become a despised character in her own neighborhood. Some of the neighborhood families give her food and blankets, but she has become part of another subculture; she now lives in the canyons that surround Westhills with the rest of the community's homeless population.

SEX

The use of drugs and alcohol is often a catalyst for sexual activity for the homegirls. Because of this, most non-gang-affiliated adolescents characterize homegirls as 'ho's (whores).

LOURDES: If you're a homegirl, it's hard to date just anybody. If you're a guy, you don't like to go out with them cause they think the worst of them.

VERONICA: They're always around the hood, you know. They'll be with any guy. They're all 'ho's, you know.

LOURDES: Or the guys are afraid they're gonna set them up.

LD: So the homegirls only sleep with guys from the hood?

LOURDES: No, they'll sleep with anybody, but most likely they end up going out with guys from the same hood.

VERONICA: The homeboys know who they are, so they're gonna try and sleep with them.

Even some of the homeboys spoke disparagingly of the homegirls' reputations.

LD: Would you ever date a homegirl?

PATO: Hell no. They been around, you know. They been around with the homeboys from different neighborhoods. You don't want to be seen with those girls.

PABLO: I don't think you could say the homeboys date them. But they hang around and drink and get stoned together and have sex, but it's more like a one-night stand, you know. Not really dating. The guys usually date girls who aren't in the gang. The girls date other guys—sometimes the guys in other gangs, or sometimes they might date drug dealers.

However, whenever I asked the homegirls about their reputations, they adamantly denied that they were sexually promiscuous, in spite of others' assertions to the contrary. The homegirls agree that some gang girls do act like 'ho's but deny that any of the homegirls from Varrio Granos are sexually promiscuous.

PAYASA: That is true of some girls; in other *varrios,* that's true. Some girls, all they do is fucking *cula caliente*—they're fucking in god damn heat. All they want to do is get high and thinking about fucking, fucking, fucking but they don't think about fucking gang banging. . . . But here it ain't true. . . . It's true we scam with them, but deep down inside, we're still family. Like if one of my homegirls slept with one of the homeboys and this and that, well, we go party. When they break up, we don't call her skenky 'ho or nothing 'cause it's like we're from the same family.

INDIA: Some girls might go out and have sex, but all the girls have their limits. Not all homegirls are 'ho's. It depends on the girl. Like some of them don't have no respect for themselves. But here, we're not like that.

Two of the homegirls, sixteen-year-old Payasa and fourteen-year-old Diabla, told me that they were still virgins. Seventeen-year-old India already had one baby and was trying to get pregnant with her current boyfriend. Fifteen-year-old Morena was currently pregnant after a night of partying and wasn't sure who the father of the baby was. Only one of the homegirls regularly used contraception. Sixteen-year-old Tiny reported that she used condoms because she felt that she was too young to have children. She felt pulled by pressure to start a family: "Sometimes I think I'm still too young, but then sometimes I think I do want to have a baby." Both her boyfriend and her mother wanted her to have children early.

While the homegirls do not gain prestige among the other gang-affiliated girls for sexual promiscuity, they do sometimes gain prestige for manipulating the homeboys by promising sex. The girls really enjoy talking about their escapades related to "playing" with several boys at the same time.

INDIA: I never used to be like this, with one guy you know. Payasa, remember when I was with all those guys? I was with like ten guys at the same time. I was always talking on the phone or something with them. [The homegirls all start laughing.] Yeah, those guys didn't know nothing.

This playing with more than one boy at a time contributes to the nongang adolescents' perceptions of the homegirls as sexually promiscuous.

Most adolescents who are not affiliated with gangs also find it difficult to believe that the homegirls can find boyfriends: "Why would somebody want to go out with them tomboys?" or, "Those girls are too mean to get a boyfriend." The homegirls also admit that some of the neighborhood boys, including the homeboys, are intimidated by them. Thus, while the homegirls enjoy the power associated with their ability to intimidate others, they do not want to be so intimidating as to be sexually undesirable. When one of the homeboys criticized Tiny as looking too masculine, Tiny changed her makeup and clothes so that she did not look as "hard" and thus was less likely to intimidate the homeboys and more likely to attract positive attention from them.

The homegirls are very conservative when it comes to some matters of sexuality, for example, homosexuality and abortion. They talk about homosexuality as "sick" or as "something you go to hell for." One homegirl admitted to me, however, after exacting a promise that I would not tell the other homegirls, that she had been involved in a lesbian relationship with a girl from outside the *varrio*: "It ain't something I'm proud of, but I was experimenting."

Almost all of the homegirls are adamantly opposed to abortion. When Tiny announced that she was going to have an abortion, India became visibly angry and called her a bitch. She told Tiny, "You ain't nobody that takes nobody's life and kills a baby. Why should the baby pay for your mistakes?" The other girls also put pressure on Tiny, presenting arguments that ranged from religious proscriptions against abortion to "if you can spread your legs you can take the responsibility." They even threatened physical violence. As it turned out, Tiny was not pregnant, but she told me: "Now I don't believe in abortion neither."

MOTHERHOOD

Pregnancy appears to restrict a girl's peer relationships (Becerra and de Anda 1984), although her social ties to the gang often continue. For example, India, who is the mother of a two-year-old, described her relationship to the gang this way:

Actually the homeboys come over like right now and they know it's like I prefer my baby before nobody. . . . A baby is the best thing that could happen to you. It's like she grew in you. . . . It's like my daughter, she makes me stand up for everything. She makes me like worry more, worry in my head about the next day. Like we had this fight with Varrio Mojado, and I didn't want to fight 'cause of my baby. I don't like looking for trouble. I don't want to risk my baby. One of my homegirls was saying that I don't kick it with them no more. I just look at them. I guess my look tells them everything. I just look at them all mean like, but then they say, you know, "I gotta respect your decision." They know that my baby's the most important.

It was interesting to watch the interaction between India and the other homeboys and homegirls. Because seventeen-year-old India had a baby and her own apartment, she had elevated herself to the status of an adult. The homeboys would ask permission to come into her house: "Mrs. India, I'm gonna go in and talk to Chato, okay?" They would also ask permission before they smoked marijuana in the front yard. The homegirls often came over to India's apartment to socialize. Many of them treated India like a big sister, asking for her advice about boys and relationships.

Motherhood is considered by the homeboys as the best way to get a girl to settle down. Girls who do not live up to an altruistic ideal of motherhood are disparaged. Homeboys who are fathers are not subject to the same kind of public and moral censure as the girls.

SERGIO: It's real bad if a girl leaves the baby at home and goes out all the time. She's supposed to take care of the baby. Sometimes a baby can make a girl change her ways.

INDIA: One of the homeboys, you know, his mom's going in jail and using drugs. She always going out and tweaking it [using crystal]. That's bad. She don't have no respect for herself. She ain't a good mom.

HUERA: Rachel ain't a mom. I know her—she was one of my homegirls, but her husband was into using the kids, pushing them through windows when they was small to do robberies or telling the kids, "Watch your mom suck that guy's dick," so they could get a smack [heroin]. She never thinks of her kids first. Her kids never had no chance.

TINY: She ain't a good mom. She's always out gang banging. She was fighting last week. That ain't no way to be a mom. She ain't even thinking about the kid.

Responsible motherhood in the *varrio* proscribes self-indulgence on the part of the mother. When a girl becomes pregnant, she is expected to change her behavior to conform to conventional expectations associated with motherhood. The good mother places the interests of her children foremost. Good mothers do not place their children at risk.

Within the gang culture, proscriptions against drug use during pregnancy are respected and affirmed by peer pressure. Boyfriends are expected to keep their girlfriends from using drugs. One homeboy beat up his girlfriend, causing her to miscarry, because he found out that she had been partying with the homegirls. In some areas, drug dealers may even deny pregnant addicts access to drugs (Moore and Devitt 1989).

Whether or not a homegirl continues to have an active affiliation with the gang after the birth of her baby depends on her individual circumstances: how involved she is with the gang, how involved she is with the father of the baby, the gang affiliation of the father of the baby. If the father of the baby is a gang member from the same neighborhood, the girl will most likely continue her association with the gang. However, when Diabla got pregnant and subsequently married a nongang member, she severed all ties to the neighborhood. As with the nongang girls, an ideology of romance that privileges male/female dyads undermines the girls' collective resistance to male authority.

Homegirls who get pregnant by a gang member from another neighborhood encounter difficulties in their *varrio*.

MORENA: If a homegirl gets pregnant with a homeboy's baby from another hood, she would move there. But a lot of times they're not together no more. She stays here, and he don't come to see the baby. At first she's an outcast, you know. All the homeboys call her a whore and tell her she ain't down for the hood. But after awhile she starts strolling the hood with the baby, and everyone forgets about that and she gets more accepted again.

LD: What gang would the baby belong to?

MORENA: The baby's gonna be from here if she lives here. There ain't no way that it could be nothing else.

India's first baby was fathered by a homeboy from Varrio B Street. She left the neighborhood and stayed with relatives until she had the baby. When she returned, the homeboys of Varrio Granos wanted her to "set up" the baby's father so that they could jump him. She refused to do that despite the fact that she and the father are no longer a couple. However, the father of her child does not come into her neighborhood to see the baby. India now has a new boyfriend from Varrio Granos who refuses to let her meet with her former boyfriend.

Mothers are revered in the *varrio* (although this does not stop homeboys and homegirls from fighting with their mothers). The homeboys often have their mothers' names tattooed on their bodies. Some of the homegirls do this also, although usually they have the names of their children tattooed on themselves. However, mothers, while they are expected to be self-sacrificing, can also be tough and exhibit characteristics traditionally associated with masculinity. Huera, the mother of Morena, makes her pack a knife before she goes out to parties.

HUERA: I make her pack when she goes out, you know . . . but she knows that she ain't gonna pull her knife unless she's gotta use it or she knows she's willing to do her time for it. But if her ass is in jeopardy and her life is on the line, she better have something there she can use. If she ain't got nothing, then she'll be shit out of luck and she'll be the one being buried, you know. . . . I can't help but think that way sometime.

During one incident at school when a teacher expelled Morena for fighting in her classroom, I watched Huera march up to the teacher, in front of all the students, and back the teacher up against the wall while she threatened the teacher with reprisals for "fucking with her kid." Morena was quite impressed with her mother's actions and even boasted about it. The homegirls whose mothers had been onetime gang members often boasted about their mothers' past exploits.

However, the younger gang members who are mothers, like India, often have difficulty reconciling their role as mother with their role as gang member.

INDIA: Look at her. [*We are sitting in front of her apartment watching a young woman walking down the street with four homeboys.*] She should settle down. She's a mom now.

CLUMSY: Look who's talking. What about you?

INDIA: That's different. It ain't like I'm throwing down and fighting the guys and shit.

I sometimes heard the girls saying that India "wasn't down for the hood" anymore, that she wasn't "kicking it" enough with the homegirls since she had her baby. However, these same girls were the first to condemn her for being a poor mother. India was often put in a position to defend her choice of participation or nonparticipation in gang activities.

Some of the homegirls do not ever plan on getting married because "you can't trust no guy to be faithful." Most of the girls plan to have a family, but they do not want to be tied down by a husband. Payasa told me that she did not want to have any children or get married. The other homegirls refused to take Payasa seriously, telling her that she would change her mind when she fell in love. It is the general opinion that girls who do not have children will become lonely old women: "The guys, they leave, but your kids—that's forever. They're always gonna be there for you."

While all of the older homegirls claim that they have an "old man," their relationships with these men are usually strained by jealousy and violence. Sometimes the homegirls admit to having a baby to "try and keep the guy interested." However, the men usually do not stay with them, and the men that do, do not assume any responsibility for child care. The men often leave for months at a time; sometimes they are incarcerated, while other times, they move in with another woman, or they "are spending time on the streets." Usually if the men return, more often than not, the homegirls take them back in. However, the majority of the time the older homegirls are left to raise their children alone, the "old man" making only intermittent appearances at home.

Most of the homegirls and homeboys said that they do not want their children or younger siblings to join the gang: "I know what it's like. Everything I been through. I wouldn't want them to go through all that." However, most of the girls are so tightly linked to the gang, through family, friends, and boyfriends, they cannot conceive of a social life that does not include gang members.

HOMEGIRLS AND HOMEBOYS

The homegirls maintain that they are independent of their male counterparts. The homeboys usually confirm the autonomous nature of the girls' activities.

PACO: There aren't that many girls that are down for the hood. They're pretty much on their own. They like to talk to the guys, and the guys treat them like they were another guy, the same handshake and stuff. Basically, they're tomboys. If the girls see someone they don't like, they'll say, "Hey, where you from?" to show the guys that they are someone, not just girls.

However, sometimes the boys talk about "using" the homegirls, much in the same way that the girls boast about manipulating the homeboys: "When we don't like some bitch, we get the homegirls to jump her for us. They do what we tell them to do."

There is a rivalry that exists between the male and female gang members. The girls would often tell me that they were better than the homeboys. They would demonstrate their superiority by regaling me with their exploits on how they manipulated the homeboys to do something for them, like stealing beer or giving them drugs or money:

INDIA: It's easy to get them to do stuff for you. You just tell them, "You ain't bad; you ain't down." Then they end up coming back with the beer. They try to do that to us. . . . We tell them we already proved ourselves, and they get mad 'cause we're not weak minded like they are. They go, "Fuck you, then. That's the last time." But they always keep on doing it. It's like the guys think that she'll think that, "Oh, he's down. He's tough." But they don't know that we're just sending him to mess with him.

The girls' relationships with the homeboys is complex. At times the girls treat the boys like rivals for prestige: "I even tell my homeboys, 'I think the homegirls are better than you guys; all they do is kick it.'" Other times the boys seem to act as their chivalrous protectors:

INDIA: [T]wo weeks ago Northcity [rival gang] came over here, and they were driving by and there were some of the homegirls right there. They [the local homeboys] pushed them down. Like that, you know. They take care of us.

Still other times, the boys are oppressive:

INDIA: Well, the way I see it is we get mad at our own homeboys 'cause they'd be like, well at first, we used to go steal cars—they'd be like that can't be, "No, you guys can't. Let the man get the job done." It's like they would say because we're girls, we can't do it. They gave us a time. One time they told us they'd give us six minutes, and we were in [the car] in three minutes. It's like that now—the homeboys kickback, and that's when the homegirls started doing their own things.

The chauvinistic behavior of the homeboys also impacted my fieldwork. For example, when one of the "shot callers," a *veterano* who had just been released from prison, decided to call a meeting with all the *varrio* gang members, I was told that I could not attend the meeting; they did not want any women at the meeting. Only India attempted to go to the meeting so that she could tell me about it the next day; however, she was kept outside of the meeting and was unable to hear much of what occurred.

For the most part, the homegirls and homeboys get along with each other, usually because the homegirls defer to their male counterparts. Although there were often small personal arguments between individual boys and girls, rarely did they escalate to form rifts in the neighborhood.

While the girls said that they would fight their male counterparts for their homegirls, I never saw this happen. When I told them that I never saw them help each other in arguments with the homeboys, the homegirls noted that fights between girlfriends and boyfriends were an exception to the rule. Usually their relationships with their boyfriends took precedence over their relationships with the homegirls. This was especially true of the older homegirls.

LD: What if there was a fight between a homegirl and a homeboy—who would you back up?

WICKED: What kind of fight? Like if they were going out [dating], I would stay out of it; it's their business. But if they were fighting over *primos* [marijuana laced with crack cocaine], I'd get in it and back up my homegirl. It's stupid to kill each other for a *primo*, but you gotta respect people's relationships.

The homegirls demanded respect from the homeboys but they were less likely to make the same demands on their boyfriends.

The girls often tolerated behavior from their boyfriends that they would never accept from other homeboys. A remark that would require a homegirl to "step up" to a guy might be ignored if it was made by her boyfriend. That is not to say that the homegirls do not fight, sometimes physically, with their boyfriends; however, they have a higher threshold for tolerating "disrespect" within their relationships. This is especially true of the older homegirls. They explained their inconsistency in behavior by saying that they were "in love and love makes you go stupid." However, boyfriends who attempt to assert their dominance over the homegirls always run the risk of confrontation.

Both the homeboys and homegirls use the threat of violence to intimidate others. The homegirls challenge boys and girls who do not give them respect. I watched on several occasions when the older homegirls, sixteen and seventeen years old, physically threatened the younger thirteen-year-old homeboys. The girls found sport in publicly emasculating the younger boys in front of others. Verbal sparring is used by the homegirls as a collective process to transform gender relations within the gang. By confronting the younger homeboys, the gang girls resist traditional male/female roles. However, while they would sometimes "talk shit" to the older homeboys, only rarely did they play the same games with them. When they did, the reprisals were often ugly and violent, sometimes including physical assaults on the homegirls. In spite of what the girls told me, I did not see or hear about a homegirl coming to the aid of another girl in these situations. Usually they justified their behavior by saying things like: "It's on her. She's gotta take care of it herself."

The homegirls do sometimes fight among themselves about boys. Because the homegirls believe that boys are at best fickle and feckless, they are extremely possessive and jealous of their boyfriends. On the one hand, they are cynical about the fallibility of marriage and conjugal relationships: "You can't trust no man." Yet they will laughingly admit to being "in check" or "whipped," a synonym for being in love and letting the boy dominate them: "When he says jump, I jump." Because of this, their roles as gang member and girlfriend often come into conflict.

Homegirls are expected to remain faithful to their boyfriends. They are also expected to perform the usual girlfriend "duties" such as cooking and cleaning for him, as well as carrying weapons and drugs. However, because homegirls are also concerned with their reputations as gang members, they often resent their boyfriends' chauvinism. I witnessed some nasty fights between the homegirls and their boyfriends, especially when the boyfriend attempted to assert control over the homegirl in public. Because both parties in the relationship frequently use violence to solve problems, the relationships between the homegirls and their boyfriends are often tumultuous.

India and her boyfriend Chato were often fighting. Most of their fights were caused by one person's attempt to dominate the other. Most often the fighting began because Chato would forbid India from going somewhere on the pretense that some of the other homeboys might try to take advantage of her. India would become angry at Chato for trying to keep her from going out with her friends, while he was out prowling around until two in the morning collecting phone numbers from other girls: "It ain't fair. He won't let me go nowhere. But I go out sometimes. He don't like it, but I do it anyway."

On one occasion India went out with friends and returned home about ten o'clock at night. The next day, when Chato asked her what time she returned home, she lied to him. Chato angrily confronted her, telling her that he had stationed one of the homeboys at the park to watch until she had returned home. They began yelling and swearing at each other; India's two-year-old daughter cried and rocked herself in the corner of the apartment. India ended the fight by throwing Chato out of the house. However, she let him come back several days later: "I got used to him being around all the time and wanted him back." India is currently trying to get pregnant with Chato's baby.

Most of the homegirls had these kinds of problems with their boyfriends. The boyfriends expected the homegirls to behave like "regular *jainas*" who stayed home and waited for their men to return. While the homegirls might sometimes play the expected role, they also chaffed under their boyfriends' attempts to control their behavior.

For the most part, the homeboys do not necessarily hold their female counterparts in high esteem. While some of the homeboys told me that they respected the homegirls, the *veteranos* characterized the homegirls as "untrustworthy and weak." A few of the homeboys called the homegirls "ho's" and told me the girls were sexually "dirty." Most of the older gang members do not believe that the homegirls were "serious" gang members. Rather, they told me that the homegirls were "just playing."

TERRITORY

Las Sureñas Locas claimed the same territory as their male counterparts. However, whereas the male gang members describe themselves as soldiers protecting the neighborhood, the girls do not. The homeboys are much more vigilant about controlling who does and does not enter their neighborhood. When I first started showing up in the *varrio*, I created a mild sensation among the homeboys. I used to come into the area to tutor Andrea. Her family's store was a favorite hangout for the male gang members. Anytime they saw my car parked out in front of the store, I could count on several of them coming by to check on me. They were very curious about me and my motivations, and often Andrea and I had to chase them away so that we could get any work done.

In comparison to the boys, the homegirls do not spend as much time kicking it in public. Small groups of homeboys are always visible in the *varrio*. Usually there are groups of six or ten boys, spending time in the park or various other areas in the *varrio*. The girls spend more time in smaller groups, usually two or three girls strolling around the neighborhood or hanging out indoors.

While the homegirls have a reputation among nongang girls as being very territorial, the girls seem to have more freedom than the boys to travel to other neighborhoods. When they do venture into other neighborhoods, the homegirls are usually escorted by the homeboys from the other neighborhood, who protect them from the other *varrio*'s homegirls. When they are visiting another neighborhood, the girls abide by a specific code of behavior:

PAYASA: Let's say we get invited to another *varrio,* right? If we go, when we're in their *varrio,* we can't throw our signs [flash the gang's hand signals]. That's like disrespecting them, you know. They invited us to their party, so we just kick it, you know. They throw their signs 'cause that's their neighborhood and they're in it. If those girls come to our neighborhood, we could throw out signs, but if they throw theirs, then we get mad.

TINY: It's different for the girls. For the guys, they would say, "Get the hell out of here." But for us, they ask us where we're from, and we tell them . . .They give us respect, you know. But if we went down there and started acting up like Locas, you know, they would slap us and all. The homeboys don't like it. They don't like that we go where we want. We go everywhere. We tell them, "Mind your own business."

While the girls often meet boys from different neighborhoods, they rarely have long-term relationships with them. Dating someone from outside the neighborhood makes for a difficult relationship: Any boy from a different neighborhood can expect to be jumped by homeboys if he is spotted inside the territory of Varrio Granos.

MORENA: Homegirls can go into the other neighborhoods, for the most part. Sometimes they will hit you up but not usually. Homegirls can go more places than the homeboys. Like this homie from Varrio B Street came to visit his *jaina* [girlfriend], and he was stupid. He came here by himself and walked right up to us, hanging out in the park. He said, "Hey I ain't packing nothing [not carrying a weapon] and I don't want no trouble. I just came to see my *jaina*." And the homeboys said, "We don't care." And they started beating the shit out of him. I ran and got his *jaina* 'cause I know her, and she was crying and shit, you know, telling them to leave him alone. It's a real bad thing to go out with Mojado, so that's on her. So after, the homies jumped me for you know getting her. I told them, "I don't care." I take my consequences—business is business. I don't take it personal, so they messed me up some, but I covered my face and it wasn't too bad.

In contrast, the Locas rarely jump a homeboy's "out-of-town" girlfriend, in spite of the fact that they have "the green light" to jump any girl that comes into their neighborhood. They explained the disparity this way: "If you got respect for the guy, you ain't gonna jump his *jaina*." Gang control of the residential neighborhood associated with Varrio Granos also impacts nongang members' relationships with individuals in other neighborhoods.

LIVING WITH THE GANGS

As Vigil (1988a) and Harris (1988) note, actual gang members are a minority in most *varrio* populations. Many of the residents of Varrio Granos are not affiliated with the gang. In fact, some of the older residents of Varrio Granos complain that they feel like "strangers" in their own neighborhood; they are intimidated by the young gang members. Others residents, however, arrange a peaceable coexistence with the gang, either because of family relationships to gang members or childhood associations:

ROSIE: I know most of the mothers of the homeboys. I grew up with them, so I'm okay with the homeboys, but I don't trust them. I don't let them in my house. They already stole two video cameras from us. I keep my kids away from them.

INDIA: We talk to some [people] that aren't gang. Some of them are my friends 'cause we're raised up with them, but they don't give them as much respect as the homegirls give to their homegirls. We give Monica respect 'cause of her brother—he's in the gang. Andrea, we probably would have messed with her if her dad didn't have a lot of respect in the *varrio*.

LOURDES: [Rosie's daughter] If you're moving stuff out of your house and they're around, they'll help you. My mom grew up with a lot of their parents, so they know us. But there's a lot of younger ones; the new ones don't have respect for no one.

ANDREA: The guy that bought our store, he's got problems with the gang members. He's been chasing them away and that causes problems. I told him, "Get a no-loitering sign and let the police chase them away." You got to be a little friendly with them, but you got to keep your distance.

CARLA: They don't mess with my family. The homeboys all think my grandma's a witch. She tells them she's gonna curse them, and they're afraid of her.

While many of the residents of Varrio Granos are not directly affiliated with the gang, most are familiar with the gang and know at least some of the gang's members. Many of the adolescents I spoke with found it inconceivable that there were not any gangs where I attended high school. One girl explained the inconsistencies between my high school experiences and her experiences in terms of ethnicity: "It's because you're white, maybe. If you were Mexican, well you couldn't be Mexican and not know about gangs; that would be impossible."

For adolescent girls in the neighborhood who want to date boys from other areas, the gangs pose a real problem. Lourdes's longtime boyfriend is from Northcity:

LOURDES: It's hard because my boyfriend can't come to my house most of the time. He has to make sure that nobody's around if he's going to pick me up. Mostly we meet at the K-Mart because it's safer.

Part of Lourdes's problem is that her previous boyfriend was a gang member who is currently in jail. She broke off all contact with him after he was incarcerated. Consequently, the homeboys often harass Lourdes for "letting down the hood."

LOURDES: The homeboys always tell me, "Get that picture [of my new boyfriend] off your notebook." They always tell me they're going to jump him and kill him. If you date the homeboys in your area, they expect you to go from homeboy to homeboy, but then you get a reputation; but if you date someone else, they get mad at you.

Arlene also had problems in the neighborhood because she ended a relationship with a homeboy. The family of the former boyfriend was no longer speaking to her, and she had been threatened with physical violence by the female cousins of the homeboy.

Sometimes just getting off the public bus in rival gang territory is enough to create problems with the local homeboys and homegirls. When Mayra was seen getting off the bus in Varrio B Street, the gang members harassed her for weeks. They followed her around the neighborhood, calling her "*rata*" (literally rat, meaning traitor).

Every girl from Varrio Granos who celebrates her *quinceañera* (fifteenth birthday) also has to contend with the problems of gangs and the threat of gang violence at her party. The parties, usually preceded by a Catholic mass, are elaborate affairs that signal the transition of a young girl into adulthood. The quinceañera's family often spends thousands of dollars on the event, including the hiring of security guards. In fact, every *quinceañera* that I attended had some type of hired security staff. Some of the girls celebrated their birthdays in Mexico or moved the reception to other cities in order to deter gang members from attending or to reduce the potential threat of a drive-by shooting.

The problem of gang violence at the parties is usually generated by the girlfriends of the *quinceañera*. The girls often move freely between rival gang territories. The girls then invite rival gang members to attend, and often before the end of the evening, a fight has broken out. When Martha celebrated her *quinceañera*, it was very obvious which boys belonged to which gang, because they all came wearing their particular gang's clothing. Before the end of the evening a fight had broken out between rival gang members, resulting in a shotgun being fired in the parking lot. The police were called, and several homeboys were taken into police custody. Martha was in tears, her party ruined. Her friend Monica, a feisty sixteen-year-old, elected not to have a *quinceañera*. She explains her reasons this way:

I didn't have a party 'cause of the problems. Homeboys have no respect. I know I told them, "How come you guys can bring girls from wherever into our hood, and if there's a problem, you back them up, but we can't bring guys in?" They said, "Because you're our girls." I told them, "I ain't your girl; I ain't a Loca." They said, "You live here." I told them, "I live here, but I ain't a Loca. Beside you think guys think you know who comes into your hood, but you don't. I got guys visiting me all the time from all over." They're like [she imitates the home-boy shoulder shrug and throws her head back, assuming a fighting stance] "Oh, yeah." [We laugh.] I told them off. I do what I want. They don't own me.

Monica can afford to reproach the homeboys because her brother's reputation in the gang protects her, although she is not afraid to fight for herself if the situation requires it. Unfortunately, not all of the girls are able to deal with the gang members as effectively as Monica does.

Graciela is a quiet sixteen-year-old who lives in the *varrio*. Her father, a conservative businessman with strong political sentiments, has chosen to confront the gangs in his neighborhood. This has had very unfortunate repercussions for his daughter and his other children. Graciela is constantly harassed by the homeboys, who catcall and insult her whenever they see her. The homegirls threaten her with physical violence; on one occasion two homegirls jumped her. With the exception of school and church, Graciela rarely goes out. Her father has to drive her to school every day because it is unsafe for her to walk through the neighborhood alone.

In spite of the homegirls' powers of intimidation, non-gang-affiliated girls are disdainful of the homegirls. They describe the homegirls alternately as "tomboys" and "'ho's," or as defective copies of their male counterparts. Most of the nongang girls perceive gang activities as something appropriate for boys but not for girls. Homegirls are always described as decidedly unfeminine.

ANA: The homegirls are like guys—but like wimpy guys. They're not really into it. The guys do the drive-bys and the girls might be in the car with them, but they don't carry no guns. When they fight, they use their fingernails and pulling hair and slapping each other. They dress like guys and fight like guys, but they only throw down with guys 'cause they don't think no guy's gonna hit them back, but they can be surprised.

MONICA: The homegirls don't get respect. The guys use them to set up other guys or get drugs for them. They share the guys. They go from one to the other guy. Some of the guys don't like the homegirls 'cause they dress like guys. They think it's ugly—like kissing another guy.

Even a few of the homegirls admit it is not always a good thing for a girl to be in a gang, because "a girl should be more like a girl." Payasa, one of four children, confided to me, "Out of my family, I'm the only one in a gang. I should've been a guy."

Conversely, homeboys do not have the same type of reputation among non-gang-affiliated girls. Homeboys are described as nice boys who are misunderstood by the general public.

MARIA: It's like they're two people. Sometimes they're acting bad when they're with their friends, but they can be real nice and treat you real good. But nobody gives them a chance, they always think the worst of them.

Girls also tend to see homeboys as "exciting."

ARLENE: Everybody wants to go out with homeboys cause they are exciting. They're always doing stuff. It's daring. They're getting you to ditch class and stuff. The other guys are too boring.

According to the girls, homeboys can "get any girl they want." Across different gang cultures, many gang-affiliated boys admit that access to girls is an important factor in their decision to join a gang (Jankowski 1991).

FEMENINIDAD AND GANG CULTURE

While some researchers indicate that involvement in gang activities may be considered improper for women (Horowitz 1983, Padilla 1992), the girls talk about being in a gang as an alternative lifestyle and a means of achieving respect. The girls achieve respect by participating in high-risk activities, traditionally associated with the male world. Most of the girls want to be, as one homeboy said, "someone, not just girls." Being a gang member confers special status on the homegirls as compared to girls who are not gang affiliated.

PAYASA: You know what I think? The girls, the ones. . . that was always at home. They don't know nothing. When you're on the streets, it opens up your eyes, and you see a lot of things out there. You have more fun. You travel more. . . . I like it the way I am. I have a lot of fun, and I think the girls—they don't realize about life 'cause they're stuck in the house and their mom won't let them out.

The homegirls feel like they have assumed control of their lives by eschewing the traditional role of girls in the *varrio*.

However, girls who affiliate themselves with gangs are confronted with an irreconcilable conflict between their gender and their gang membership. The homegirls cite their desire for respect as the primary reason that they participate in gang activities, but the gang's construction of respect is one that prizes high-risk, traditionally masculine behaviors and denigrates femininity and all behaviors perceived as feminine. In the *varrio* there are two means of achieving respect, a distinctly feminine version and a masculine version. The feminine code of respect idealizes sexual purity, fidelity, cooperation, and nurturing characteristics. The masculine code of respect, also known as *machismo*, emphasizes loyalty, aggression, courage, chauvinism. The homegirls pursued the masculine version of respect.

MORENA: Homegirls act like guys to get respect. The only way for most girls to get respect is by taking her old man's shit, having his kid. The guys, when they need drugs or shit, they're like, "Oh baby you know I love you." But then they go fuck around, you know. The only way girls get respect is by having the old man's baby. The homegirls ain't into all that. They're more like I can do the shit as good as the guys can.

GIGGLES: It's more like you get respect. If somebody says shit to you, you gotta step up to them. If you show weakness, they take advantage of you.

Their adherence to the masculine code of respect places homegirls in a tenuous position. In actual fact, the homegirls do not receive much respect from anyone other than themselves. They do not receive respect from nongang members; other girls and women were especially critical of them. Even the male gang members do not afford the homegirls unconditional respect: "The homegirls, they're just playing like tomboys." For the more conventional residents of the *varrio*, the homegirls are a symbol of improper femininity; in effect, they mark the boundaries of femininity and masculinity.

Research on adolescent male groups indicates that masculine subcultures traditionally construct themselves in opposition to femaleness and femininity (Brake 1980; Cohen 1955; Jankowski 1991; Vigil 1988a, 1988b; Willis 1977, 1981b). The male gang associated with Varrio Granos is exceptionally chauvinistic in orientation. Thus, Las Sureñas Locas have to manage their femininity in order to better reconcile their female status with their gang member status.

One way that the homegirls manage the conflict between their gender and their gang affiliation is by adopting masculine clothing styles and mannerisms. Gang-affiliated girls can be distinguished from their nongang female counterparts in terms of their dress, language, and mannerisms/behavior. Homegirls traditionally wear masculine clothes, mostly jeans and khakis with oversized Pendletons. They choose dark or neutral colors, favoring gray, black, and khaki. They use language peppered with swear words and crude expressions, and they have reputations as sexually promiscuous, aggressive, and confrontational people. They are most frequently described by *varrio* adults and adolescents as tomboys or poor imitations of male gang members.

However, in spite of the overt masculinity associated with gang membership, the homegirls do not reject all feminine behaviors. They spend great amounts of money and time on their makeup, hair, and jewelry. Girl gang members perceive themselves as liberated from many of the constraints of traditional feminine behavior, yet they still want to be accepted by the homeboys as essentially feminine, sexually attractive girls. The homegirls walk a fine line between their desire for parity with the male gang members and their desire to be sexually attractive to them.

Female gang members appear to be expanding their roles within the gang; however, their male counterparts are still dominant in many ways. Although the homegirls purport to be independent of their male counterparts, there are times when the homeboys do control the girls' activities. For example, all access to firearms in the *varrio* is controlled by the boys. The homegirls have to ask permission to borrow a gun. The boys also revel in their role as protectors of the homegirls, but this protection often carries the price tag of oppression. The homegirls vacillate between agreeing that the homeboys "take care" of them and arguing that the homeboys are "nothing but a bunch of punks" who take credit for their escapades.

The homeboys talk about the girls in the neighborhood as possessed sexual objects, a sentiment the homegirls often challenge. Part of the reason that the homegirls are not able to challenge their status as sex objects successfully is that they often look to their male counterparts for validation. Because the homegirls subscribe to values of femininity that emphasize the domestic role of girlfriends, wives, and mothers, they do not develop a truly collective or effective counter-culture.

The girls' relationships with their homegirls conflict at times with their boy/girl relationships. Incompatibility between femininity and gang affiliation is especially acute for homegirls who were girlfriends of male gang members. As Payasa told me, "Being in love fucks you up for the gang." When Payasa violated parole, India allowed her to stay in her apartment. However, when India's boyfriend said that he did not want Payasa in the apartment, India complied. She did this in spite of the fact that Payasa is her best friend, and she did not have any other place to stay.

The homegirls struggle in their efforts to reconcile the two contradictory role choices that they feel are available to them: gangster or *jaina*. Most of them identify closely with both of these roles. Thus, while they will brag about going out with ten different guys at the same time—"Just like the *vatos* [guys] do"—they are also concerned about their reputations, vehemently denying sexual promiscuity: "It wasn't like I was like a 'ho or nothing like that. I'm only *really* with one guy at a time." Even gang-affiliated girls are expected to subscribe to expectations of sexual fidelity. Faithfulness is also something they want from their boyfriends but find difficult to enforce. A few of the girls did not resign themselves to their boyfriends' infidelities and responded by either continuously confronting their boyfriend or assaulting the other girls.

The homegirls of Varrio Granos are trying to empower themselves. Unfortunately, they do not see education or political activism as a means of empowerment. The girls are alienated from many of conventional society's institutions and trapped between two cultures. None of the homegirls who comprised the core of the Las Sureñas Locas attend school. Instead of pursuing conventional middle-class means of empowering themselves, through work, politics, or education, these girls have chosen the gang.

However, while the gang lifestyle rejects some conventional values associated with *femeninidad*, such as little-girl passivity and softness, it incorporates others. The one conventional means of empowerment that the homegirls do pursue is motherhood. Babies confer social prestige as well as some financial independence, through welfare benefits, to the girls. As with many of the other adolescent girls in the *varrio*, some of the homegirls believe that children will provide them with the love and adult social status they so desperately want: "Babies give you a reason to get up in the morning."

The girls often make the choice of gang membership when they are very young, before they are fully aware of the repercussions of their decision. When asked directly about the problems of gang affiliation, however, the younger girls tended to romanticize the gang lifestyle, depicting high-risk delinquent activities as adventures. Any time that I confronted them with the realities of death or serious injury, they would tell me, "Well, everybody's got their time. You gotta die sometime."

Although some of the girls are enthralled with the gang—"I want to be a gangster bitch forever"—the older gang members seem to be more cynical about the gang. They overwhelmingly told me that they did not want their children to be in gangs because "the gang brings you problems." Unfortunately, some of the older girls and women who want to get out of the gang are so intimately bound to the gang, through family and social networks, that they find it nearly impossible to do so. Some of these girls and women harbor escape fantasies that centered around finding "a white boy, probably a marine with lots of money, so I can move from here."

However, in spite of their disenchantment with the gang, older gang members also downplay the risks associated with gang membership. This acceptance of personal risk conforms with the gang ethos. Whenever I tried to ask them about the problems associated with gang membership, every homegirl remained silent. Some of them even went so far as to deny a bad side to gang membership, since talking about the problems of the gang is seen as disloyal.

The homegirls describe themselves as superior to non-gang-affiliated girls. They told me they were stronger than other girls. To demonstrate, they often cited their freedom and self-determination: "I can do whatever I want without nobody telling me I can't."

PAYASA: The other girls, they let the guys push them around and talk about them. But when it comes back to us, it's like, "Fuck you!"

INDIA: Well, the way I see it, if you put a girl from a gang and another girl that's never been in a gang, the way I see it, I think the girl from the gang will survive more.

And in some respects, they are correct. Las Sureñas Locas are survivors. Many of them have been effectively on their own since they were twelve and thirteen years old, some even younger. Many of them have also been the victims of child abuse and molestation. The world they inhabit is a world where it is difficult to find someone they can trust, so they learn to rely on themselves and their homegirls.

PAYASA: I been on the streets since I was nine. I had family problems. India here is my dog. I love her. She took me in. I would die for her. I always tell her when me and her go out, if we get caught, I'll take the blame. I have love for my homegirls; for them I'd get locked up—you know what I mean? Especially if they had kids.

GIGGLES: The homegirls, they're like my sisters. If I need clothes or something, they give me theirs. It's the same with me: If they need something, I give it to them. We share every-thing.

The homegirls of Varrio Granos turn to each other for support. For most of these girls, there is no one else who is going to take care of them. In many ways the hard-core homegirls are just young women who are looking for love and acceptance in a world that offers them little of either.

Unfortunately, the empowerment that the homegirls seek by joining the gang more often than not traps them into a lifetime of poverty. They often join the gang to gain some control over their lives, to escape family problems and gain independence. However, their independence usually translates into motherhood at an early age, unstable family and marital relationships, drug addiction, police records, and dependence on government assistance. For the most part, these girls are unable to envision a future for themselves that does not involve the gang.

The homegirls are not exclusively responsible for their circumstances, nor are they exclusively the victims of their social milieu. The members of Las Sureñas Locas are aware that conventional society sees them as deviant. They know that many of their gang activities are not considered proper behavior, especially for girls. However, they perceive their deviance as conforming to the gang lifestyle, rather than deviating from conventional behavior (Campbell 1990; Harris 1988). Because of this, they face serious role conflicts when they attempt to follow gang norms that dictate one type of behavior for gang members and another for the girlfriends of male gang members. In general, the girls find it impossible to reconcile these two conflicting norms of behavior. Thus, as they mature, they usually choose to curtail their activities as gang members in order to fulfill the obligations of motherhood and wife/girlfriend. Some of the homegirls may eventually become *veteranas*, who maintain their ties to the gang through their children and boyfriends.

Gender-related issues act as an impetus for gang affiliation. The members of Las Sureñas Locas have joined the gang in an attempt to escape conventional expectations associated with their female status. While the girls do not explicitly identify themselves as feminists (they equated feminism with lesbianism and "selfish," childless women), they do often use feminist rhetoric to describe their lives. The homegirls are stretching gender-specific roles in order to cope with other issues related to gang affiliation, such as poverty, discrimination, and cultural alienation.

NOTE

1. When the homegirls reviewed this manuscript, they took exception to my description of their clothing style. They argued that they did not always "dress down." Sometimes the homegirls would dress in gang-style clothes when I took them out to lunch, although other times they would wear their "undercover" clothes. While it is true that they did not always put on their makeup and gang-style clothing, they did dress like this when they were going "cruising" or "gang banging."

Chapter 11

Conclusion

The ethnographic evidence presented in this text provides a strong counterargument to the Culture of Poverty. The Culture of Poverty assumes that dominant cultural values (i.e., Anglo middle-class values) are natural and universal and that cultural values that deviate from their normative standard are pathological. From this perspective, the behavioral choices made by many of these girls—unprotected sexual intercourse, early pregnancy, gang-affiliation—are understood as the outcome of individual irresponsibility and lack of moral fortitude. However, the girls' behavioral decisions are also linked to the structural and material realities of their lives. Thus, while in some respects the girls' behaviors do reflect irresponsibility, it is an irresponsibility born out of their lack of social power and status. Social institutions, such as schools, communities, and social services, that fail to provide support for these girls must also bear some of the responsibility for the consequences of the girls' choices.

What looks like social deviance and poor judgment from an outsider's point of view looks very different from the perspectives of the girls. Decisions about joining gangs, engaging in unprotected sex, becoming a mother, and dropping out of school make sense given an environment that offers few options to these young women. Gang-affiliated girls are attempting to assert some control over their lives by rejecting a passive construction of femininity. Adolescent girls who become mothers seek a more conventional, domestic route in their attempts to achieve some semblance of self-determination and adulthood. The "deviant" life choices made by many of the girls have at their root the logic of conventional society. In many instances, they are simply seeking a means of attaining love, dignity, and social prestige in a world that offers them limited means for achieving these goals. Often the deviant behavioral choices they make—early motherhood and gang-affiliation—are alternate routes to access success and social prestige.

The girls are aware of the discrepancies between the reality of their lives and the lives of the people whose houses their mothers clean, whose cars their brothers wash, and whose lawns their fathers tend. While they have positive views of middle-class goals—family, house, car, well-paying job—they are also aware that it will be a struggle for them to achieve the things that seem to come so easily to others. The economic, institutional, and cultural obstacles confronted by girls who entertain visions of attending college illustrate the difficulties for girls who attempt to pursue a more conventional path toward self-determination.

The Culture of Poverty argument is insidiously seductive because it allows us to blame the victim for her own problems: Poor people are poor because they choose not to work; girls become single mothers because they are sexually irresponsible. It effectively divorces an individual's decisions from the social and economic context in which they were made. Social policy that identifies these girls as immoral and deviant, and ignores the social and economic circumstances that severely limit the options of these girls, results in misguided legislation which may even exacerbate the conditions associated with the social problems of gang violence, teen pregnancy, and school dropouts.

During my research, I found that what these girls needed most was an advocate—someone to help them fight the internal and external obstacles that impeded their social and economic advancement. So many of the girls were either unaware of their options or overwhelmed by confusion and frustration in attempting to achieve their goals. What these girls need is hope for a future. They need dedicated mentoring, meaningful after-school activities, career training, and access to well-paying jobs. What they often find in their communities is a segmented labor force, limited access to all but minimum wage work, lack of subsidized child care, inflexible and overburdened schools, chronic economic hardships that contribute to increasing stress and violence within their homes, and a social welfare system that is overburdened, underfunded, and disorganized.

In this context, many of the girls' decisions make sense: They appear to offer liberation to these girls, a means of achieving dignity and value, and a direct route to freedom and "respect." Unfortunately, too late they often find out that the liberation promised by early motherhood and/or gang affiliation is a chimera. Rather than liberating them, these alternatives further restrict their options. Young mothers are bound more closely to their homes because of the requirements of caring for a child. Gang-affiliated girls also find their access to conventional society limited because of the stigmatism associated with their delinquency. Also, because many young mothers fail to complete their education, it is difficult for them to find well-paying jobs that will allow them to support themselves and their children.

These adolescents are not making good, well-informed, well-though-out decisions about their lives. However, we must ask ourselves, Who bears the blame for this? It is easy to blame the individual adolescents. After all, they are the ones making these decisions. It is also easy to blame their families or their communities. It is much more difficult to blame ourselves. We must examine the ways in which our social institutions, whether through benign neglect or through intentional discrimination, produce teen pregnancy and juvenile delinquency.

Epilogue

LYDIA

Lydia graduated from Westhills High School and found employment working as a receptionist. She is currently attending community college part-time. Lydia lives at home. She continues to date her boyfriend who is currently unemployed.

ANDREA

Andrea graduated from Westhills High School and is currently working as a sales representative at a retail store. She lives at home and attends community college. She also continues to date her longterm boyfriend, who is studying to get his GED after serving time at California Youth Authority for burglary.

MORENA

Morena became pregnant and gave birth to a little boy. Her mother died when the baby was five months old. Morena's relatives did not want to assume responsibility for her and the baby. Sixteen-year-old Morena felt that she had no alternative but to move in with her abusive boyfriend. During her pregnancy she attempted to pursue high school credits with an independent study program; however, after the death of her mother, she decided she was no longer able to continue with the program. She is no longer attending school.

CARLA

Before the end of her tenth-grade year of high school, Carla dropped out of school.

MONICA

Monica got pregnant her junior year of high school. The same summer that her fourteen-year-old brother was killed in a gang-related incident, she gave birth to a little girl. Monica dropped out of Westhills High School to enroll in an alternative school, which provided on-site child care. She graduated and is currently working at a retail store.

INDIA

By the end of the summer 1995, India's boyfriend was in jail. She became involved with a member of a rival gang and was soon pregnant with his child. Consequently, she and her daughter have moved from the *varrio* and found an apartment in neutral territory between the two rival gangs.

LOURDES

Lourdes graduated from Westhills High School early. She is currently attending school to become a medical assistant. She and her longtime boyfriend had planned to marry by the end of summer 1995; however, her boyfriend's brother was shot and killed during a robbery attempt during the summer. Consequently, the wedding plans have been delayed.

Bibliography

Abu-Lughod, L. 1990. "The Romance of Resistance: Tracing Transformation of Power through Bedouin Women." *American Ethnologist* 17(1): 41-56.

Adler, F. 1974. *Sisters in Crime: The Rise of the New Female Criminal*. New York: McGraw-Hill.

Alan Guttmacher Institute. 1994a. *Sex and America's Teenagers*. New York: AGI.

————. 1994b. "Sexually Transmitted Diseases in the United States." In *Facts in Brief*. New York: AGI.

Althusser, L. 1971. "Ideology and Ideological State Apparatuses." In *Lenin and Philosophy and Other Essays*, translated by B. Brewster, 127-186. London: New Left Books.

Andrade, S. 1982. "Social Stereotypes of the Mexican American Woman: Policy Implications for Research." *Journal of Behavioral Sciences* 4(2): 223-244.

Apple, M., ed. 1982. *Cultural and Economic Reproduction in Education*. Boston: Routledge & Kegan Paul.

Ardener, E. 1975. "Belief and the Problem of Women." In *Perceiving Women*, edited by S. Ardener, 1-27. London: Malaby Press.

Arnot, M., and Weiner, K., eds. 1987. *Feminism and Social Justice in Education: International Perspectives*. London: Falmer Press.

Baca-Zinn, M. 1975a. "Chicanas: Power and Control in the Domestic Sphere." *Aztlán* 2(3): 19-31.

————. 1975b. "Political Familism: Toward Sex Role Equality in Chicano Families." *Aztlán* 6: 13-26.

————. 1978. "Marital Roles, Marital Power and Ethnicity: A Study of Changing Chicano Families." Ph.D. diss.,University of Oregon.

————1979. "Chicano Family Research: Conceptual Distortions and Alternative Directions." *Journal of Ethnic Studies* 7(Fall): 59-71.

————1982. "Chicano Men and Masculinity." *Journal of Ethnic Studies* 10 (Summer):29-44.

Baer, B. 1975. "Stopping Traffic: One Woman's Cause." *The Progressive* 39(9): 38-44.

Baer, B., and Matthews, G. 1974. "The Women of the Boycott." *The Nation,* February 23, 1974, 232-238.

Barret, M. 1980. *Women's Oppression Today: Problems in Marxist Feminist Analysis.* London: Verso Editions.

Barthes, R. 1967. *Elements of Semiology.* Translated by A. Lavers and C. Smith. New York: Hill and Wang, Inc.

Becerra, R., and de Anda, D. 1984. "Pregnancy and Motherhood Among Mexican American Adolescents." *Health and Social Work* 9: 106-123.

Becker, H. 1963. *Outsiders: Studies in the Sociology of Deviance.* New York: Free Press.

Berger, B. 1995. *An Essay on Culture: Symbolic Structure and Social Structure.* Berkeley: University of California Press.

Bourdieu, P. 1977a. "The Economics of Linguistic Exchange." *Social Science Information* 16(6): 646-668.

———. 1977b. *Outline of a Theory of Practice.* Cambridge: Cambridge University Press.

———. 1984. *A Social Critique of the Judgement of Taste.* Translated by R. Nice. Boston: Harvard University Press.

Bourdieu, P., and Passeron, J. 1977. *Reproduction in Education, Society and Culture.* London: Sage Publications.

Bowker, L., ed. 1981. *Women and Crime in America.* NewYork: Macmillan Publishing.

Bowker, L., Gross, H., and Klein, M. 1980. "Female Participation in Delinquent Gang Activities." *Adolescence* 15(59): 509-519.

Bowles, S., and Gintis, H. 1976. *Schooling and Capitalist America.* Boston: Routledge & Kegan Paul.

Brah, A., and Minkas, R. 1985. "Structural Racism or Cultural Difference: Schooling for Asian Girls." In *Just a Bunch of Girls,* edited by G. Weiner, 14-25. Philadelphia: Open University Press.

Brake, M. 1980. *The Sociology of Youth Culture and Youth Subcultures: Sex and Drugs and Rock 'n Roll.* London: Routledge & Kegan Paul.

Bray, W. 1991. *The Everday Life of the Aztecs.* New York: Peter Bedrick Books.

Brown, G., Rosen, N., and Hill, S. 1980. *The Condition of Education for Hispanic Americans.* National Center for Education Statistics. United States Department of Education. Washington, D.C.: U.S. Government Printing Office.

Brindis, C., and Jeremy, R. 1988. "Adolescent Pregnancy and Parenting in California: A Strategic Plan for Action." Center for Population and Reproduction Health Policy, Institute for Health Policy Issues, University of California, San Francisco.

Brumberg, J. 1992. "Something Happens to Girls: The Changing Experience of Menarche." Paper presented at the Alice in Wonderland Conference, Amsterdam.

Butler, J. 1990. *Gender Trouble.* New York: Routledge, Chapman and Hall, Inc.

California Basic Education Data Systems. California Department of Education Statistical Reports made available for 1980-1994.

California Department of Corrections. 1993. Statistical Reports made available. California Department of Health Services, San Diego County.

———.1993a. "Births to Teenage Mothers in San Diego County by Race/Ethnicity and Subregional Area: 1992." San Diego, County Office of Health Services, September.

———. 1993b. Statistical Reports made available.

California Department of Justice. 1989. "The Juvenile Justice System in California: An Overview." *BCS Reports: Office of the Attorney General.* Sacramento: Department of Justice.

———. 1993. *Gangs 2000: A Call to Action.* Sacramento: California Department of Justice.

Campbell, A. 1984. *The Girls in the Gang: A Report from New York City*. New York: Basil Blackwell, Inc.

————. 1990. "Female Gang Participation in Gangs." In *Gangs in America*, edited by C. R. Huff, 163-183. Newbury Park, CA: Sage Publications.

Centers for Disease Control. 1992. *National Profile Tables and Statistics*. Washington, D.C.: U.S. Government Printing Office.

————. 1993. *National Profile Tables and Statistics*. Washington, D.C.: U.S. Government Printing Office.

Candelaria, C. 1980. "La Malinche, Feminist Prototype." *Frontiers* 5(2): 1-6.

Carter, B. 1973. "Reform School Families." *Society* 12(1): 36-43.

Chafetz, J. 1978. *Masculine, Feminine or Human?* Itasca, IL: F. S. Peacock Publishers, Inc.

Chamot, A., and O'Malley, J. 1986. *A Cognitive Academic Learning Approach: An ESL Content Based Curriculum*. Wheaton, IL: National Clearing House for Bilingual Education.

Chapa, J., and Valencia, R. 1993. "Latino Population Growth, Demographic Characteristics and Educational Stagnation: An Examination of Recent Trends." *Hispanic Journal of Behavioral Science* 15(2): 165-187.

Chesney-Lind, M. 1981. "Judicial Paternalism and the Female Status Offender: Training Women to Know Their Place." In *Women and Crime in America*, edited by L. Bowker, 354-365. New York: Macmillan Publishing.

————. 1989. "Girl's Crime and Woman's Place: Toward a Feminist Model of Female Delinquency." *Crime and Delinquency* 35(1): 5-29.

Chilton, R., and Datesman, S. 1987. "Gender, Race and Crime: An Analysis of Urban Arrest Trends 1960-1980." *Gender and Society* 1: 152-171.

Clark, R. 1983. *Family Life and School Achievement: Why Poor Black Children Succeed or Fail*. Chicago: University of Chicago Press.

————. 1990. "Economic Dependency and Divorce: Implications for the Private Sphere." *International Journal of Sociology of the Family* 20(Spring): 47-65.

Clarke, J.; Hall, S.; Jefferson, T.; and Roberts, B. 1976. "Subculture, Culture and Class: A Theoretical Overview." In *Resistance through Rituals: Youth Subcultures in Postwar Britain*, edited by S. Hall and T. Jefferson, 9-75. London: Hutchinson and Co.

Cloward, R., and Ohlin, L. 1960. *Delinquency and Opportunity*. Glencoe, IL: Free Press.

Cloward, R., and Piven, F. 1979. "Hidden Protest: The Channeling of Female Innovation and Resistance." *Signs* 4(4): 651-669.

Cockburn, C. 1991. *The Way of Women*. New York: Macmillan Publishing Co.

Cohen, A. 1955. *Delinquent Boys: A Culture of the Gang*. Glencoe, IL: Free Press.

Conly, C.; Kelly, P.; Mahanna, P.; and Warner, L. 1993. *Street Gangs: Current Knowledge and Strategies*. U.S. Department of Justice, NCJ 143290. Washington, D.C.: U.S. Government Printing Office.

Cortez, C. 1983. "Chicanas in Film: A History of Image." *Bilingual Review* 10: 94-108.

"Court Rules Photos For Police 'Gang Books' Are Illegal." *San Diego Union-Tribune*, December 5, 1993, A8.

Cowie, C., and Lees, S. 1981. "Slags or Drags." *Feminist Review* 9: 17-31.

Crime and Delinquency in California. 1991. Office of the Attorney General. Sacramento: Department of Justice.

Cromwell, V., and Cromwell, R. 1978. "Perceived Dominance in Decision Making and Conflict Resolution among Anglo, Black and Chicano Couples." *Journal of Marriage and Family* 40(4): 749-759

Curry, G. D.; Ball, R. A., and Fox, R. J. 1994. *Law Enforcement Records and Gang Crime Problems*. Morgantown: West Virginia University Press.

Curry, G. D., and Spergel, I. 1992. "Gang Involvement and Delinquency among Hispanic and African-American Adolescent Males." *Journal of Crime and Delinquency* 29(3): 273-291.

David, M. 1993. "Theories of Family Change, Motherhood and Education." In *Feminism and Social Justice in Education: An International Perspective*, edited by M. Arnot and K. Weiler, 10-31. London: Falmer Press.

De Certeau, M. 1984. *The Practice of Everyday Life*. Translated by S. Rendall. Berkeley: University of California Press.

Deem, R., ed. 1978. *Schooling for Women's Work*. London: Routledge & Kegan Paul.

DeJong, A.; Hervada, A.; and Emmet, G. 1983. "Epidemiological Variations in Childhood Sexual Abuse." *Child Abuse and Neglect* 7: 155-162.

Delgado, A. 1974. "Machismo." *La Luz*. 3(9): 6.

De Saussure, F. 1959. *Course in General Linguistics*. Translated by W. Baskin. London: Peter Owen.

Diaz-Guerrero, N. 1975. *Psychology of the Mexican*. Austin: University of Texas Press.

Donato, R., Menchaca, M., and Valencia, R. 1991. "Segregation, Desegregation and Integration of Chicano Students: Problems Prospects." In *Chicano School Failure and Success*, edited by R. Valencia, 27–63. New York: Falmer Press, Taylor and Francis, Inc.

Douglas, M. 1984. *Purity and Danger: An Analysis of the Concepts of Pollution and Taboo*. 1966 Reprinting, London: Ark.

Espinosa, R., and Ochoa, A. 1986. "Concentration of California Hispanic Students in Schools with Low Achievement: A Research Note." *American Journal of Education* 95: 77-95.

Fagan, J. 1990. "Social Processes of Delinquency and Drug Use among Urban Gangs." In *Gangs in America*, edited by C. R. Huff, 183-222. Newbury Park, CA: Sage Publications.

Faludi, S. 1991. *Backlash: The Undeclared War against American Women*. New York: Anchor Books, Doubleday.

Federal Bureau of Investigation. 1987. *Crime in the United States 1986*. Washington, D.C.: U.S. Government Printing Office.

———. 1992a. *Crime in the United States 1991*. Washington, D.C.: U.S. Government Printing Office.

———. 1992b. *National Crime Index*. Washington, D.C.: U.S. Government Printing Office.

———. 1993. *Uniform Crime Reports*. Washington, D.C.: U.S. Government Printing Office.

Fellmeth, R.; Kalemkiarian, S.; and Reiter, R. 1994. *California Children's Budget 1994-1995*. San Diego: Children's Advocacy Institute.

Fine, M. 1988. "Sexuality, Schooling and Adolescent Females: The Missing Discourse of Desire." *Harvard Educational Review* 58(1): 29-53.

———. 1991. *Framing Dropouts: Notes on the Politics of an Urban Public High School*. Albany: State University of New York Press.

Fordham, S. 1988. "Racelessness as a Factor in Black Students' School Success: Pragmatic Strategy or Pyrrhic Victory?" *Harvard Educational Review* 58(1): 54-84.

Fordham, S., and Ogbu, J. 1986. "Black Students' Schooling Success: Coping with the Burden of Acting White." *Urban Review* 18(3): 176-206.

Forste, R., and Heaton, T. 1988. "Initiation of Sexual Activity among Female Adolescents." *Youth and Society* 19(3): 250-268.

Foucault, M. 1979. *Discipline and Punish*. Translated by A. Sheridan. 1977. Reprint, New York: Vintage Books.

———. 1990. *The History of Sexuality*. Vol. 1. Translated by R. Hurley. 1978. Reprint, New York: Vintage Books.

Fox, L. 1983. "Obedience and Rebellion: Revision of Chicana Myths of Motherhood." *Women's Studies Quarterly* 6(2): 20-22.

Fuller, M. 1980. "Black Girls in a London Comprehensive School." In *Schooling for Women's Work*, edited by R. Deem, 52-65. London: Routledge & Kegan Paul.

Garcia, A. 1989. "The Development of Chicana Feminist Discourse 1970-1984." *Gender and Society* 3(2): 217–238.

Gaskell, J. 1985. "Course Enrollment in the High School: The Perspective of Working Class Females." *Sociology of Education* 58: 48-59.

Gibson, M. 1987. "The School Performance of Immigrant Minorities: A Comparative View." *Anthropology and Education Quarterly* 18: 262-275.

———. 1988. *Accommodation without Assimilation*. Ithaca, NY: Cornell University Press.

Gibson, M., and Ogbu, J., eds. 1991. *Minority Status and Schooling: A Comparative Study of Immigrant and Involuntary Minorities*. New York: Garland Press.

Gilmarten, K. 1980. "The Status of Women and Minorities in Education: A Social Feasibility Study." *Journal of Educational Equity and Leadership* 1(1): 3-27.

Giordano, P., and Cernkovich, S. 1979. "On Complicating the Relationship between Liberation and Delinquency." *Social Problems* 26: 467-481.

Giroux, H. 1981. *Ideology, Culture, and the Process of Schooling*. Philadelphia: Temple University Press.

———. 1983. "Theories of Reproduction and Resistance in the New Sociology of Education: A Critical Analysis." *Harvard Educational Review* 53(3): 257-293.

Glick, R., and Moore, J. 1990. *Drugs in Hispanic Communities*. New Brunswick, NJ: Rutgers University Press.

Goldstein, B. 1986. "In Search of Survival: The Education and Integration of Hmong Refugee Girls." *Journal of Ethnic Studies* 16(2): 1-27.

Gomez, N. 1973. "La Feminista." *Encuentro Femenil* 1: 34–47.

Gonzalez, A. 1982. "Sex Roles of the Traditional Mexican Family: A Comparison of Chicano and Anglo Students' Attitudes." *Journal of Cross Cultural Psychology* 13(3): 330-339.

Gonzalez, J. 1988. "Dilemmas of the High Achieving Chicana: The Double-Bind in Male/Female Relationships." *Sex Roles* 18(7–8): 367–379.

Gramsci, A. 1989. *Selections from the Prison Notebooks*. Translated by Q. Hoare and G. Smith. 1971. Reprint, New York: International Publishers.

Grebler, L., Moore, J., and Guzman, R. 1970. *The Mexican American People*. Glencoe, IL: Free Press.

Griffin, C. 1987. "Young Women and the Transition from School to Un/Employment." In *Gender Under Scrutiny*, edited by G. Weiner and M. Arnot, 213-221. London: Open University Press.

Hagan, J.; Simpson, J.; and Gillis, A. R. 1979. "The Sexual Stratification of Social Control: A Gender Based Perspective on Crime and Delinquency." *British Journal of Sociology* 30(1): 25-38.

———. 1987. "Class in the Household: A Power Control Theory of Gender and Delinquency." *American Journal of Sociology* 92: 788-816.

Hagendorn, J. 1988. *People and Folks: Gangs, Crime and the Underclass in a Rustbelt City*. Chicago: Lake View Press.

Hargreaves, A. 1982. "Resistance and Relative Autonomy Theory: Problems of Distortion and Incoherence in Recent Marxist Analysis of Education." *British Journal of Sociology* 3(2): 107-126.

Harris, M. 1988. *Cholas, Latino Girls and Gangs*. New York: AMS Press, Inc.

Hawkes, G., and Taylor, M. 1975. "Power and Structure in Mexican and Mexican American Farm Labor Families." *Journal of Marriage and Family* 37(4): 807-811.

Hebdige, D. 1987. *Subculture and the Meaning of Style*. 1979. Reprint, London: Routledge & Kegan Paul.

Heller, C. 1966. *Mexican American Youth: Forgotten Youth at the Crossroads*. New York: Random House.

Hertz, R. 1986. *More Equal Than Others: Women and Men in Dual Career Marriages*. Berkeley: University of California Press.

Hoffman-Bustamante, D. 1973. "The Nature of Female Criminality." *Issues in Criminology* 8(Fall): 117-136.

Holland, D., and Eisenhart, M. 1990. *Educated in Romance: Women, Achievement and College Culture*. Chicago: University of Chicago Press.

Holland, D. C., and Skinner, D. 1987. "Prestige and Intimacy: The Cultural Models behind Americans' Talk about Gender Types." In *Cultural Models in Language and Thought*, edited by D. C. Holland and N. Quinn, 78–111. Cambridge: Cambridge University Press.

Horowitz, R. 1975. "Honor, Convention and Violence: The Social World of Youth in a Chicano Community." Ph.D. Diss., University of Chicago.

———. 1981. "Passion, Submission and Motherhood." *Sociological Quarterly* 22 (Spring): 241-252.

———. 1983. *Honor and the American Dream*. New Brunswick, NJ: Rutgers University Press.

———. 1990. "Sociological Perspectives on Gangs: Conflicting Definitions and Concepts." In *Gangs in America*, edited by C. R. Huff, 37-55. Newbury Park, CA: Sage Publications.

Hudson, B. 1984. "Femininity and Adolescence." In *Gender and Generation*, edited by A. McRobbie and M. Nava, 31-53. London: Macmillan Publishers, Ltd.

Hudson Institute. 1987. *Workforce 2000: Work and Workers for the 21st Century*. Indianapolis: Hudson Institute.

Huff, C. R. 1990. "Denial, Overreaction and Misidentification: A Postscript to Public Policy." In *Gangs in America*, edited by C. R. Huff, 310-317. Newbury Park, CA: Sage Publications.

Jankowski, M. 1986. *City Bound*. Albuquerque: University of New Mexico Press.

———. 1991. *Islands in the Street: Gangs and American Urban Society*. Berkeley: University of California Press.

Kelley, P. 1990. "Delicate Transactions: Gender, Home and Employment among Hispanic Women." In *Uncertain Terms: Negotiating Gender in American Culture*, edited by F. Ginsburg and A. Tsing, 183-198. Boston: Beacon Press.

Kennedy, L., and Baron, S. 1993. "Routine Activities and a Subculture of Violence: A Study of Violence on the Street." *Journal of Research in Crime and Delinquency* 30(1): 88-112.

Kerber, L. 1988. "Separate Spheres, Female Worlds, Woman's Place: The Rhetoric of Women's History." *Journal of American History* 75(June): 9-39.

Kessler, S.; Ashendon, D. J.; Connell, R. W.; and Dowsett, G. W. 1985. "Gender Relations in Secondary Schooling." *Sociology of Education* 58: 34-45.

Klein, M. 1971. *Street Gangs and Street Workers*. Englewood Cliffs, NJ: Prentice-Hall.

Klein, M., and Maxon, C. 1989. "Street Gang Violence." In *Violent Crime, Violent Criminals*, edited by N. Weiner and M. Wolfgang, 198-235. Newbury Park, CA: Sage Publications.

Krashen, S. 1982. *Principals and Practices of Second Language Acquisition.* Oxford: Pergammon Press.

Lamphere, L. 1974. "Strategies, Cooperation and Conflict Among Women in Domestic Groups." In *Women, Culture and Society*, edited by M. Rosaldo and L. Lamphere, 97-118. Stanford: Stanford University Press.

Lawhn, J. 1989. "El Regidor and La Prensa: Impediments to Women's Self Definition." *Third Woman* 4: 134-142.

Lees, S. 1986. *Losing Out: Sexuality and Adolescent Girls*. London: Hutchinson and Co.

————. 1993. *Sugar and Spice: Sexuality and Adolescent Girls*. New York: Penguin Books.

Leonard, E. 1982. *Women, Crime and Society: A Critique of Criminological Theory.* New York: Longman, Inc.

Leong, L.W.T. 1992. "Cultural Resistance: The Cultural Terrorism of British Male Working-Class Youth." *Current Perspectives in Social Theory* 12: 29-58.

Leon-Portilla, M. 1963. *Aztec Thought and Culture*. Norman: University of Oklahoma Press.

Lesko, N. 1988. "The Curriculum of the Body: Lessons from a Catholic High School." In *Becoming Feminine: The Politics of Popular Culture*, edited by L. Roman and L. Christian-Smith, 123-143. London: Falmer Press.

Lewis, D. 1977. "A Response to Inequality: Black Women, Racism and Sexism." *Signs* 3(2): 339-361.

Lewis, O. 1959. *Five Families: Mexican Case Studies in the Culture of Poverty.* New York: Basic Books.

Liebow, E. 1969. *Tally's Corner: A Study of Negro Streetcorner Men*. Boston: Little, Brown.

Lipstiz, G. 1988. "The Struggle for Hegemony." *Journal of American History* 75(1): 146-150.

Lizarraga, S. 1985. "Images of Women in Chicano Literature by Men." *Feminist Issues*. 5(2): 69-88.

Lombroso, C., and Ferrero, W. 1898. *The Female Offender*. New York: D. Appleton and Company.

Long, J. M., and Vigil, J.D. 1980. "Cultural Styles and Adolescent Sex-role Perceptions." In *Twice a Minority: Mexican American Women*, edited by M.B. Melville, St. Louis: C. V. Mosby

Macleod, A. 1992. "Hegemonic Relations and Gender Resistance: The New Veiling as Accommodating Protest in Cairo." *Signs* 17(31): 533-557.

Macleod, J. 1987. *Ain't No Makin' It: Leveled Aspiration in a Low Income Neighborhood*. Boulder, CO: Westview Press.

Madsen, W. 1973. *Mexican Americas of South Texas*. 1967. Reprint, New York: Holt, Rinehart and Winston, Inc.

Marini, M. and Brinton, M. 1984. "Sextyping and Occupational Socialization." In *Sex Segregation in the Workplace*, edited by B. Reskin. Washington, D.C.: National Academy Press.

Markus, E. 1990. "Does It Pay for a Woman to Work Outside Her Home?" *Journal of Comparative Family Studies* 21(3): 397-413.

Marynik, J., Vickery, K., Jones, C., Murray, W., and Luca, R. 1993. *Gangs 2000: A Call to Action*. Sacramento, California: Department of Justice, Division of Law Enforcement.

Matuti-Bianchi, M. 1986. "Ethnic Identities and Patterns of School Success and Failure among Mexican-Descent and Japanese American Students in a California High School: An Ethnographic Analysis." *American Journal of Education* 95(1): 233-255.

———. 1991. "Situational Ethnicity and Patterns of School Performance among Immigrant and Non-immigrant Mexican-Descent Students." In *Minority Status and Schooling*, edited by M. Gibson and J. Ogbu, 205-248. New York: Garland Publishing, Inc.

Maxon, C., and Klein, M. 1990. "Street Gang Violence: Twice as Great or Half as Great." In *Gangs in America*, edited by C. R. Huff. Newbury Park, CA: Sage Publications.

Mckenna, T., and Ortiz, F., eds. 1988. *The Broken Web: The Educational Experiences of Hispanic American Women.* Berkeley: Floricanto Press.

McRobbie, A. 1978. "Working Class Girls and the Culture of Femininity." In *Women Take Issue: Aspects of Women's Subordination.* London: Hutchinson and Co.

———. 1991. *Feminism and Youth Culture: From Jackie to Just Seventeen.* Boston: Unwin Hyman.

McRobbie, A., and Garber, J. 1976. "Girls and Subcultures." In *Resistance through Rituals*, edited by S. Hall and T. Jefferson. London: Hutchinson and Co.

McRobbie, A., and Nava, M. 1984. *Gender and Generation.* London: Macmillan Publishers, Ltd.

Meier, K., and Stewart, J. 1991. *The Politics of Hispanic Education.* Albany: State University of New York Press.

Menchaca, M., and Valencia, R. 1990. "Anglo-Saxon Ideologies and Their Impact on the Segregation of Mexican Students in California, the 1920's-1930's." *Anthropology and Education Quarterly* 21: 222-249.

Merton, R. 1938. "Social Structure and Anomie." *American Sociological Review* 3(October): 672-682.

Miller, Walter. 1958. "Lower Class Culture as the Generating Milieu of Gang Delinquency." *Journal of Social Issues* 14: 5-19.

———. 1973. "The Molls." *Society* 11: 32-35.

———. 1980. "Gangs, Groups and Serious Youth Crime." In *Critical Issues in Juvenile Delinquency*, edited by D. Schickor and D. Kelley. Lexington, MA: Lexington Books.

Mirandé, A. 1982. "Machismo: Rucas, Chingasos y Chagaderos." *De Colores* 6: 17-31.

———. 1985. *The Chicano Experience.* Notre Dame: University of Notre Dame Press.

———. 1988. "*Qué Gacho es Ser Macho*: It's a Drag to Be a Macho Man." *Aztlán* 17 (2): 63-89.

Mirandé, A., and Enriquez, E. 1979. *La Chicana.* Chicago: University of Chicago Press.

Mirza, H. S. 1992. *Young Female and Black.* London: Routledge & Kegan Paul.

———. 1993. "The Social Construction of Black Womanhood in British Educational Research: Toward a New Understanding." In *Feminism and Social Justice in Education International Perspectives*, edited by M. Arnot and K. Weiler. London: Falmer Press.

Modelski, T. 1991. *Feminism without Women.* London: Routledge & Kegan Paul.

Montiel, M. 1971. "The Social Science Myth of the Mexican American Family." In *Voices: Reading from El Grito,* edited by O. Romano V. 40-47. Berkeley: Quinto Sol.

———. 1973. "The Chicano Family: A Review of the Research." *Social Work* 8(2): 22-31.

Moore, H. 1988. *Feminism and Anthropology.* Minneapolis: University of Minnesota Press.

Moore, J. 1976. *Mexican American.* Englewood Cliffs, NJ: Prentice Hall.

———. 1978. *Homeboys: Gangs, Drugs, and Prison in the Barrios of Los Angeles.* Philadelphia: Temple University Press.

———. 1985. "Isolation and Stigmatization in the Development of an Underclass: The Case of Chicano Gangs in East Los Angeles." *Social Problems* 33(1): 1-12.

————. 1990. "Mexican American Women Addicts: The Influence of Family Background." In *Drugs in Hispanic Communities*, edited by R. Glick and J. Moore. New Brunswick, NJ: Rutgers University Press.

————. 1991. *Going Down to the Barrio: Homeboys and Homegirls in Change.* Philadelphia: Temple University Press.

Moore, J. and Devitt, M. 1989. "The Paradox of Deviance in Addicted Mexican American Mothers." *Gender and Society* 3(1): 53-70.

Moore, J., and Pinderhughes, R. 1993. *In the Barrios: Latinos and the Underclass Debate.* New York: Russell Sage Foundation.

Moore, J., and Vigil, J. D. 1989. "Chicano Gangs: Group Norms and Individual Factors Related to Adult Criminality." *Aztlán* 18(2): 27-44.

Moore, J.; Vigil, J. D.; and Garcia, R. 1983. "Residence and Territoriality in Chicano Gangs." *Social Problems* 31(2): 182-194.

Morales, P. 1985. "Feminismo Chicano." *Fem* 8(39): 41-44.

Morales, S. 1983. "Chicano Produced Celluloid Mujeres." *Bilingual Review* 10: 89-93.

Moran, J., and Corley, M. D. 1991. "Sources of Sexual Information and Sexual Attitudes and Behaviors of Anglo and Hispanic Adolescent Males." *Adolescence* 26(104): 857-864.

Morash, M., and Rucker, L. 1989. "An Exploratory Study of Connection of Mother's Age at Childbearing to her Children's Delinquency in Four Data Sets." *Crime and Delinquency* 35(1): 45-93.

Murphy, S. 1978. "A Year with the Gangs of East Los Angeles." *Ms.* 7(1): 56-64.

Nathanson, C. 1991. *Dangerous Passage: The Social Control of Sexuality in Women's Adolescence.* Philadelphia: Temple University Press.

National Education Goals Panel. 1992. *The National Education Goals Report: Building a Nation of Learners.* Washington, D.C.: U.S. Government Printing Office.

NiCarthy, G. 1983. "Addictive Love and Abuse: A Course for Teenage Women." In *The Second Mile: Contemporary Approaches in Counseling Young Women*, edited by S. Davidson. Phoenix: New Directions for Young Women, Inc.

Oakes, J. 1985. *Keeping Track: How Schools Structure Inequality.* New Haven, CT: Yale University Press.

Ogbu, J. 1974. *The Next Generation.* New York: Academic Press.

————. 1981. *Schooling in the Ghetto: An Ecological Perspective on Community and Home Influence.* ERIC Document Reproduction Service No. ED 252 270. Washington, D.C.: National Institute of Education.

————. 1987. "Variability in Minority School Performance."*Anthropology & Education Quarterly* 18: 312-334.

————. 1991a. "Immigrant and Involuntary Minorities in Comparative Perspective." In *Minority Status and Schooling,* edited by J. Ogbu and M. Gibson. New York: Garland Publishing, Inc.

————. 1991b. "Minority Coping Responses: A School Experience." *Journal of Psychohistory* 18(4): 433-456.

Olson, H. 1985. "La Mujer, El Amor y el Poder." *Fem* 8(39): 17-21.

Olson-Raymer, G., Jefferson, P., and Ortega, M. 1989. "The Oceanside Police Department Gang Study." Oceanside Police Department, Oceanside, CA. Duplicated.

Ong, A. 1990. "State Versus Islam: Malay Families, Women's Bodies, and the Body Politic in Malaysia." *American Ethnologist* 17(2): 257-275.

Orfield, G. 1988a. "The Growth and Concentration of Hispanic Enrollment and the Future of America's Education." Paper Presented at the National Council of La Raza Conference. Albuquerque, NM, July.

————. 1988b. "School Desegregation in the 1980's." *Equity and Choice* 4: 25-28.

Ortiz, S., and Casas, J. 1990. "Birth Control and Low Income Mexican American Women: The Impact of Three Values." *Hispanic Journal of Behavior* 12: 83-91.

Orum, L. S. 1986. "The Education of Hispanics: Status and Implications." Washington, D.C.: National Council of La Raza, Duplicated.

————. 1988. "Making Education Work for Hispanic Americans: Some Promising Community-based Practices." Washington, D.C.: National Council of La Raza, Duplicated.

Padilla, F. 1992. *The Gangs as an American Enterprise*. New Brunswick, NJ: Rutgers University Press.

Pardo, M. 1990. "Mexican American Women Grassroots Community Activists: Mothers of East Los Angeles. *Frontiers* 11(1): 1-6.

Paz, O. 1961. *The Labyrinth of Solitude.* Translated by L. Kemp. New York: Grove.

Peng, S., and Takai, R. 1983. *High School Dropouts: Descriptive Information from High School and Beyond*. National Center for Education Statistics Bulletin.Washington D.C.: U.S. Government Printing Office.

Pennel, S., Evans, E., Melton, R.,and Hinson, R. 1994. *Down for the Set: Describing and Defining Gangs in San Diego.* San Diego: San Diego Association of Governments.

Perez, S., and Salazar, D. 1993. "Economic, Labor Force, and Social Implications of Latino Education in Population Trends." *Hispanic Journal of Behavioral Sciences* 15(2): 188-229.

Pesquera, B. 1984. "Having a Job Gives You Some Sort of Power: Reflections of a Chicano Working Woman." *Feminist Issues* 4(2): 79-96.

Phoenix, A. 1987. "Theories of Gender and Black Families." In *Gender under Scrutiny,* edited by G. Weiner and M. Arnot, 50-64. London: Open University Press.

Pierce, J. 1984. "The Implications of Functionalism for Chicano Family Research." *Berkeley Journal of Sociology* 29: 93-117.

Pollak, O. 1961. *The Criminality of Women.* 1950. Reprint, Philadelphia: University of Pennsylvania Press.

Powell, R. 1993. "Hire-a-Youth Has a Job Explaining Extra Expenses." *San Diego Union-Tribune,* August, 18, 1993, B-1.

Ramos, R. 1982. "Discovering the Production of the Mexican American Family Structure." *De Colores* 6(1–2): 121-134.

Rendon, A. B. 1972. *Chicano Manifesto*. New York: Macmillan.

Riddell, S. 1992. *Gender and the Politics of Curriculum*. London: Routledge.

Rogers, S. 1974. "Female Forms of Power and the Myth of Male Dominance: A Model of Female/Male Interaction in Peasant Society." *American Ethnologist* 2: 727–756.

Roman, L., and Christian-Smith, L., eds. 1988. *Becoming Feminine: The Politics of Popular Culture.* London: Falmer Press.

Romo, H. 1984. "The Mexican Origin Populations' Different Perceptions of Their Children's Schooling." *Social Science Quarterly* 65(2): 635-650.

Rosaldo, M. 1974. "Woman, Culture and Society: a Theoretical Overview." In *Woman, Culture and Society,* edited by M. Rosaldo and L. Lamphere. Stanford: Stanford University Press.

Rose, M. 1990a. "From the Fields to the Picket Lines: Huelga Women and the Boycott, 1965-1975." *Labor History* 31(3): 271-293.

————. 1990b. "Traditional and Nontraditional Patterns of Female Activism in the United Farm Workers of America, 1962-1980." *Frontiers* 11(1): 26-32.

Rosenbaum, J. 1989. "Family Dysfunction and Female Delinquency." *Crime and Delinquency* 35 (1): 31-44.

Rubel, A. 1966. *Across the Tracks: Mexican Americans in a Texas City*. Austin: University of Texas Press.

Ruiz, R. 1992. *Triumphs and Tragedy: A History of the Mexican People*. New York: W.W. Norton, Co.

Rumbergers, R. 1991. "Chicano Dropout: A Review of the Research and Policy Issues." In *Chicano School Failure and Success*, edited by R. Valencia. New York: Falmer Press.

Sadker, M., and Sadker, D. 1994. *Failing at Fairness: How America's Schools Cheat Girls*. New York: Charles Scribner's Sons.

Sanday, P. 1981. *Female Power and Male Dominance*. Cambridge: Cambridge University Press.

San Diego County Offices of Health Services. 1993. Statistical reports made available. San Diego, CA. Duplicated.

Schlossman, S. 1989. "The California Experience in American Juvenile Justice: Some Historical Perspectives." *BCS Forum*. Offices of Attorney General. Sacramento: Department of Justice.

Schmitt, C., and Pulat, M. 1993. *Trends in Enrollment in Higher Education by Racial/Ethnic Category: Fall 1982-Fall 1991.*"U.S. Department of Education, Office of Educational Research and Improvement NCES 93-448. Washington, D.C.: U.S. Government Printing Office.

Schulz, M. 1990. "The Semantic Derogation of Women." In *The Feminist Critique of Language*, edited by D. Cameron, 134-147. New York: Routledge.

Scott, J. 1985. *Weapons of the Weak: Everyday Forms of Peasant Resistance*. New Haven, CT: Yale University Press.

———. 1991. *Domination and the Arts of Resistance*. New Haven, CT: Yale University Press.

Segura, D. 1984. "Labor Market Stratification: The Chicana Experience." *Berkeley Journal of Sociology* 29: 57-91.

———. 1989. "Chicana and Mexican Immigrant Women at Work: The Impact of Class, Race and Gender on Occupational Mobility." *Gender and Society* 3(1): 37-52.

Sheldon, W. 1949. *The Varieties of Delinquent Youth*. New York: Harper.

Shorris, E. 1992. *Latinos: A Biography of a People*. New York: Aron Books.

Simon, R. 1975. *Women and Crime*. New York: Lexington Books.

Simon, R., and Baxter, S. 1989. "Gender and Violent Crime." In *Violent Crime, Violent Criminal*, edited by N. Weiner and M. Wolfgang. Newbury Park, CA: Sage Publications.

Slonim-Nevo, V. 1992. "First Premarital Intercourse among Mexican American and Anglo American Adolescent Women: Interpreting Ethnic Differences." *Journal of Adolescent Research* 7(3): 332-351.

Smith, D. 1987. *The Everyday World as Problematic*. Boston: Northeastern University Press.

Sosa-Riddell, A. 1974. "Chicanas and El Movimiento." *Aztlán* 5(1): 155-165.

Soto, S. 1986. "Tres Modelos Culturales: la Virgen de Guadalupe, la Malinche y la Llorona." *Fem* 10(48): 13-16.

Sparrow, D. 1970. *Women Who Murder*. London: Arthur Barker Ltd.

Spelman, E. 1988. *Inessential Woman*. Boston: Beacon Press.

Spender, D. 1980. *Man Made Language*. London: Routledge & Kegan Paul.

Spender, D., and Sarah, E. 1980. *Learning to Lose: Sexism and Education*. London: Women's Press, Ltd.

Stack, C. 1974. "Sex Roles and Survival Strategies in an Urban Black Community." In *Woman, Culture and Society*, edited by M. Rosaldo and L. Lamphere, 113-128. Stanford: Stanford University Press.

————. 1975. *All Our Kin: Strategies For Survival in a Black Community*. New York: Harper & Row.

Stafford, A. 1991. *Trying Work*. Edinburgh: Edinburgh University Press.

Stanley, J. 1973. "Paradigmatic Woman: The Prostitute." Paper presented at the South Atlantic Modern Language Association.

Stoddard, E. 1973. *The Mexican Americans*. New York: Random House.

Strong, S. 1993. "All the School's a Stage: Drama as Discourse Across Curriculum." Master's Thesis, University of California at San Diego.

Suarez-Orozco, M. 1986. "In Pursuit of a Dream." Ph.D. Diss., University of California at Berkeley.

————. 1989. "Psychosocial Aspects of Achievement Motivation among Recent Hispanic Immigrants." In *What Do Anthropologists Have to Say About Dropouts?*, edited by H. Trueba, G. Spindler, and L. Spindler, 99-116. New York: Falmer Press.

————. 1991. "Immigrant Adaptation to Schooling: A Hispanic Case." In *Minority Status and Schooling*, edited by M. Gibson and J. Ogbu, 37-62. New York: Garland Publishing, Inc.

Sutherland, E. 1947. *The Professional Thief*, 1937. Reprint, Chicago: University of Chicago Press.

Taylor, C. 1993. *Girls, Gangs, Women and Drugs*. Ann Arbor: University of Michigan Press.

Tevis, Y. 1991. "Feminism and the Mexican American Woman." *University of California MEXUS News* 28(Summer): 1-7.

Thornberry, T., Krohn, M., Lizotte, A., and Chard-Wierschem, D. 1993. "The Role of Delinquent Gangs in Facilitating Delinquent Behavior." *Journal of Research in Crime and Delinquency* 30(1): 55-87.

Thrasher, F.M. 1928. *The Gang*. Chicago: Chicago University Press.

United States Bureau of the Census. 1990. *Current Population Reports*. Washington, D.C.: Government Printing Office.

————. 1992. *Current Population Reports*. Washington, D.C.: Government Printing Office.

————. 1993. *Census Information and Population Housing Estimates for 1993.* Washington, D.C.: Government Printing Office.

U. S. Department of Commerce. Bureau of the Census. 1986. "Projections of the Hispanic Population: 1983-2080." In *Current Population Reports*. Series P-25, No. 995. Washington, D.C.: Government Printing Office.

————. 1990. "What's it Worth? Education Background and Economic Status: Spring 1987." In *Current Population Reports*. Series P-70, No. 21. Washington, D.C.: Government Printing Office.

————. 1991a. "Educational Attainment in the United States: March 1989 and 1988." In *Current Population Reports*. Series P-20, No. 451. Washington, D.C.: Government Printing Office.

————. 1991b. "The Hispanic Population of the United States: March 1990." In *Current Population Reports*. Series P-25, No. 995. Washington D.C.: Government Printing Office.

————. 1992. "Money Income of Families and Persons in the United States." In *Current Population Reports*. Series P-60. Washington, D.C.: Government Printing Office.

U. S. Department of Education. 1992. "A Progress Report to the Secretary of Education from the President's Advisory Commission on Educational Excellence for Hispanic Americans." Washington, D.C.: Government Printing Office.

Valdez, D. 1982. "Mexican American Family Research: A Critical Review and Conceptual Framework." *De Colores* 6(1–2): 48-63.

Valdez, T. 1980. "Organizing as a Political Tool for the Chicana." *Frontiers* 5(2): 7-12.

Valdez, R. 1984. "Understanding School Closure: Discriminatory Impact on Chicano and Black Students." In *Policy Monograph Series* No. 1. Stanford: Stanford University, Stanford Center for Chicano Research.

―――. 1991. *Chicano School Failure and Success: Research and Policy Agendas for the 1990's.* New York: Falmer Press.

Valenzuela, A. 1993. "Liberal Gender Role Attitudes and Academic Achievement among Mexican-Origin Adolescents in Two Houston Inner-city Catholic Schools." *Hispanic Journal of Behavioral Science* 15(3): 310-323.

Valli, L. 1986. *Becoming Clerical Workers*. London: Routledge & Kegan Paul.

Valverde, S. 1987. "A Comparative Study of Hispanic High School Dropouts and Graduates: Why Do Some Leave School Early and Some Finish?" *Education and Urban Society* 19(3): 320-329.

Vigil, J. D. 1988a. *Barrio Gangs*. Austin: University of Texas Press.

―――. 1988b. "Group Processes and Street Identity: Adolescent Chicano Gang Members." *Ethos* 16(4): 421-445.

Vigil, J. D., and Yun, S. 1990. "Vietnamese Youth Gangs in Southern California." In *Gangs in America,* edited by R. Huff, 146-162. Newbury Park, CA: Sage Publications.

Votaw, C. 1986. "Influencias Culturales y Femeninismo en la Mujer Chicano." *Fem* 10(48): 27-30.

Ward, J., and Taylor, J. 1994. "Sexuality Education for Immigrant and Minority Students: Developing a Culturally Appropriate Curriculum." In *Sexual Cultures and the Construction of Adolescent Identities*, edited by J. Irving, 50-70. Philadelphia: Temple University Press.

Weiler, K. 1988. *Women Teaching for Change: Gender, Class and Power*. South Hadley, MA: Bergin and Garvey.

Weiner, G. 1985. *Just a Bunch of Girls*. Philadelphia: Open University Press.

Weiner, G., and Arnot, M., eds. 1987. *Gender Under Scrutiny*. London: Open University Press.

Weiner, N., and Wolfgang, M., eds. 1989. *Violent Crime, Violent Criminals*. London: Sage Publications.

Weis, L. 1990. *Working Class without Work: High School Students in a De-Industrializing Economy*. New York: Routledge, Chapman and Hall, Inc.

Whatley, M. 1994. "Keeping Adolescents in the Picture: Construction of Adolescent Sexuality in Textbook Images and Popular Films." In *Sexual Cultures and the Construction of Adolescent Identities,* edited by J. Irvine, 183-205. Philadelphia: Temple University Press.

Whyte, W. 1955. *Street Corner Society*. Chicago: University of Chicago Press.

Williams, N. 1988. "Rolemaking among Married Mexican American Women: Issues of Class and Ethnicity." *Journal of Applied Behavioral Sciences* 24(2): 203-217.

―――. 1990. *The Mexican American Family*. New York: General Hall, Inc.

Willis, P. 1977. *Learning to Labor: How Working Class Kids Get Working Class Jobs*. New York: Columbia University Press.

―――. 1981a. "Cultural Production is Different from Cultural Reproduction is Different from Social Reproduction is Different from Reproduction." *Interchange* 12(2/3): 48-67.

―――. 1981b. *Learning to Labor: How Working Class Kids Get Working Class Jobs*. Rev. ed. New York: Morningside.

Wilson, D. 1978. "Sexual Codes and Conduct: A Study of Teenage Girls." In *Women, Sexuality and Social Control,* edited by C. Smart and B. Smart. London: Routledge & Kegan Paul.

Wolf, N. 1991. *The Beauty Myth*. New York: Anchor Books/Double Day.

Wood, J. 1984. "Groping Toward Sexism: Boys' Sex Talk." In *Gender and Generation*, edited by A. McRobbie and M. Nava. London: Macmillan Publishers Ltd.

Ybarra, L. 1982. "Marital Decision-making and the Role of Machismo in the Chicano Family." *De Colores* 6: 32-47.

Zatz, M. S. 1985. "Los Cholos: Legal Processing of Chicano Gang Members." *Social Problems* 33 (1): 13-30.

Zavella, P. 1987. *Women's Work and Chicano Families*. Ithaca, NY: Cornell University Press.

Zelnik, M., and Kim, Y.J. 1982. "Sex Education and Its Association with Teenage Sexual Activity, Pregnancy, and Contraceptive-Use." *Family Planning Perspectives* 14(3): 117-126.

Index

About the Author

LISA C. DIETRICH received her Ph.D. in cultural anthropology from the University of California, San Diego in 1996. She is presently preparing to relocate to Santiago, Chile with her husband and son to continue her research.